MAHA YOGA

OR

THE UPANISHADIC LORE
IN THE LIGHT OF THE TEACHINGS OF
BHAGAVAN SRI RAMANA

By
"WHO"

SRI RAMANASRAMAM
Tiruvannamalai
2009

© Sri Ramanasramam
  Tiruvannamalai

First Edition	:	*1937*
Second Edition	:	*1942*
Third Edition	:	*1947*
Fourth Edition	:	*1950*
Fifth Edition	:	*1961*
Sixth Edition	:	*1967*
Seventh Edition	:	*1973*
Eighth Edition	:	*1984*
Ninth Edition	:	*1996*
Tenth Edition	:	*2002*
Eleventh Edition	:	*2006*
Twelfth Edition	:	2009
		1000 Copies

Price: Rs.80/-

CC No: 1027

ISBN: 81-88018-20-1

Published by

V.S. RAMANAN
President, Board of Trustees
Sri Ramanasramam
Tiruvannamalai 606 603
Tamil Nadu
India

Tel: 91-4175-237200 / 9244937292
Fax: 91-4175-237491
Email: ashram@sriramanamaharshi.org
Website: www.sriramanamaharshi.org

Designed and typeset at
Sri Ramanasramam

Printed by
Sudarsan Graphics
Chennai - 600 017

Foreword

In this book the author passes the philosophical portion of Sri Ramana Maharshi's teaching through the Advaitic acid-test, and then declares the teaching to be genuine coin of the Advaitic realm. For the author is a keen and uncompromising upholder of the doctrine that the world, God and the individual soul are really a unity and that their seeming separateness is but an illusion.

I am not sufficiently competent a metaphysician to pass judgement upon his conclusions, but I perceive that he states his case and rallies the Master's statements to his support with a convincing and unhesitating pleading that must be difficult to refute. At any rate he has added many true points about other aspects of Sri Ramana Maharshi's teaching — such as the nature of the personal ego and the necessity of devotion in some form or other — and he writes with such clearness of thought and expression that I have frequently admired both his mind and his literary style. It is with some pleasure that I recommend this book to the notice of those interested in the metaphysical side of the Maharshi's writings and sayings.

PAUL BRUNTON

Preface to the Eighth Edition

Maha Yoga or *The Upanishadic Lore in the Light of the Teachings of Bhagavan Sri Ramana* is both a profound exposition of Sri Ramana's teachings and a lucid summary of the whole Vedantic philosophy, the ancient lore of the Upanishads. Before an aspirant embarks upon the practice of Self-enquiry, which is the cornerstone of Sri Ramana's teachings and the essence of the Upanishadic lore, it is extremely useful — if not essential — for him to have a clear and well-founded understanding of the theoretical background upon which the practice of Self-enquiry is based, and such an understanding is possibly not made available to aspirants anywhere so clearly as in this book, which elucidates many important aspects of Sri Ramana's teachings.

The author of this book, Sri K. Lakshmana Sarma ('WHO'), was amply qualified to write such an exposition, because he spent more than twenty years in close association with Bhagavan Sri Ramana and he made a deep study of His teachings under His personal guidance. One day in 1928 or 1929 Sri Bhagavan asked Lakshmana Sarma, "Have you not read *Ulladu Narpadu?*" Lakshmana Sarma replied that he had not, because he was unable to understand the classical style of Tamil in which it was composed, but he eagerly added that he would like to study it if Sri Bhagavan would graciously teach him the meaning. Thus began the disciple's close association with his Master. Sri Bhagavan started to explain to him slowly and in detail the meaning of each verse, and Lakshmana Sarma, being a lover of Sanskrit, started to compose Sanskrit verses embodying the meaning of each Tamil verse as it was explained to him. After composing each verse in Sanskrit, Lakshmana Sarma submitted it to Sri Bhagavan for correction and approval, and if Sri Bhagavan's approval was not forthcoming he would recompose the verse as often as was necessary until His approval was obtained. In this way all the verses of *Ulladu Narpadu* were rendered into Sanskrit within a few months. But Lakshmana Sarma was unable to stop with that. He was so fascinated by the profound import of *Ulladu Narpadu* that he felt impelled to go on revising his Sanskrit rendering any number of times until he was able to make it an almost perfect and faithful replica of the Tamil original. For two or three years he went on repeatedly revising his translation with the close help and guidance of Sri Bhagavan, who always appreciated his sincere efforts and who once remarked, "It is like a great *tapas* for him to go on revising his translation so many times." Because of his repeated efforts to make such a faithful Sanskrit rendering of *Ulladu Narpadu*, Lakshmana Sarma was blessed with the opportunity of receiving long and pertinent instructions from Sri Bhagavan about the very core of His teachings.

At first Lakshmana Sarma had no idea of publishing his Sanskrit rendering of *Ulladu Narpadu*, which he was preparing for his own personal benefit, and he had even less idea of writing any lengthy exposition upon Sri Bhagavan's teachings. However, towards the end of 1931 a certain book was published which purported to be a commentary on Sri Bhagavan's teachings, but when Lakshmana Sarma read it he was distressed to see that it gave a very distorted picture of the teachings, so he approached Sri Bhagavan and said in a prayerful attitude, "If your teachings are misinterpreted like this in your very lifetime, what will become of them in future? Will not people think that you have approved this book? Should not such a wrong interpretation be openly condemned?" But Sri Bhagavan replied, "According to the purity of the mind (*antahkarana*) of each person, the same teaching is reflected in different ways. If you think you can expound the teachings more faithfully, you may write your own commentary." Prompted thus by Sri Bhagavan, Lakshmana Sarma began to write a Tamil commentary on *Ulladu Narpadu*, which was first published in 1936, and *Maha Yoga*, which was first published in 1937. In later years Sri Bhagavan once remarked that of all the commentaries on *Ulladu Narpadu* which then existed, Lakshmana Sarma's Tamil commentary was the best.

Maha Yoga is based largely upon two Sanskrit works, namely *Sri Ramana Hridayam* and *Guru Ramana Vachana Mala*, extracts from which are given in appendices A and B. *Sri Ramana Hridayam* is Lakshmana Sarma's Sanskrit rendering of *Ulladu Narpadu* (The Forty Verses on Reality) and *Ulladu Narpadu Anubandham* (The Supplement to the Forty Verses on Reality), which are two of the most important Tamil works composed by Sri Bhagavan, while *Guru Ramana Vachana Mala* is a work consisting of 350 verses composed by Lakshmana Sarma, about 300 of which are translations of selected verses from Sri Muruganar's *Guru Vachaka Kovai* (The Garland of Guru's Sayings) and all of which embody the oral teachings of Sri Bhagavan.* Just as Lakshmana Sarma had composed *Sri Ramana Hridayam* with the help and guidance of Sri Bhagavan, he composed *Guru Ramana Vachana Mala* with the help of both Sri Bhagavan and Sri Muruganar, and in doing so he had a further opportunity to study Sri Bhagavan's teachings deeply and to receive pertinent instructions from Him. On one occasion when Lakshmana Sarma was asked why he had written *Maha Yoga* and his Tamil commentary on *Ulladu Narpadu* under the pseudonym 'WHO', he replied, "I wrote in those books only what I had learnt from Sri Bhagavan and Sri Muruganar, so I felt 'Who wrote it?'"

In addition to the many verses of *Sri Ramana Hridayam* and *Guru Ramana Vachana Mala* which are quoted throughout this book, the author also quotes numerous other sayings of Sri Bhagavan and conversations with Him, particularly in the last chapter. These other sayings and conversations were

---

* The complete Sanskrit text of *Sri Ramana Hridayam* together with an English translation is published by us in a book called *Revelation*, and an English translation of the whole of *Guru Ramana Vachana Mala* is published by us in a separate book. For details about these and other books in English on the life and teachings of Sri Bhagavan, the reader may refer to the bibliography given at the end of this book.

heard and recorded by the author himself, and proof of their authenticity lies in the fact that most of them have also been recorded either in *Maharshi's Gospel* or in *Talks with Sri Ramana Maharshi*, both of which were published after this book.

In his foreword to the first edition of *Maha Yoga*, which is reproduced once again in this edition, Paul Brunton writes that "in this book the author passes the philosophical portion of Sri Ramana Maharshi's teaching through the Advaitic acid-test, and then declares the teaching to be genuine coin of the Advaitic realm." However, in his preface to that edition the author explains that his intention was rather the other way round, because in his view Sri Bhagavan's teachings are the primary authority and they confirm, rather than are confirmed by, the ancient lore of the Upanishads. To cite the author's own words:

"The ancient lore — the Upanishads — has received a striking confirmation from the life and teachings of the Sage of Arunachala, known as Bhagavan Sri Ramana. To his disciples, both eastern and western, the written and oral teachings of the Sage are the *primary* revelation, and the ancient lore is of value because it is found to be in full accord with those teachings. But even for those who look upon the ancient lore as of primary authority, the teachings of a living Sage must be profoundly interesting. In these pages a synthetic presentation of the old and new revelations is sought to be given."

When the first edition of *Maha Yoga* was published, it quickly met with a warm response from the intelligent public, and it was soon translated into

French by Jean Herbert, who looked upon it as a "most remarkable book". This French translation was published first in 1939 and again in 1940 as the first volume of a series entitled *Études sur Ramana Maharshi,* and Swami Siddeswarananda, the founder-President of Sri Ramakrishna Mission in France, wrote a lengthy preface for it,* which he concluded by saying:

". . . But this mysticism of the Maharshi has its basis in a profound and intelligent comprehension of life and its problems. And to understand that, it is necessary to place the Maharshi in His philosophical and cultural milieu. From this point of view, no work is as powerful and as faithful to the heritage of India as the beautiful study presented here. Its author, Dr K. Lakshmana Sarma, is one of our friends. He has spent years with the Maharshi exercising himself always to his best to understand Him in the light of the words spoken by the Sage on the philosophical problems and on this life of illumination which, like the great fire lit on the Hill of Arunachala, is a veritable light-house for those who wish to see in modern India the revivifying effect of the Upanishadic teachings consecrated by time."

Since the first edition of *Maha Yoga* met with such warm appreciation, Lakshmana Sarma was encouraged to revise and enlarge upon it for the second edition, which was published in 1942. The

---

* A condensed English translation of Swami Siddheswarananda's preface to the French version of Maha Yoga *is published as an appendix to Maharshi's Gospel.*

present edition is substantially the same as the second edition, except for a few alterations which were made by the author in the third and fourth editions, and except for appendix C, which was printed in the first edition and which we have decided to include again in this edition.* Since the time when the second edition was published, *Maha Yoga* has been translated and published in a number of other European languages such as German and Portuguese.

Finally a word might be said about the title of this book. At the end of chapter nine the author writes, "The Sage once told this writer that the Quest is the Great Yoga — Maha Yoga — and the reason is that, as shown here, all the Yogas are included in the Quest", and this is why he called this book *Maha Yoga*. Once, some years after the publication of this book, Sri Bhagavan came across a verse in the *Kurma Purana* (2.11.7) in which Lord Siva declares, "That (yoga) in which one sees the Self (*atman*), which is Me, the one immaculate and eternal bliss, is considered to be the Maha Yoga pertaining to the Supreme Lord." Since this verse thus confirmed His statement that Self-enquiry, the practice of attending to the Self, is the 'Maha Yoga', Sri Bhagavan transcribed it in His own copy of *Maha Yoga* at the end of chapter nine.

---

* In the first edition of *Maha Yoga* this appendix was prefaced with the remark: "The following passages are extracts from a letter written by a critically minded visitor, which once appeared in the *Vedanta Kesari* (Mylapore, Madras)." However, from the French translation of *Maha Yoga* we come to know that the unnamed visitor who wrote it was Swami Tapasyananda, a distinguished member of Sri Ramakrishna Mission.

We are happy to bring out yet another edition of this valuable book, and we are sure that it will continue as ever before to provide guidance and inspiration to all seekers of truth.

SRI RAMANASRAMAM   T.N. VENKATARAMAN
14th April 1984.   PUBLISHER.

Author's Note

MAHA YOGA is the Direct Method of finding the Truth of Ourselves, It has nothing in common with what is commonly known as 'Yoga', being quite simple — free from mysteries, — because it is concerned with the utter Truth of our Being, which is Itself extremely simple.

MAHA YOGA frees its follower from his beliefs, not to bind him with new beliefs, but to enable him to pursue with success the Quest of the True Self, which transcends all creeds.

MAHA YOGA has been described as a process of *unlearning*. Its follower has to unlearn all his knowledge, because, being in relativity, it is ignorance, and therefore a hindrance.

This true Yoga is the subject-matter of the Upanishads. But the Truth that is to be found by this Yoga is eternal and needs to be testified to by *living* witnesses from time to time. This book starts with the very reasonable assumption that only a living Teacher can tell us the Upanishadic Truth, not the Upanishads themselves, because they are just words and little more, while the Living Teacher is an Incarnation of the Truth we seek. The Living Teacher of our age was the Sage of Arunachala, Bhagavan Sri Ramana, of whose life a brief sketch is given in the first Chapter. His teachings are treated in this book as the *primary* authority, and the Upanishadic lore as next in value — as amplifying and supplementing it. The reader need not accept anything that is set forth here, unless he finds it to be in consonance with the actual teachings of the Sage.

Contents

Foreword by Paul Brunton iii

Preface to the Eighth Edition. v

Author's Note xiii

1. The Sage of Arunachala 1
2. Are We Happy? 19
3. Ignorance .. .: 26
4. Authority 41
5. The World 53
6. The Soul 88
7. God 108
8. The Egoless State 117
9. The Quest 161
10. The Sage 181
11. Devotion 200
12. Some more Sayings of the Sage 219

Appendix A 243

Appendix B 251

Appendix C 256

Index 261

Bibliography 273

Chapter I

The Sage of Arunachala

THERE IS A profound Truth in us, the truth of ourselves, the practical knowledge of which will make us free; but he that would be free must seek, and reverently question one that is himself free. So says the ancient lore.* Thus it emphasises the need of resort to a *living* teacher of the Truth of the real Self, if one such can be found. The knowledge that comes by the study of the sacred lore is of little value; one can learn more, and more quickly, from this *silence* of a living teacher than he can gather by a lifetime of the study of the books.

We are told by the great teacher Sri Ramakrishna Paramahamsa that there are two kinds of Sages, namely those who are born with the mission to teach and elevate other men, and those who have no such mission; the former are from birth untainted by worldly desires; they win the state of Deliverance about the time they cease to be boys; and they do so

---

* तद्विद्धि प्रणिपातेन परिप्रश्नेन सेवया ।
उपदेक्ष्यन्ति ते ज्ञानं ज्ञानिनस्तत्त्वदर्शिनः ॥

—*Bhagavad Gita*, 4.34.

with little or no effort; the latter are born in subjection
to worldly desires and weaknesses and have to go
through a long period of sustained and well-directed
effort in order to reach the same goal. The former
kind of sage is naturally very rare. Whenever such a
one appears, multitudes of disciples and devotees are
drawn to him, and they profit greatly in his presence.
Bhagavan Sri Ramana is such a one. He is the last of
a long line of great Sages, who have renewed and
confirmed the teaching of the ancient Revelation.

He was born in the south of India in the village
of Tiruchuzhi about thirty miles from Madura, and
received the name of Venkataraman. His father died
when he was twelve years old and after that he was
brought up by his mother and uncles. The boy was
sent for education, first to Dindigul and then to
Madura, which is a great centre of pilgrimage. His
guardians had no suspicion of what he was destined
to become. They tried their best to fashion him after
their own idea of what he should become; they sought
to equip him for the life of the world by giving him a
'good education.'

The boy was not at all wanting in intelligence.
But he was incorrigibly indifferent to his studies; he
would put forth no personal effort to learn and
remember; in so far as he did learn something, he did
so in spite of himself. The reason was that he had no
'will to get on in the world,' which every boy has, who
is above the average. We now know that he was one of
those rare beings who bring with them an endowment
of spirituality. That perfection which was to make him
the revered Master of millions of men existed in him
already in a latent state; and it is a law of nature that

a spiritual endowment makes one indifferent to worldly gains. It is because the average man is poorly endowed in a spiritual sense, that he falls an easy prey to worldly desires; urged by these desires he takes great pains to achieve what he calls success in life. We know that Sri Ramakrishna also had an incorrigible aversion to "this bread-winning education."

Thus the boy Ramana gained hardly any knowledge while at school. But destiny put in his hands a copy of an ancient sacred book in Tamil, which gives detailed narratives of the sixty-three Saints of the cult of Siva. He read it through with fervour. We have reason to believe that he had already been a Saint of the same high degree of excellence, and had *passed* this stage of spiritual evolution; he had in him the potentiality of something far higher, namely the status of a *Sage*; when we come to the chapter on Devotion we shall be able to see the difference between a Saint and a Sage. For the present we need only say that the Sage differs from the Saint as the ripe fruit does from the flower. Saintliness is no more than the *promise* of sagehood, which alone is perfection; when Jesus told his disciples: 'Be ye perfect even as your Father in Heaven is perfect,' he had in mind the Sage, not the Saint.

Even as a little boy, Ramana was continually aware of something supremely holy, whose Name was Arunachala; this we learn from a poem composed by the Sage later for the use of his disciples. We see that he brought over from his past lives a fully ripe devotion to that mysterious Being, which most of us call God, but which may be more justly described as the Spiritual Centre of life. This was seen on one

occasion in his boyhood, when an uncle of his spoke
to him harshly; he then went for consolation and
peace, not to his earthly mother, but to the Divine
Mother in the temple of the village. Sometimes also
he would fall into what seemed to be an exceptionally
profound sleep, a sleep from which nothing could
awake him; if we may judge from the perfection which
he attained later, and which he enjoys in the waking
state also, we may surmise that this seeming sleep
was in fact a spiritual experience on an elevated plane
of being.

Thus continued his life, a double life on parallel
lines — a life in the world which he led mechanically
and without interest, as one that did not really belong
to the world, and a life in the spirit, of which the people
around him had not even the faintest suspicion. This
lasted till the end of the sixteenth year of his life. He
was then in the highest class in the high school course,
and it was expected that at the end of the course he
would sit for the matriculation examination of the
University of Madras; but this was not to be; for then
something happened, which brought the boy's
schooling to an abrupt end.

The age-period of sixteen and seventeen is a
critical one for all. In the average man the mind is
then overrun by imaginations and desires, which
revolve round the sense of sex. But for a few
exceptional souls it is the time of the awakening to
the *true* life — compared to which this thing that we
call life is death — the life that begins with the
blossoming of the spiritual perfections which are
already latent in them. This we find to be the case in
the lives of all the Saints and Sages of the world.

It is also a fact, appearing in the lives of the Sages of the past, that this awakening begins as a rule with a sudden fear of death. It is true that the fear of death is not unfamiliar to common men; for it comes often enough to them; but there is a difference in the reaction to this fear; to the common man it makes very little difference; he is led to think of death when he sees a funeral procession; sometimes he begins to philosophise, more or less on traditional lines; but this mood lasts only until his next meal; afterwards he becomes 'normal' again; the current of his life runs on the same lines as before.

The born Sage reacts differently to the thought of death. He begins to reflect coolly, but with all the force of his intelligence, on the problem of death; and this reflection is the starting point of a concentrated effort to transcend the realm of death. Thus it was in the case of Gautama Buddha.* Thus it was also in the case of Ramana.

Thus he reflected: "Who or what is it that dies? It is this visible body that dies; the kinsmen come and take it away and burn it to ashes. But when this body dies, shall *I* also die? That depends on what *I* really am. If *I* be this body, then when it dies, *I* also would die; but if *I* be not this, then *I* would survive."

Then there arose in his mind an overpowering desire to find out, then and there, whether he — the real Self of him — would survive after death. And it occurred to him that the surest way to find it out would be to enact the process of death. This he did by

---

* 'Buddha' means 'a sage'. The Sage was also called Sugata which means one that has attained the State of Deliverance.

imagining that the body was dead. A dead body does not speak nor breathe; nor has it any sensation; all this he imagined with such perfect realism, that his body became inert and rigid just like a corpse; his vital energies were withdrawn from it, and gathered into the mind, which now turned inwards, animated by the will to find the real Self, if any. At this moment a mysterious power rose up from the innermost core of his being and took complete possession of the whole mind and life; by that power he — that is to say, his mind and life — was taken inwards. What then happened is a mystery; but we can gather some idea of it from the teachings of the Sage himself. We must take it that, possessed by this power — which is identical with what devotees call 'grace' — the mind plunged deep into the Source of all life and mind and was merged in *It*. All this happened while he was wide awake, and therefore he became aware of his own Real Self, free from all thought-movement; this Self was free from the bondage of desires and fears and therefore full of peace and happiness. The state which he now reached was just the Egoless State described in a later chapter — the state in which the Real Self reigns alone, and in serene calmness. Thus Ramana became a Sage. We shall never know what that state is like, until we ourselves shall reach it and abide in it; but with the help of his Revelation we shall be able to understand what it is *not*.

From this we see that a sustained and one-pointed resolve to find the real Self —which is the highest and purest form of devotion — is the means of winning that Self. This is in accord with a text of the ancient Revelation which says: "He alone shall find this Self, who is powerfully attracted to Him in complete devotion; to him that Self reveals Himself as He really is."* This is the highest truth of all religions; it was differently expressed by Jesus, who said: "Ask, and *It* shall be given; knock and *It* shall be opened."

It is this very path that the Sage teaches in his answers to disciples and in his writings. In one of the latter he calls it 'the Direct Path for all'† by which all the problems of life are transcended. The state that is won by pursuing this path is called the Natural State — *Sahajabhava*. It is so called because therein the Self is manifest as He really is, and not as He appears to the ignorant. It is also described as the Egoless State and the Mindless State. The truth of that State as revealed by the Sage and by ancient Revelation is the subject of a later chapter. Here it is enough to say that the Natural State is the highest there is — that for one that has attained that State there is nothing else to be striven for. For him the pilgrimage of life is at an end.

Ramana had by this Experience become a 'Sage', or rather the Sage that was always in him became unveiled. For him, therefore, there could be no further evolution in spirituality. Mind and body are by this Experience completely dissociated from the Self. That is to say, the mind no longer identifies the body with the Self. Ignorance being just this identification and nothing more, and the mind itself — as will be seen

---

* यमेवैष वृणुते तेन लभ्यस्तस्यैष आत्मा विवृणुते तनूं स्वाम् ॥
— *Katha Upanishad*, 1.2.23.

† The passage referred to occurs in *Upadesa Saram*, verse 17.

later — being an outcome of this ignorance, this great
Event is also called the destruction or dissolution of
the mind. Hence it is strictly true that for the Sage
there is no mind nor body nor world. But that does
not mean that body and mind are destroyed in the
sense that other people will cease to see them; for
them the Sage's body and mind will continue to
appear, and they would appear to be affected by
events, and hence there can be a further history of
the Sage. The Sage himself may seemingly be active
in diverse ways, though these actions are not really
his. Hence the course of events that occurred after this
great Event — some of which are narrated here — do
not really belong to the Sage; they do not affect him
in any way.

Because Ramana had never read about nor heard
of the Nameless, Formless, Indescribable known to
the learned as Brahman, he had no doubts as to the
nature of the State which he won by this Event. Later,
when he came to know that the sacred books described
the State of Deliverance as that in which the Self is
experienced as identical with that Reality, he had not
the least difficulty in understanding that he himself
had attained that State.*

---

* It is said of one of the Sages of yore, namely Suka, the son of Vyasa,
that the great Event occurred for him without any effort on his
part, but that a doubt arose in his mind afterwards as to whether
the State that had thus come to him was or was not the final Goal.
He asked his father, who told him that it was. But seeing that the
boy was not convinced, Vyasa advised him to go to Janaka to get his
doubt cleared. From Janaka the boy learnt that there was nothing
more for him to strive for. It is noteworthy that in the case of Ramana
this doubt did not arise.

Whatever occurred in the life of the Sage after this great Event concerns only the body and the mind that apparently survived the Event, and not the Sage himself. The divine qualities and powers which are inherent to the Natural State became soon manifest, since their exercise was necessary for the fulfilment of the Sage's mission in the world.

Thus it happened that immediately after this great Event, in the intervals when his mind was not wholly absorbed in the Natural State, it began to feel a need of some object to take hold of. The only object that was acceptable was God, in Whose love the sixty-three Saints had found their highest happiness.

So Ramana began to frequent the temple oftener than before. And there, in the presence of God, he would stand, while floods of tears streamed from his eyes — such tears as can flow only from the eyes of the most ardent of devotees. It is ever the earnest prayer of all devotees that they may have such profound devotion as this; for they consider that a copious flow of tears is a manifestation of the highest devotion, which itself is the fruit of divine grace. We can understand this manifestation in Ramana only if we suppose that in a previous life he had been such a great devotee. Also these floods of tears might have, in this case, fulfilled some divine purpose; for the tears of divine love are purifying and those that shed them are exalted thereby; the vehicles of consciousness are thereby transformed. So we may presume that in this way the body and the mind of Ramana underwent changes which made them worthy to serve as the abode of a great Teacher, a Messenger of God.

Along with these manifestations there was also at the time an acute sensation of heat in the body. All these manifestations continued until the Sage arrived at Tiruvannamalai and found himself in the Presence in the temple there. We are told of a similar sensation of heat in the case of Sri Ramakrishna.

We saw that as a student Ramana was annoyingly backward. Now he became worse than ever; for he was frequently lapsing into that mysterious state which he had won by his effortless quest of the real Self; when he was out of it, he had not the least inclination for studies. His elders could not understand what it was that had occurred to the boy. They had always been inclined to be angry with him for his aversion to study; and now they were provoked more than ever. His elder brother, who was himself a student then, was greatly irritated by these new ways of his. One day, about six weeks after his first experience of the Egoless State, the brother saw him going into it, when he ought to have been learning his lessons; this provoked a stinging remark from the elder one: "What is the use of these things (books and other things that belong to a student) to one that is thus?"

The words went home. But the effect they produced was not what the speaker intended. At the time the boy just smiled and resumed his book. But inwardly he began to think: "Yes, he is right. What is the use of books and school for me now?" Immediately the idea took shape in his mind that he must leave his home and go and live far away, unknown to those that claimed him as their own.

He had learned before this that his beloved 'Arunachala' is the same as Tiruvannamalai, a well-known place of pilgrimage. He had learned this from a relative; the latter on returning from a pilgrimage had told him in answer to his question that he had been to 'Arunachala'. This was a great surprise for the lad, who had never imagined that Arunachala was a place on this earth; the relative then explained to him that Arunachala is only another name for Tiruvannamalai.*

This place was far enough away from Madura for his present purpose, but not too far for him to reach. So he decided to leave home secretly and go there, and thereafter do as he may be guided by Providence. Fortune favoured his enterprise; his elder brother's school-fee for the month had not yet been paid; and the latter gave him five rupees, which he was told to pay to the school. Out of this he took just three rupees, thinking that this would suffice for his journey by rail; the remainder he left with a letter expressing his decision to go away in quest of his Divine Father, and insisting that no search should be made for him.

He purchased a ticket and got into the train at Madura; but as soon as he had taken his seat, he fell into the Egoless State, and was in it nearly all the time. He had hardly any appetite during the journey and ate next to nothing. He had made a mistake in planning his journey; but this was providentially set right; he had to walk a part of the way, because he

---

* 'Arunachala' is the Sanskrit name of the hill, which is itself regarded as God's image; the Tamil form of it is 'Annamalai'; 'Tiru' is prefixed to the name, to show that the place is holy; thus the Tamil name of the place is Tiru-Annamalai, which is pronounced as Tiruvannamalai.

had not money enough left. But on the way he
obtained some money by pledging his golden ear-
ornaments, and reached Tiruvannamalai by rail.

At once he went to the Presence in the temple
and cried in ecstasy, "Father, I have come just
according to Thy command." And at once the burning
heat in the body disappeared, and therewith the sense
of something being lacking. Also, there was not any
more flow of tears after this except once, when, much
later, he was composing a devotional hymn for the
use of his disciples, which is one of his 'Five Hymns
to Arunachala.'

Going out of the temple he made a complete change
in his externals: but this he did in a mechanical way,
without thinking and making decisions. A barber's
services were offered; and presently the lad had a
complete shave on his head. He reduced his dress to a
kaupina — or cod-piece — and he threw on the steps
of a tank the remainder of the cash, clothes and
whatever else he had brought with him from his last
place of halt on the journey. All this was done with the
conviction that the body was not himself and did not
deserve to be treated as of any importance. He even
omitted the bath that invariably follows a shave. But
a sudden shower of rain drenched him on his way back
to the temple.

For long after this he had no fixed place of abode;
he just sat in any place in which he could remain in
the Egoless State without disturbance from curious
or mischievous people. For long periods he was totally
unconscious of the body and its environment. The
people who observed his ways took it that he was a
recluse who had taken a vow of silence; and so they

did not try to make him speak; and he did nothing to undeceive them; he remained silent. And this accidental silence continued for many years, so that in course of time he lost the ability to speak; later, when disciples came to him and he had to answer their questions, he had to write his answers; but after a time he recovered speech, not without some effort.

He never lacked food; for the people recognised his exalted spirituality and were eager to supply his needs, so that they might gain the merit of serving a holy one. But he had, in the beginning, some trouble with mischievous boys, which however did not disturb his inner peace.

Soon after coming to Tiruvannamalai, as a result of his continuous experience of the Egoless State, he realised the truth of the highest of the ancient Revelation: 'I and my Father are one.' Thus he became a perfect Sage. Now he no longer needed to enter into himself in order to enjoy the happiness of the real Self; he had it all the time, whether he was aware of the world or not. He thus became able to fulfil his mission in the world as a Messenger of God — or rather of the real Self, there being no God but that Self. It is this state of uninterrupted experience of the real Self, which is known as the Natural State (*Sahajabhava*).*

---

* It is next to impossible not to make mistakes in seeking to understand the true nature of this State. The descriptions given in the books are mostly tentative, incorporating the ignorance of the disciple; they are subject to correction by other descriptions. The truth of this State may be understood to some extent by the discussion of it in Chapter VIII.

The vigorous search for the missing boy that was made by his family proved a failure. But some years after his flight they came to know by mere accident that he was at Tiruvannamalai. First his uncle, and then his mother, came to him and importuned him to come back and live near them, if he would not live *with* them. But they could make no impression on him; it was as if he did not recognise their claims on him; such claims were founded on the assumption that his body was himself.

Much later his mother and younger brother — at that time the sole surviving brother — came to live with him, and he let them do so. He took advantage of this opportunity to instruct and guide his mother on the path to spiritual perfection.

On various occasions during the early part of his life at Tiruvannamalai the Sage passed through many kinds of trials. But nothing could ruffle his peace of mind. He exemplifies in himself the truth expressed in the *Gita* and other sacred books, that the man who is firmly established in the Egoless State will not be moved from it by the severest trials.* The correct explanation seems to be that the events of the external world, including even what happens to the body, are not real to the Sage; for he dwells in the State of unassailable happiness, a happiness which is so abundant, that it radiates around him, draws to him disciples and devotees and attaches them to him for life. Indeed many of them look upon him as God in human form.

---

* यस्मिन्स्थितो न दुःखेन गुरुणापि विचाल्यते ॥

— Bhagavad Gita, 6.22.

It is a curious fact about this Sage that he had never had any book-knowledge concerning the real Self. The ancient lore, which reveals as much of the truth of that Self as can be expressed in words, never came his way; nor was he initiated by anyone into the secrets of that lore; nor did he even know that there was any such lore, till long after he had won the State which is their subject-matter. But when disciples came to him, and some of them wanted light on the inner sense of certain obscure passages in the sacred lore, he had to read those books; and he understood their hidden meanings with perfect ease, because those books described just that very state — the Egoless State — which he was constantly enjoying as his own; thus he was able to give out the correct sense of those passages,— a sense that is beyond the grasp of the most diligent students of that lore. Thus it happens that this Sage is an exception to the general rule of the ancient lore, that every aspirant to the State of Deliverance must become a disciple of a competent Teacher and be initiated by him into the mysteries. The competent Teacher is termed a 'Guru.'*

Another instructive feature of the Sage is that he teaches more by Silence than by word of mouth. Visitors come to him from far and near with bundles of questions; but when they take their seats in his presence after making due obeisance, they forget to put their questions; and after a time they find that the questions have evaporated. The would-be questioner either realises that the questions need no answer, or finds the answers in himself.

---

* 'G' in this word is pronounced as in 'gain.'

The Sage however quite readily answers any question that is not purely worldly; and when he does answer, his words are clear, but brief. And as a rule his teachings are free from the technical terms that abound in most of the books. And as he speaks, so he writes. That may be taken as a proof that he speaks from his own experience — not from a knowledge of books. The learned man cannot talk without using the phraseology of the books he has studied; it may be said that the books master the man, and not man the books.

The Sage has written a few books, which are all very brief, but full of meaning. But these he wrote, not because he himself wanted to write books, but because he was importuned by certain disciples, who were eager to have a Revelation from the Sage himself — not being content with the extant sacred lore. He has also, at the request of disciples, translated some of the older sacred lore into Tamil. The disciples of this Sage are in a stronger position than those who have to rely on the sacred lore of the past. Answers that the Sage has given orally to questions put to him have also been recorded by disciples.

Disciples come to the Sage from all over the world, and they profit by his silent influence as well as his teachings, according to the intensity of their desire for deliverance from bondage. Their impressions about him vary according to their mentality. But all recognise that he is a unique person, worthy of profound veneration. What is the secret of this power in him? The answer is that he has attained that state of Deliverance which everyone aspires to, more or less earnestly; some also find in his presence a foretaste of that state of being.

One particular trait that marks him out as unique is the fact that neither praise nor censure has any effect on him; he is neither pleased to hear praise of himself, nor pained by words of censure or detraction. This may not seem to be very important; but the fact is that other perfections of character are to be seen in varying degree in almost any good man, but not so this particular trait; indeed this is the one trait by which the Sage can be recognised; it is pointed out that even the most saintly of men — if they have not won the Egoless State — react just like common men to praise and blame.* So long as even a trace of ego remains, it is impossible not to be affected by praise or blame; only the Sage in the Egoless State is unaffected by them.

Being egoless the Sage sees no distinction between himself and others, nor between one person and another. For him neither sex, nor fortune, nor social status has any existence; his sense of equality is absolute; even animals — dogs, cats, birds, squirrels — he treats as if they were human. And — incredible as it seems — in his eyes no one is ignorant or a sinner.

Many maintain that a Sage alone can recognise a Sage, and that therefore no one can positively assert that this one is a Sage. This is not altogether true; he that is in earnest to find a competent guide — a Guru — on the path of deliverance has to decide somehow whether the person he would elect be a Sage or not; and if he be of pure and devout mind, he will be aided by divine grace to make the right choice. It is also a help for him, to understand the profound truths taught in the

---

* Refer to *Ulladu Narpadu Anubandham* verse 37 (see also page 188 and appendix A, verse 83).

Sage's Revelation; we have already noticed a few of
the marks of a real Sage. A few more will be set down
later on.

The mission of a born Sage or Messenger of God
is twofold. He renews and confirms the essentials of
the old Revelation. He also serves as a centre of divine
grace to his disciples — especially to those who,
intuitively or through understanding of the sacred
teaching, recognise him as an embodiment of God,
and therefore bear unto him the same devotion that
they formerly bore to God, seeing no distinction
between the two. This is in accordance with the spirit
of the ancient sacred lore, which is expressed in the
following verse.

ईश्वरो गुरुरात्मेति मूर्तिभेदविभागिने ।
व्योमवद्व्याप्तदेहाय दक्षिणामूर्तये नमः ॥ *

"Obeisance to the Lord of Divine Wisdom, infinite
like the sky, who is three in one, as God, the Guru
and the Real Self." It seems that for one who
understands this truth and becomes a disciple and
devotee of the Sage it may not be quite necessary to
go to the Sage and live near him always. The Sage
transcends time and space and is therefore
everywhere.

We shall now make a study of the teachings of
all the Sages, always giving special prominence to
those of this Sage.†

---

* Sureshvaracharya in his *Vartika* on Sri Sankaracharya's
Dakshinamurti Stotra.
† The reasons for doing so are discussed in some detail in the chapter
on Authority.

Chapter 2

Are We Happy?

THIS WORLD is to us a means to an end, namely happiness; at least it is so for most of us. Some there are who maintain that we are here for the sake of the world, not for our own sake. What they mean is that we ought not to live for ourselves, but for the world. But that is quite another matter. The fact is that we live for ourselves in the first place, and for the world also in so far as the good of the world happens to be also our own. That being the case, we shall have to consider, some time or other, whether we have found happiness, and if not, then why; we shall have to think over the question whether, in seeking happiness in and through this world, we have not made some false assumptions.

We begin life with the belief that happiness can be had in and through this world. And most people go on believing thus to the very end. They never pause and think; they do not take notice of the fact that their hopes of happiness have not been realised. How then can they consider the further question, why those hopes have been falsified?

Not all the religions and philosophies of the world can do for us what *we* can do for ourselves, *if* we pause and think; for what we get from these is just so much

mind-lumber — mere fashions of thought and speech
which do not fit in with what we really are; for only
what we find out for ourselves from our own experience
can be of real use to us. Further, we can find nothing
of real value, even from our own experience, if we do
not pause and think. If these religions and philosophies
just hasten the day when we shall pause and think,
they shall have done quite enough for us.

What keeps us from pausing and thinking is the
belief that we are getting — or shall soon get — from
life the thing we want, happiness. The one thing that
can possibly shake this belief is experience of the tragic
side of life. We are told by the Sage of Arunachala that
this is Nature's way; and he gives us the analogy of
dreams to prove it; when we are dreaming of pleasant
things we do not awake: but we do so as soon as we see
visions of a frightful nature. A life of placid enjoyment
is naturally inimical to serious thinking on serious
subjects; and here the religious-minded are no better
than the rest of us.

Let us suppose that we have found life
disappointing, if not quite intolerable — that we have
found it so either on our own account, or as
representatives of the whole race of men. We must
suppose so, since these inquiries are only for those
that have so found it. In fact many of us have found
it so, and that not once, but again and again.

What have we done each time? We have consulted
priests or astrologers, or prayed to God; these are the
popular patent remedies for the disease that afflicts
us all. And these have only postponed the crisis. And
this will be so till we pause and think.

We sought happiness through all the weary years; again and again we were on the point of winning it and making it ours for ever; but each time we were deceived; but without pausing to think — as we shall now do — we simply went on in the same old way. If now we pause and think,— the thought will occur to us, that probably we set out on the quest of happiness without a right understanding of the true nature and source of it.

First let us look at happiness itself and find out what it *is*. What we mean by happiness is something constant — something that will abide with us in all its freshness and purity so long as we ourselves exist. What the world has given us is not that, but something transient and variable, and its rightful name is pleasure. Happiness and pleasure are two entirely different things. But we assume that pleasures are the very texture of happiness; we assume that if we can provide for a constant stream of pleasures for all time we shall secure happiness.

But it is the very nature of pleasure to be inconstant; for pleasure is just our reaction to the impact of outside things. Certain things give us pleasure, and we seek to acquire and keep hold of them; but the same objects do not give equal pleasure at all times; sometimes they even give pain. Thus we are often cheated of the pleasure we bargained for, and find that we are in for pain at times; pleasure and pain are in fact inseparable companions.

The sage of Arunachala tells us that even pleasure is not from things. If the pleasure that we taste in life were really from things, then it must be more when one has more things, less when one has less, and none when one has none; but that is not the case. The rich, who have an abundance of things, are not exactly happy; nor are the poor, who have very little, exactly unhappy. And all alike, if and when they get sound, dreamless sleep, are supremely happy. To make sure of the undisturbed enjoyment of sleep we provide ourselves with every available artificial aid — soft beds and pillows, mosquito-curtains, warm blankets or cool breezes and so on. The loss of sleep is accounted a grievous evil; for its sake men are willing to poison the very source of life, the brain, with deadly drugs. All this shows how much we love sleep; and we love it, because in it we are happy.

We are thus justified in suspecting that true happiness is — as many wise men have told us — something belonging to our own inner nature. Sages have ever taught that pleasure has no independent existence; it does not reside in external objects at all; it appears to do so because of a mere coincidence; pleasure is due to a release of our own natural happiness, imprisoned in the inner depths of our being; this release occurs just when, after a rather painful quest, a desired object is won, or when a hated one is removed. As a hungry street-dog munching a bare bone, and tasting its own blood, might think the taste is in the bone, so do we assume that the pleasures we enjoy are in the things that we seek and get hold of. It may be said that desire is the cause of our being exiled from the happiness that is within us, and its momentary cessation just allows us to taste a little of that happiness for the time being.

Because we are most of the time desiring to get hold of something, or to get rid of something, we are most of the time unhappy. The desire to get rid of something is due to fear. So desire and fear are the two enemies of happiness. And so long as we are content to remain subject to them, we shall never be really happy. To be subject to desire or fear is itself unhappiness; and the more intense the desire or the fear, the keener is the unhappiness.

Desire tells us, each time, 'Now get thou this, and then you shall be happy.' We believe it implicitly and set about getting it. We are unhappy for wanting it, but we forget the unhappiness in the effort. If we do not get it, we have to suffer. Neither are we happy if we get it; for desire then finds something *else* for us to strive for, and we fail to see how desire is fooling us all the time. The fact is, desire is like a bottomless pit which one can never fill up, or like the all-consuming fire which burns the fiercer, the more we feed it.*

As desire is without end, so is fear; for the things that fear tells us to avoid are without end.

Thus we come to this conclusion; so long as desire and fear have sway over us, we shall never reach happiness. If we be content to remain in bondage to them, we must, as rational beings, renounce all hope of happiness.

---

* न जातु काम: कामानामुपभोगेन शाम्यति ।
हविषा कृष्णवर्त्मेव भूय एवाभिवर्धते ॥

— *Mahabharatam.*
See also *Guru Vachaka Kovai* vv. 371 & 592 (appendix B, vv.44 & 181).

But knowing that desire and fear are our
enemies, can we not put them away by sheer will-
power? The answer that experience gives is 'No'. We
may, like the Stoics, wrestle with them and succeed
in overcoming them for a time. But the victory does
not last, and finally we give up the fight. Without
help from someone else, we feel, we cannot hope to
achieve lasting deliverance. And who can help us, but
one that has himself conquered desire and fear, and
won for himself perfect happiness?

Such a one we must seek and find, if we are
sincerely and earnestly resolved to become free from
these our foes — the foes of happiness. He alone
can show us the path, and also give the power to
tread the path; for he knows both the goal and the
path. The ancient lore tells us — and we can now
see that it does so rightly — that one that is in
earnest for freedom must seek and reverently
question one that is himself free. He that feels
acutely the need for a remedy for the ills that are
inseparable from life cannot help seeking someone
who is competent to guide him aright; he can no
more help it, than a sick man can help going in
search of a healer.

There have been men in the past, who had won
true happiness for themselves and were thus able
to help others also; what they taught their own
disciples is recorded, more or less faithfully, in the
scriptures of the religions they are supposed to
have founded. But the records as we now find them
are incomplete, and more or less distorted by the
want of clarity of those that wrote them down; the
teachings were given orally; they were not written

down till long after the Teachers had passed away.* They cannot have for us the same value as the words heard from a living Teacher; and this not only because we can be sure that the teaching is genuine, but also — or chiefly — because the living Teacher is a centre of spiritual power, which we lack. Such a Teacher is the Sage of Arunachala.

---

* The incompleteness of the Christian Gospels appears from this: there is next to nothing in that revelation about freedom and the way to it. There is just one stray sentence in it, which shows that Jesus *must* have given such teaching to at least one disciple. In answer to the question how one can become free, the Master said: "Know the Truth and let It make you free." But there is nothing else in all the four Gospels and the rest of the New Testament, which could be of any help to the seeker of freedom. Evidently those disciples to whom Jesus taught this wisdom had no hand in the writing of the Gospels.

Chapter 3

Ignorance

THE SAGE ALONE can rightly diagnose our ills and prescribe the right remedy; he alone can unravel the tangled skein of right and wrong knowledge which fills our minds.

The first thing that the Sages tell us is that the cause of all our sufferings is in ourselves alone, not outside. The Buddha is reported to have said: "You suffer from yourselves alone; no one compels you." The Sage of Arunachala says the same thing; in answer to a question whether there is something radically wrong in the world-scheme itself, he said: "The world is all right as it is; it is we that are to blame, because of our own mistaken way of thinking; what we have to do is to trace the initial error that is at the back of our minds and pluck it out; then it will be all right."

This finding and plucking out of our fundamental error is the only radical cure there is; all other remedies are only palliatives; the utmost that can be said for them is that in their own way they help to lead us on to the right remedy. The religious faiths and practices that divide the world are of value only to this extent. Often they only enthral and weaken the mind and thus postpone the day of deliverance.

In fact from this point of view a sincere and earnest sceptic may be far better off than the bigoted believer — the kind of believer that has not the sense to see that all these religions are for humanity, not humanity for the religions; such a one holds his beliefs, not lightly and tentatively, as something that may possibly be falsified by the actual experience of the Truth — to which it is only a means, — but as the veritable Truth itself. The so-called sceptic is in truth no sceptic if he believes that there is something which is true, and that it alone matters; it is safe to say that he that is devoted to the truth is the best of all devotees. No believer is worthy of regard if he fails to perceive that truth is all in all, and that beliefs should be held sacred for the sake of the truth alone, and not otherwise. Such a one is in a much worse position than the honest and earnest sceptic, because in the first place he is very unlikely to take up the inquiry that is sketched in these chapters. In the second place, if he goes to a living Sage and seeks guidance from him, he is very likely to misunderstand what the Sage might tell him; for this reason it happens that Sages as a rule do not give out all the teachings they have in them to all questioners alike; they withhold the deeper truths from those whose minds are unopened; for a truth that is misunderstood is more fatal than sheer ignorance.* Whoever,

---

* Tradition tells us that Gautama Buddha once gave an answer by which the questioner was unsettled in his faith, as he was too immature to understand the answer aright; on another occasion, when a question was put to him by another immature visitor, he kept quiet; he later explained to a disciple that he did so, because any answer that he could give was sure to be misinterpreted.

therefore, is willing to be fully instructed by a Sage
must be prepared to put aside his own beliefs; he must
not be fanatically attached to any creed. The open-
minded disciple who has little or no book-knowledge
is thus in a better position than the learned ones with
minds enslaved by their creeds.

With open minds, then, we go to the Sage and
ask him why we are in bondage to desires and fears.
He replies that it is so, because we do not know
ourselves aright — that we think ourselves to be
something that we are not.

At the first thought it may appear that this
answer is doubly wrong. We are unable to see how a
right knowledge of ourselves can be necessary to the
business of life; we want to know how to bend this
world to our wills, or as the next best thing, how to
adjust ourselves to the world, so that we may be able
to make the best of the world, bad as it is. We do not
see how knowing ourselves aright can be of any help
to us in all this. In the second place we are fully
persuaded that we do know ourselves all right.

We believe that knowledge is of great value and
seek to know the truth about everything that we
might possibly come across in life; we are even so
fanatical in this that we want to make the acquisition
of knowledge compulsory for all. And all this
knowledge concerns the world — not ourselves. In
the course of centuries every single nation or group
of nations had piled up vast heaps of knowledge —
history, geography, astronomy, chemistry, physics,
ethics, theology, biology, sociology, and even what goes
by the proud name of philosophy or metaphysics. If
all this be knowledge, then along with the piling up

of these heaps of it there must have been a steady increase of human happiness. But this is not the case. It may be claimed that increase of knowledge has given us a greater mastery over the blind forces of Nature, and that this is all to the good. But it is not so. For this mastery has been placed by an untoward fate in the hands of a few, and the greater this mastery becomes, the deeper is the degradation and despair into which the masses sink. And the sense of their unrelieved misery cannot but poison the cup of happiness — or seeming happiness — for those among the fortunate few who are not wholly self-centred. The millennium, which the scientists of a now forgotten age prophesied, is now farther off than ever. In fact science has now brought the world to a state in which the very life of the human race is being seriously threatened. No; it is sheer wickedness — unworthy of one that aspires to a pure and untainted happiness — to contend that all this knowledge has been to the good. And this should lead us to suspect that this is no knowledge at all. We may at least suspect that happiness is not to be had through this kind of knowledge. The teaching of the Sages confirms this suspicion. The Sage of Arunachala goes even so far as to characterise all this knowledge as ignorance.

Once a young man fresh from his university — one who had studied science as his special subject — came to the Sage and asked him about the "blank wall of ignorance" which faces the scientist in his quest of the ultimate truth of the universe; investigating the infinitely small, he was just able to guess at the existence and behaviour of certain mysterious entities called electrons, protons, positrons

and neutrons, but could not get at them and know
them at first hand, not to speak of finding the *one*
ultimate substance, the cause of all; on the other hand
in his researches into the infinitely large he could
not get beyond the nebulae or star — dust, supposed
to be the raw material of creation; nor could he
discover the secret of the fundamentals of all
objectivity, namely time and space.

The Sage replied that questioning the outside
world can never lead to anything but ignorance; he
said that *when one seeks to know anything other than
himself, without caring to know the truth of himself,
the knowledge he obtains cannot possibly be right
knowledge.**

This might seem to us a very strange reason for
discrediting all human knowledge at one stroke. But
a little dispassionate thinking will make it clear that
the Sage is right. In the first place, as seen above,
this knowledge is already suspect, because it has
failed to promote human happiness. In the second
place there is nothing like a real unanimity among
those whom we regard as knowing ones. Often this
want of unanimity does not come to the knowledge of
the general public, because the great majority of those
who are supposed to know are agreed, and they make
all the noise, while the more knowing ones — who
strongly disagree from the majority — are practically
silent; and it does often happen that these are in the
right, and not the vocal majority, who are mostly
mediocre minds. The common man assumes that there
is such a thing as science apart from the scientist.

---

* See *Ulladu Narpadu* verse 11 (appendix A, verse 16).

But, as in religion or philosophy, so in science there are differences of opinion due to differences in natural intelligence and character. It was observed by Mr. Bernard Shaw that the conversion of a savage to Christianity is really the conversion of Christianity to savagery; for the savage does not cease to be one by being baptised and taught a catechism. The pursuit of truth demands on the part of a seeker certain perfections of head and heart which are certainly rare; universal education has certainly not succeeded in increasing the number of really competent investigators. Hence it is that with the same data different people come to different conclusions. Hence we must be willing to concede that the Sage may be right after all.

The reason given by the Sage is that he that would know the truth of anything whatever must first know himself aright. He means that he that does not know himself begins with an initial error, which falsifies all the knowledge he gains by his inquiries; from this error the Self-knower is free, and hence he alone is competent to find the truth of the world or of the things in the world. The quality of the would-be knower is an inescapable element in the knowledge gained by him; it would be right knowledge only if the would-be knower were rightly equipped for the quest of knowledge.

This is the true explanation of the fact — though many might deny it — that science has failed. The scientist assumes that he does not *need* to know himself aright. In any case, he starts on his enquiry into objective reality with certain notions about the self that are wrong.

But do we not know ourselves? We think we do. The average man is very positive that he knows himself aright; and it may not be possible for him to realise that he does not, even if he listens to a Sage. For it requires a very advanced and greatly purified mind even to perceive and acknowledge the fact that we do not know ourselves — that those notions about ourselves that we have cherished all along are mistaken. Sages tell us that our notions of ourselves are a mixture of truth and error.

Once a few followers of a faith which very vehemently condemns the use of 'idols' came to the Sage and started questioning him. Their aim was to obtain from him an admission that it is wrong to worship God in an idol. Their spokesman asked the Sage: "Has God any form?" The Sage said in reply: "Who says that God has form?" The questioner then said: "If God is formless, then is it not wrong to worship Him in an idol?" The Sage said: "Let God alone: tell me if *you* have a form or not." The questioner promptly answered: "Yes, *I have* a form, as you see." The Sage said: "What! Are you this body, which is about three and a half cubits in height, dark in colour and moustached and bearded?" "Yes," came the answer. "Are you this in your dreamless sleep also?" "Of course; for on waking I find myself to be the same." "Also when the body dies?" "Yes." "If so, why does not the body say to the people, when they are preparing to take it away for burial, 'No, you must not take me away. This house is mine and I want to remain here?'" Then at last the disputant realised his error; he said: "I was wrong; I am not the body; I am the life that dwells in it." Then the Sage explained:

"Look here; until now you quite seriously believed that this body is yourself; but now you see that you were wrong in this; understand that this is the initial ignorance, out of which grows inevitably *all* the ignorance that enslaves men; so long as this primal ignorance remains, it does not matter much whether you regard God as with form or formless; but when this primal ignorance goes, then with it will go all the rest." The Sage, we thus see, diagnoses the disease — bondage to desire and fears — as due to ignorance of our true selves, and the consequent false assumption that the body is the self. And this is confirmed by the observation that desire and fear arise because of the body.

Most of us are no wiser than the disputant in this dialogue. We are all of us fully persuaded that the body — which is so constantly in our thoughts and which is the object of all our anxious care — is the self. The above dialogue shows also that in this belief we are wrong.

In the above dialogue the disputant believed in the immortality of the Self and hence he could not but acknowledge that he had been mistaken. But there are the materialists and the atheists who contend that there is no Self other than the body. But when we have a Sage for our instructor, the arguments of these people do not prevail with us. For the Sage speaks with the authority of direct experience, and we are far more ready to believe him than these half-philosophers. But the Sage does not say in so many words: 'You *must* believe me, because I have first-hand knowledge of this fact'; on the contrary, he seeks to persuade us by means of

arguments based on our own experience. The full force
of these arguments may possibly be difficult to realise
until the whole of his Revelation is mastered; we shall
for the present be satisfied with a brief statement of
them. In the first place the Self has a continuous
existence in all the three states of being known to us,
namely waking, dream and sound sleep, while the
body exists only in the first two and not in the third;
this will not be quite convincing, especially to those
whose minds are deeply entangled in materialistic
ways of thinking; but even they can see that there is
a state — namely sleep — in which the Self exists
without the body.

Another argument is that the Self is the one
indubitable reality, while the reality of all other
things, — including the body and even the mind — is
in doubt; this argument will become understandable
when we go through the chapter on the world. When
we realise the full force of these arguments we shall
no more be troubled by the arguments of the
materialists.

But then one may ask: 'What about those
devotees and philosophers who profess to know that
the body is not the self, who cannot possibly believe
that the body and the self are identical, being
steadfast believers in the existence of a Self distinct
from the body? These maintain that the soul is an
extremely subtle being who inhabits the body as one
inhabits a house, using it for a time, and leaving it
afterwards to inhabit another body. Are they not, by
their steadfastness in this belief, protected from this
illusion? Are they, too, ignorant, like the disputant
in the dialogue set forth above?' It is true that they at

first believe that by their belief they are raised to a
level above the common people. But in due course
they are disillusioned; they come to see that their
knowledge is purely theoretical — not practical —
and that they are in no way better than the rest; they
find themselves still confounding the body — gross
or subtle — with the self, just as others do. If the
body be short, *they* are short; if it be tall, *they* are tall;
if it be fair, *they* are fair; if it be weak and diseased,
they themselves are so, and if it be improved and made
healthy, they themselves are made so. In the same
way they treat the mind as the self; if the mind be
alert or joyous or clear, or the opposite, they
themselves are so. The bondage to desire and fear is
not even less than before; it is perhaps even tighter
than before, on account of the added elements of self-
esteem.

We are told by the Sages that we shall cease to
identify ourselves with these bodies — and thus be
free once for all from the sufferings that come through
them — only when we attain direct experience of the
real Self. Just as we now have direct experience of
the body as the Self, so we must have direct experience
of that Self as he really is.* This ignorance is an
ingrained habit of thought, which has been bred in
the mind through a long course of wrong acting and

---

* आत्मानं चेद्विजानीयादयमस्मीति पूरुष: ।

किमिच्छन् कस्य कामाय शरीरमनुसंज्वरेत् ॥
                                — *Brihadaranyaka Upanishad*, 4.4.12.
"If one becomes conscious of the Self by the experience 'I am He,'
then for whose sake, and for desire of what thing, shall he be
fevered through the body?"

thinking. Out of it have arisen numerous attachments
to things. These thought habits form the very
structure of the mind; and the mere introduction of a
contrary thought — which is a very weak one, just
like a newly-born infant, — will make very little
difference. The mind will still flow along the same
habit-channels; it will still be subject to the same
attractions and repulsions. And this will be so
because, while it may be possible for the book-learned
philosopher to be able to feel at *times* that he is not
the body, he cannot with equal facility come to feel
that he is not the mind. And this double ignorance
will cease only when the Self is known — not
theoretically, but practically, that is, by actual
experience of the Self.

Until that realisation dawns, the philosopher
cannot be said to have thrown off his ignorance; it
survives in all its vigour. His philosophical lore does
not even make any difference in his character. In fact,
as the Sage points out,* the book-taught philosopher
is even worse off than other men; his egoism is swelled
by the pride of knowledge; his heart is beset with new
attachments — from which the illiterate are free —
which leave him no time for the enterprise of finding
the real Self; often he is even unaware of the very
urgent necessity of preparing himself for that
enterprise, by harmonising the contents of his mind,
and directing its energies towards the Self, instead
of the world. Hence it follows that he that knows the
Self from books alone, knows it no more than humbler
folk; for this reason the Sage likens him to a

---

* See *Ulladu Narpadu Anubandham* v. 36 (appendix A, v. 82).

gramophone; he is no better for his book-lore than the gramophone is for the good things it repeats.*

Books, we should remember, are no more than signposts on the road to the wisdom that makes us free; that wisdom is not in the books themselves. For the Self that we need to know is *within*, not outside; if and when the eye of wisdom is opened, the Self will be found shining in all its glory, directly, without any medium; but the study of books engenders the notion that the Self is something outside, needing to be known as an object, through the medium of the mind.

The vast confusion that prevails in philosophical and theological speculations is due, says the Sage, to this ignorance. Everyone is fully persuaded that the abstruse questions concerning the world, the soul and God can be settled finally and satisfactorily by intellectual speculation sustained by arguments drawn from *common* human experience, which is what it is because of this ignorance. Philosophers and theologians have disputed from the very beginning of creation — if there was a creation — about the first cause, the mode of creation, the nature of time and space, the truth or otherwise of the world, the conflict of fate and freewill, the state of deliverance, and so on without end; but no finality has been reached. The Sage explains to us that there can be no final conclusion — such that it cannot be upset by new, or seemingly new, arguments advanced by fresh disputants — unless and until the real Self is realised; for him that has realised that Self these controversies come to an end; but for others they must continue,

---

* See *Ulladu Narpadu Anubandham* v. 35 (appendix A, v. 81).

unless they hearken to the advice of the Sage, which is to the effect that they should leave all these questions on one side and devote themselves whole-heartedly to the quest of the Self. Either we must accept the teaching of Sages on these matters at least tentatively, so that we shall no more be diverted from the quest by these disputes, or we should recognise the profound truth that these questions are of no importance at all, and need no answer — that the one thing needed is to find the Self; for these questions arise, if at all, only to those that look upon the mind or the body as the Self.*

We thus understand that all our sufferings are due to our ignorance of the real Self. This ignorance must be removed, if we are ever to enjoy real happiness; for removal of the cause is the only radical cure there is; all else is only palliative treatment, which may even do harm in the long run by actually adding to the disease. And we can get rid of this ignorance only by actual experience of the Self.

This is no easy task; for the instrument by which we must work at it is the mind; it has to be turned aside from all else and towards the true Self; but the mind does not readily turn aside from its customary preoccupations; if forcibly turned aside it does not stay so, but soon turns back to them. This is because the mind is full of notions which are the progeny of this ignorance; and these notions naturally rise up in arms to defend the life of their parent, this ignorance; for its life is also their own. We have therefore to liquidate all these notions.

---

* See *Ulladu Narpadu* v. 34 (appendix A, v. 39).

Because these notions are the progeny of this primary ignorance, they are presumably false. And it stands to reason that false knowledge is inimical to the dawn of the Truth. Therefore also it is needful for us to examine these notions and reject them if they are found to be incorrect, or even if only doubtful; thus alone shall we be secure against traitorous outbreaks behind us, when we are engaged in the quest of the real Self.

In this examination we must be guided by absolute devotion to the Truth; the *Gita* tells us: "He that loves the Truth and subdues his whole being to the love of the Truth, shall find it."* This condition is very important. Surely there can be no partial love of the Truth; such love implies a love of untruth in greater or less degree. Perfect love of the Truth means a perfect readiness to renounce whatever shall be found to be untrue, as a result of an impartial examination. It also implies ability to submit to a thorough examination all the beliefs we now have about the world, the soul and God, without attachment to those beliefs. It is the mark of the Truth-lover that he is no more attached to his own beliefs than to those of another; he holds those beliefs tentatively and can calmly contemplate the possibility of finding that they are untenable and worthy to be renounced. It is the freedom from attachment to one's own beliefs that enables him to make an impartial examination of their validity. And if as a result of such examination he finds that they are invalid, he not only renounces them, but is ever on his guard

---

* श्रद्धावाँल्लभते ज्ञानं तत्पर: संयतेन्द्रिय: ॥   — *Gita*, 4.39.

against their possible return, until they lose their power on him. Therefore we must see to it, that we shall be devoted to the Truth and the Truth alone, untainted by errors. And for its sake we must renounce the love we bear to our present beliefs, so that the Truth may reign supreme in our hearts when we have found it.

What is known as philosophy is just this impartial scrutiny of all our notions — of the entire contents of our minds. This alone is true philosophy. All else is pseudo-philosophy; and it is safe to say that pseudo-philosophers are those who have either not understood the fact they are ignorant of the Self, or are quite content to remain in subjection to that ignorance.

We shall now consider how to make sure that in our philosophising we shall avoid the pitfalls that lurk in our path and arrive at notions which shall not be inimical to our pursuit of the Quest of the true Self.

Chapter 4

Authority

WE HAVE SEEN that before taking up the Quest of the real Self — whereby we shall become free from bondage to desire and fear — we have to prepare ourselves for it by revising our ideas and casting off those that are at all likely to hamper the pursuit of the Quest. This revision of our present ideas — as a preparation for the Quest — is called philosophy; for philosophy is a means, and not an end in itself.

But there are philosophies and philosophies. Unless it is of the right kind, it will, instead of leading us to the Quest, actually lead us deeper into the ignorance that is the cause of all our ills. The right kind of philosophy is an impartial criticism of all our present notions about the three things, the world, the soul and God. Those philosophies whose aim is to confirm these notions are inimical to success in the Quest; they are to be avoided.

Philosophy, therefore, to be really helpful, must begin with a recognition of the primary ignorance that is pointed out in the foregoing chapter. This means that all our present ideas are suspect, for the reason given by the Sage, and explained in the same chapter. They must be subjected to a thorough criticism, and replaced by other ideas which shall be unobjectionable and helpful to the Quest.

In the course of this criticism we shall need to consider the evidence for or against the validity of our ideas. But the evidence we are to rely upon must be of the right kind.

What is the right kind of evidence? Is it the common experience of men? That experience is the outcome of the primary ignorance! To rely on such evidence would only result in giving the stump of philosophical truth to the ideas we criticise. We require evidence of a different kind.

We can now understand how it happens that philosophy has earned a name for futility. It is undeniable that philosophies have as a rule failed to give us any real help in solving the riddle of life. This has been particularly so in the West. This failure was evidently due to their use of evidence of the wrong kind. They used as evidence the common experience of mankind, which, as we have seen, is bad as being the offspring of our ignorance. And they used this wrong kind of evidence, because they began their philosophies without a recognition of this ignorance. Naturally they arrived at conclusions which confirmed that ignorance and barred the way to Deliverance.

Some tell us that the body is the Self. Others say that the mind is the Self. Both agree in asserting that the world is real, and that the Self is an individual, one of a vast multitude of selves. Some there are who admit that the Self is neither the body, nor the mind as we know it, but imagine that there is a superior kind of mind which is the real Self. All these views agree in making it out that the Self is finite. But finiteness is the cause of bondage. If, as these philosophers say, the Self is really finite — finite in its very nature — then we must bid good-bye to all hope of becoming free. Thus there is no vital difference among these views. These philosophies cannot at all help us in getting rid of our primary ignorance.

He that would philosophise aright must avoid the mistakes of these philosophers. He must choose his evidence aright. He must seek and find evidence of experience which is *not* the outcome of the ignorance.

Reliable evidence, therefore, is not the experience of ignorant men, but that of the Sages, who are wholly free from this ignorance. Only on the basis of *their* experience can we build up a philosophy that would relax the grip that this ignorance now has on us, and thus make it possible for us to start on the Quest and pursue it to the very end, so that we may win similar experience for ourselves.

That the truth cannot be reached without evidence other than the experience of common humanity was felt by Prof. James of America. He sought to supply that need to the best of his power in his book *Varieties of Religious Experience*. In that book he made free use of the contents of another book, namely *Cosmic Consciousness* by Dr. Bucke. The evidence gathered into these books is that of exceptional men. But all this evidence has been treated uncritically, because the authors had no clear notion of the primary ignorance. There are at least three classes of exceptional men, and all of them are not of the same grade. That is to say, those who have given evidence of exceptional experiences belong to one of three classes,

namely Yogis, Saints and Sages. We need to
discriminate among them and find out which of these
are the proper witnesses in our inquiry.

The evidence of the Yogis is unreliable, because
they have not transcended the realm of ignorance.
This is seen in the fact that they differ among
themselves. The same is the case with the Saints. The
Sages do not differ among themselves, because they
have transcended the ignorance.

No Sage ever contradicts another Sage. Revelation
tells us that all Sages are one; we shall be able to
recognise the correctness of this teaching later on.

As between the Yogis and the Saints the latter
are far more worthy to be followed than the former,
though we need to discriminate between Saint and
Saint, because — as we shall see in the chapter on
Devotion — their views differ according to the degree
of their ripeness; the nearer they are to sagehood, the
wiser are their utterances. And there are Saints whose
utterances are of a mischievous tendency. We also find
that the Saints have moods, or rather that moods have
them, which is not the case with the Sages.

The experiences of the Yogis are highly complex
and therefore their descriptions have an irresistable
fascination for us. But the fact is, they are not even
conscious of the empire that the ignorance has over
them. Their goal is *not* the ending of the ignorance,
but the attainment, *within* the realm of the ignorance,
of a glorious status that seems to them worthy of being
striven for. They are persuaded that the mind itself
is the Self. And this is the case even when they deny
it. They believe in a blissful existence in which the
mind shall survive, though infinitely glorified and

endowed with wonderful powers. This they consider to be the highest possible gain. Some of them are more ambitious still. They hope to be able, after winning these powers, — which they wrongly call Deliverance — to obtain control over the world and then to change it beyond recognition — to erect a tangible heaven on earth. The Saints are free from these ambitions.

That neither Yogis nor Saints can have a right vision of the Truth was clearly pointed out by the Sage Sankara. In his *Viveka Chudamani* (verse 365) he tells us that the vision of the Truth obtained by non-Sages is apt to be distorted by the interference of the mind, which is not the case with the Sages.*

According to the Sages this glorified mind of the Yogis is but a body of a subtler kind. The notion that this is the Self is simply the primary ignorance in a more dangerous form. The common man is in fact in a much better state than the Yogi; for the latter has only gone deeper into the ignorance and postponed the day of Deliverance.

With all due respect, therefore, to the Yogis, we must reject their evidence. The Saints as a class are worthy of reverence. But *for the present* we must put on one side their evidence also, and build up our philosophy on the evidence of the Sages alone. But after we shall have done this, we may take up the evidence of the Saints and make a study of it in the light of the teachings of the Sages. This study has a great value for us, as we shall see in due course.

---

* निर्विकल्पसमाधिना स्फुटं ब्रह्मतत्त्वमवगम्यते ध्रुवम् ।
नान्यथा चलतया मनोगते: प्रत्ययान्तरविमिश्रतं भवेत् ॥

There have been Sages in every age down to the
present. Their testimony has come down to us
enshrined in certain books called Upanishads or
Vedantas. There are many passages in the books
which carry conviction straight to the heart. In fact it
is the Heart of all life, the Real Self, that speaks to us
in them. The student is thus simultaneously aware
of two things — that the teaching is true, and that
the teacher is a Sage.

But there can be no doubt that the earnest
disciple would prefer to these books the words of a
living Sage, if he can find one. There can be honest
doubt about the genuineness of the texts of the ancient
Revelation. But we can have none whatever of the
genuineness of the teachings of a living Sage. And
we are on much stronger ground if the Sage has
himself written down his teachings. There is also this
further advantage; if we happen to be in doubt about
the correct meaning of any passage, we can apply to
the best possible commentator, namely the giver of
the Revelation, the Sage himself.

The disciples of the Sage of Arunachala are
therefore in a much better position than those that
rely on the older books, or on pandits who have
studied those books. The Sage has written down his
teachings, and has himself explained the meanings
of some of the passages. He has also given oral
answers to a great many questions that have been
put to him from time to time, and these answers have
been recorded fairly accurately by disciples.* Of

---

* e.g. *Maharshi's Gospel*, Books I & II and *Talks with Sri Ramana
Maharshi*, etc. (— Publisher).

course, apart from these considerations, it is a great thing to attach oneself to a living Sage, as the older Revelation tells us. Those that fail to do so are losing a great chance. It is not possible for a teacher who is not a Sage — who is just a pandit and nothing more — to understand the *spirit* of the ancient Revelation. Still less is it possible for him to rouse the spiritual energies that are latent in the disciple, for the reason that he himself has not had them roused. It is necessary that the Guru or Master that is to teach us should himself be the embodiment of that Wisdom which he is to impart to us.

The teaching of our Sage is therefore for us the new Revelation. And for the reasons pointed out, this Revelation is the most authoritative for us. We should take it as the chief basis of our philosophy, and utilise the older Revelation also, in so far as it may serve to explain or complete the teaching.

There is, of course, the unexpressed view of orthodox pandits, namely that the ancient Revelation is the primary authority, and that the words of a living Sage are authoritative only as echoes of that Revelation. We shall come to this view later on. Just now we shall seek to obtain a clear and rational notion of what is known as *authority*.

Authority is just the testimony of the Sages, giving us an idea of their own experience of the True Self, transcending the ignorance. It is called authority, because it is the only reliable evidence we can have about the True Self and the state of deliverance, so long as we ourselves are subject to that ignorance.

There is an apparent conflict between authority and reason. A European student of philosophy who for some

years sat at the feet of the Sage once remarked to the
Sage that, as *history* shows, this is the 'age of reason,'
and hence it is necessary that the teaching we shall
listen to and accept must be in accordance with reason.
The Sage replied as follows: "*Whose is the intellect?* You
must answer '*My* intellect.' So the intellect is *your* tool,
You use it for measuring variety. It is not yourself, nor
is it something independent of yourself. *You* are the
abiding reality, while the intellect is just a phenomenon.
You must find and get hold of yourself. There is no
intellect in dreamless sleep. There is none in a child.
The intellect develops with age. But how could there be
any development or manifestation of the intellect
without the seed of it in sleep or childhood? Why go to
history to discover the fundamental fact? The degree of
truth in history is the same as the degree of truth in the
historian."

We may put it this way. The usefulness of the
intellect is limited by its origin, namely the primary
ignorance. To those that are unaware of their subjection
to this ignorance, and to those also who are content to
remain in subjection to it, the intellect is a good enough
tool for all their purposes. That is to say, it is an
excellent tool in the service of that ignorance. But for
the purpose of transcending it, it is of little use. The
utmost that the intellect can do for us is to recognise
its own limitations and cease to hinder our Quest of
the Truth. This it can do as soon as it begins to realise
the fact of its own tainted origin and of the necessity of
relying on the evidence of the Sages as a step in aid of
the Quest, by which an authentic Revelation of the
True Self can be won. Thus the conflict between reason
and Revelation is only apparent.

Our reliance on the testimony of the Sages is not unreasonable, also because such reliance is only *tentative*. The Sages tell us about the real Self and the way to obtaining the direct Experience of that Self, *not* that we may blindly believe whatever they tell us, but that we may verify their teaching by our own Experience of the truth of that Self. The essential part of their teaching is not what they tell us about the State of Deliverance or the true nature of the Self, but what they tell us about the *method* of winning that State. That is why this Sage always tells the disciple, to begin with, that he must find the Self by means of the Quest taught by himself. Whatever else he teaches is auxiliary to the Quest. And we are to accept all this teaching only tentatively, so that we may be able to take up the Quest and carry it through to the point of success.

All sense of conflict between reason and faith in the Guru will vanish as we proceed in the study of the teaching. The Sages as a rule appeal to our own experience as worldly men; and the Sage of Arunachala is no exception. It is true, as we saw already, that our experience is discredited as the offspring of the primary ignorance. But even out of it the Sages are able to pick out facts that make it easier for us to accept their teaching, revolutionary as it seems to be at almost every step. The light that they shed on our own past experience enables us to see that, in truth, there is no real conflict between faith and reason.

This being the true nature of what has been called authority, it follows that in the last resort everyone is his own authority. Before accepting the teaching of a Sage as authoritative, he must decide for himself

whether or not he *is* a Sage — a person having
intimate Experience of the Real Self, and established,
by virtue of that Experience, in the State of
Deliverance, which he himself wants to attain. He
must come to the conclusion that the person in
question is in the enjoyment of unalloyed and
uninterrupted happiness, due to his freedom from
desire and fear, the two enemies of happiness. The
disciple is not asked to surrender his reason, until he
finds one to whom he can surrender it with the
prospect of incalculable gain. The Sage to whom he
makes this surrender becomes his Guru or Master.

It is not possible to lay down clear rules to guide
the novice in the delicate business of recognising a
Sage. And it may be said that no rules are really
necessary. He that is destined to find a Sage and to
become his disciple will find no practical difficulty in
recognising him when he finds him. For those that are
not so destined, rules will be of little use. Divine Grace
plays a decisive part in the process by which the Sage
is recognised as such and accepted as one's own Guru.
But when once the choice is made, the disciple can use
the available tests of sagehood, in order to *confirm* his
choice. The chief test is serenity and unruffled
happiness, which is the same as perfect peace. Another
test is egolessness, and this is proved chiefly by
indifference to praise and censure, as noted before.
Other tests will appear in the course of this exposition.

We shall now discuss the notion of authority,
which is upheld by the orthodox pandit, who has not
sat at the feet of a Sage. This notion is as follows.
There are certain books which are unquestionably
authoritative in their entirety, because they are of

divine origin. Every sentence or clause of a sentence
in them is divine, and it is not permissible to us to
doubt their authenticity and authority. It is said that
the books 'prove themselves' — that they are
'*svatahpramanam.*' In this sense authority is a kind
of spiritual dictatorship imposed from without. The
subservience of the seeker of the Truth goes further
still. Not only must he accept the sacred lore as
authoritative, but he must also bind himself in
advance to accept the interpretations of disputed
passages which these pandits offer.

This notion is one of the many untoward effects
of the organisation of religions into churches or
hierarchies. It must be said that this notion is good
enough for the man who is content to live and die in
ignorance. He that wills to rise above it needs
authority of a different kind.

Even the sacred lore is of relative value* and
needs evidence of some kind to prove its worth. There
is only one thing that proves itself, namely the Self.

The upholders of the orthodox view do not recognise
the testimony of a living Sage as having any authority
of its own. They believe that a special sacredness
attaches to the ancient lore, and that no additions can
be made to it.

But the truth is the other way about. The reason
for the authoritative nature of the ancient lore is the
fact that it contains passages, which are more or less
faithful records of the testimony of Sages that lived
in the past. And Sages are the same at all times. As
the ancient lore itself tells us, they are not in time,

---

* See *Guru Vachaka Kovai* verse 147 (appendix B, verse 82).

but transcend it. Further in the sacred lore we have
the injunction that we should receive instruction from
a living Sage. The truth is that the Sage is not a
person, but an embodiment of Divinity, as the *Gita*
(7.18) tells us in the words ज्ञानी त्वात्मैव, "The Sage is
Myself"; and this — which is one of the fundamental
teachings of the ancient lore — seems to be
insufficiently understood by the pandits.

Besides, the most natural way for us is to start with
the teaching of a living Sage; for we are able to determine
by our intuitive perception whether the teacher is a Sage
or not. We cannot thus judge any Sage of the past.

Besides, we can never be *quite* sure that the books
as we now find them are a faithful record of what the
Sages had said. It seems probable that these books
are made up of the actual utterances of Sages *and*
other passages composed by philosophers who were
not Sages. It would seem that the evidentiary texts
remained unrecorded for a long time before they were
incorporated into the books. During the interval the
texts must have been preserved by oral tradition,
which may account for the fact that the same passages
occur in different books, but with variations.

The claim that is made for the ancient lore is
based on its being prior in time. But priority in time
is no consideration at all in any inquiry in which the
validity of time itself as an objective reality is in
question, as we shall see in due course.

Our first reliance therefore shall be on the
testimony of the Sage of Arunachala; we shall make
use of the ancient lore by way of amplification or
commentary.

Chapter 5

The World

WE HAVE SEEN that the truth of the Self will reveal Itself when the mind persists in the Quest of the Self, actuated by the resolve to find that Truth. This the mind can do if it be not deflected from the Quest by extraneous thoughts. The mind that is not so deflected is an apt instrument for finding the Self. In the case of the Sage of Arunachala the mind was such an apt instrument, because it was untainted by desires or attachments which could raise a current of thoughts diverting the mind from the Quest. For such a one it is unnecessary to engage in discussions about the world. Says the Sage: *"Of what use are disputes about the world, saying that it is real, that it is an illusory appearance, that it is conscious, that it is insentient, that it is happy, that it is miserable? All men alike love the Egoless State, which is won by turning away from the world and knowing the untainted real Self which transcends the assertions that It is one or that It is manifold.**

Here the Sage makes a statement which at first would seem to be inaccurate. He says that *all* of us are lovers of the Egoless State, which is to be won by

---

* *Ulladu Narpadu* verse 3 (see appendix A, verse 8).

turning aside from the world; and since we are to turn
our backs on the world after all, it does not matter to
us what the world may be. But few are the persons
who have heard of the Egoless State. And still fewer
are those that *want* that State. What then does the
Sage mean by saying that all men without exception
are devotees of that State?

The Sage himself has furnished the explanation,
which is in perfect harmony with the teachings of
the ancient lore. It is as follows. It is true that not all
are *conscious* lovers of the Egoless State. But
unknowingly they do love that State. And they show
that love by their great partiality to a state which
has great resemblance to the Egoless one, namely the
state of dreamless sleep. This state is far inferior to
the Egoless State, as we shall see later. It is a happy
state, but its happiness bears no comparison at all
with that of the Egoless State. However, it is exactly
similar to the Egoless State in being egoless and
worldless. It will be seen later that its egolessness is
imperfect. Because it is egoless, it is also worldless;
and this it is that makes it happy. The Sage tells us
that one that is in love with sleep, in spite of its
imperfection, cannot be heard to say that he does not
love the Egoless State. For this reason, if only we knew
what it is that we really want, it would be unnecessary
for us to discuss the world. It is the Self that should
interest us, not the not-Self. Therefore, says the Sage,
it is absurd to investigate the not-Self, as it would be
absurd for a barber to scrutinise the heaps of shorn
hair, instead of putting it in the dust-bin.*

_____

* See *Guru Vachaka Kovai* verse 1076 (appendix B, verse 212).

All inquiries about the not-Self are vain, if not mischievous, because it delays the main enterprise, the Quest of the Self. And this is so, even if one arrives at the correct conclusion about the nature of the world, if he does not then at least commence that Quest.

But for those that are in earnest to find the Self, without being able to pursue the Quest with one-pointed mind, this inquiry is neither unnecessary nor undesirable. The necessity arises thus. Most men, even those that are in earnest to be delivered from bondage, are hindered in the pursuit of the Quest by unwanted thoughts that arise and fill the mind.

The habitual flow of the mind is towards the world, not towards the Self; even when one succeeds in turning the mind away from the world and concentrating it on the Self, it breaks loose and wanders back to the world.

But why do thoughts intrude into the mind even when they are not wanted? The Sages say it is because we have the belief that the world is real.

The Sage of Arunachala tells us in one of his compositions that but for our belief that the world is real, it would be quite easy for us to obtain the Revelation of the Self.[†] The greatest wonder, says the Sage, is this — that, being always the real Self, *we* are striving to *become* one with Him.[*] He tells us that a day will dawn when we will have to laugh at our present efforts to that end. But that which will be realised on that day of laughter exists even now as the Truth. For we are not to *become* that Self; we are He.

---

† See Appendix B, Verse 4.
* See *Guru Vachaka Kovai* verse 622 (appendix B, verse 96).

It may be asked what this belief of ours has to do with the Quest. One reason is this. Whatever we hold to be real has an unquestionable right of entry into the mind; thoughts regarding realities cannot be denied admittance by a mere fiat of the will. But that is not all. We now regard the world as real in a sense in which it is not real. And by so regarding it we make it impossible for ourselves to realise the Self, until we give up our false belief. It so happens that the very thing that obscures the Self for us is the world itself.

How can that be? The Sages tell us that the Self is the Reality underlying the world; just as, when a rope is mistaken for a snake, the snake obscures the rope, so the world obscures the Self. There is only one Reality, which in our ignorance appears to us as the world, and will appear as it really is, as the Self, when we transcend the ignorance. When we shall Experience the Truth, we shall find that what now appears to us as this multiple world of names and forms in time and space is just the real Self, who is the indivisible Reality, nameless, formless, timeless, spaceless and changeless. And it is axiomatic that appearance excludes the reality; as long as the rope is supposed to be a snake, it cannot appear as the rope it really is; the false snake effectually conceals the real rope. The same is the case with the Self. So long as the Self appears to us as the world, we shall not realise Him as the Self; the world-appearance effectually conceals the Self; and it will do so until we get rid of the appearance; and we cannot do so unless we understand that the world-appearance is unreal. For this reason the Reality — which is also the Self — is practically non-existent for him that believes the world to be real, just as the rope is non-existent for him that sees it as a snake. For this reason he is a *nastika* (atheist), even though he may honestly believe that there is a Reality.

Thus it happens that, because of this false belief, the Self, who is infinitely great and blissful, and who is our dearest possession, if we may call Him a possession, is for the time being lost to us. And what greater loss can there be?

But the idea of a self is innate to us. It is not open to us even to doubt the existence of a self of some sort. The Self is the only indubitable reality there is; if anyone questions the reality of the Self, he would at once put himself out of court; to be able to raise any question at all, he must admit he exists. Therefore it happens that, feeling the void due to the obscuring of the real Self, we fill it up with a false self.

But since the world is taken as real, and we are unable to think of any reality beyond the world, we have to locate this hypothetical self *in* the world. And this can be only by identifying the Self with the body. And as there are two bodies, the physical or gross one and the mental or subtle one, we cannot escape taking one or both of them as the Self. It needs to be understood that in both ways we fall into ignorance; the real Self is neither the body nor the mind, as we shall see later. By this ignorance we are disabled from conceiving of a real Self transcending both mind and body. Thus unless we are willing to renounce the belief that the world is real *as such* — that is, as the *world* — we shall never realise the real Self that the Sages have testified to. And this means that to get rid of the primary ignorance we must renounce the belief that

the world is real, unless our minds are of such
exceptional purity and harmony that we can put away
all thought about the world and the body while
engaged in the Quest. Therefore we need to listen to
what the Sages tell us about the world, and accept
their teaching at least as tentatively true.

The Sage of Arunachala tells us that the world
is both real and unreal; and he tells us also that there
is no self-contradiction in this. The world is real in
one sense and unreal in another. The world is real
because that which appears as the world is the
Reality, which is the real Self; it is unreal, because,
considered as world, it is a mere appearance of the
Reality. Apart from the Reality the world has no
existence. But its appearance as the world does not
affect the Reality; for It never really became the world,
just as the rope never really became a snake.

Thus we are taught that the world *as such* is
unreal. It is not wholly unreal, because there is
something — the Reality, the Self — behind the false
appearance. The meaning is that the Reality, being
obscured by the world, does not appear to us as It
really is. This teaching is briefly referred to as *maya-
vada*; the world is declared to be *maya*, an illusory
appearance of the Reality. *Maya* may be defined as
that mysterious Power which makes the Real appear
as something which It is not.

This teaching has come in for a great deal of
violent criticism. It is asserted that the teaching is
not to be found in the Upanishads — that it is an
invention of more recent writers, which was adopted
by Bhagavan Sri Sankara. For us, the controversy is
set at rest by the testimony of the Sage of Arunachala.

The teaching that the world is *maya* only states a principle known to and admitted by all, namely that *things are not what they seem.* Modern science, especially physics, has gone far towards confirming it as the fundamental principle of matter. Whereas the Reality is One, indivisible, unchangeable, untainted, formless, timeless and spaceless, our minds picture It as manifold, broken up into an infinite number of fragments, subject to change, tainted by desire, fear and sorrow, confined in forms, and limited in time and space. This rather long and complicated statement is summarised by the statement that *all this is maya.* The school of Vedanta which accepts this teaching is called *Advaita.*

Those that are repelled by this teaching are not asked to accept it. It is offered *only* to those that have realised that the cause of bondage is ignorance, and earnestly desire to get rid of it. Their point of view is fundamentally different from that of other people, and the teaching given to them is naturally different.

The merit of this teaching lies in its giving us a synthesis of two apparently unconnected teachings of the ancient lore, namely that the Reality is the material Cause of the world, and that it remains unaffected, transcending all duality. Those that are determined to believe that the Reality has *really* become all this multiplicity are not called upon to accept the teaching; for them the ancient lore and Sages have provided other ways of spiritual progress. The Sages are not at all annoyed if these people assert that *their* way is alone the right way. But if ignorance is to be transcended, there is no escape from accepting this teaching; for if the world be real as such, there

would be no unchangeable Reality, without which
there can be no Deliverance.

Thus the teaching about the world is really twofold. But that part of the teaching which says that
the real Self is the Truth underlying the world
appearance, is separable from the other part. Besides,
the latter part — namely that the world is not real as
such — is of greater value to us to begin with, because
it serves as an antidote to the false belief that the
world is real as such. The former part of the teaching
is also more difficult of comprehension. Hence the
Sages recommend the cultivation of the belief that
the world is unreal, even though it is not the *whole*
truth about the world. Those who are unable to
assimilate the whole teaching would be on the safe
side if they accept that part of it which says that the
world is unreal.

This will be the safe course, because the
alternative to the view of the world's unreality often
is that the world is real as world. For the average
mind is so made that it cannot be held in suspense on
any question that is raised; it must have an answer
one way or other to any question that is raised.

Reasons for the view that the world is unreal as
such are given in ample measure. We shall now
consider these.

The first reason is the fact of the ignorance that
is at the root of all our experience. Once the Sage was
asked the following question: "How can I accept the
teaching that the world — which I am sensing all the
time in so many ways — is not real?" The Sage
answered: "This world, which you try to prove to be
real, is all the time mocking at you for seeking to know

it, without your first knowing yourself!" If once we realise that we do not know ourselves aright, how can we pretend that we know the world aright? The Sage has expressed this argument as follows: *"How can the knowledge of objects arising in relative existence to one that knows not the truth of himself, the knower, be true knowledge? If one rightly knows the truth of him named 'I', in whom both knowledge and its opposite subsist, then along with ignorance (relative) knowledge also will cease."**

To one that can feel the full force of this argument no further discussion is needful. The teaching that the world is not real as such will become self-evident as soon as one comes to feel that ignorance of the Self is the one source of all worldly knowledge. But meanwhile some more detailed discussion of the question will be useful.

The second reason is that our belief that the world is real as such is *not* based on any reliable evidence. We shall presently discuss the evidence offered in proof of the reality of the world. But first we need to meet an objection that may be raised.

It may be objected that in asserting that there is no satisfactory proof of the reality of the world we are simply throwing the burden of proof on the other side — on him that says that the world is real. The answer to this is that the burden of proof *does* lie on him that asserts the existence of the world; the burden of proof does *not* lie on him that denies its existence. In courts of law it is a rule of evidence that the burden of proof lies on him that *asserts* something, not on him that is

---

* *Ulladu Narpadu* verse 11 (see appendix A, verse 16).

content with a denial of the assertion; and this is a
perfectly sound rule. There is no reason why a
different rule should be observed in philosophy. The
reason for this rule is that a denial is usually
incapable of proof, while an assertion of something
positive — as that something exists — is capable of
proof. The one that denies is thus entitled to win his
case if the assertor is not able to let in clear evidence
of the existence of the thing asserted by him. If the
assertor fails to adduce clear and unobjectionable
evidence to prove his case, the judgement will go
against him. Thus the burden of proof is rightly
thrown on those that contend that the world is real
as such. We shall examine the evidence that is
adduced by them, and if the evidence be inconclusive,
we shall have to conclude that their case is baseless.

Of course there is the clear evidence of the
Sages which is decisive; but we need not refer to it
for the present.

Before we begin this discussion we need to set up a
standard of reality which shall be rigorously applied.
We cannot make use of the standard of reality that is in
common use, because it is an instrument of the primal
ignorance that vitiates all our knowledge. We must go
to the Sages for a standard of reality that would guide
us aright. This standard of reality is thus expressed:
*That alone is real which exists unchanged and without
intermission.* This means that things whose existence
is limited by time or space, are not real. This test of
reality has been handed down from time immemorial
and is found recorded in the *Bhagavad Gita* (Ch. II, 16)
as follows: नासतो विद्यते भावो नाभावो विद्यते सत: "Existence
never belongs to the unreal, nor does non-existence

The unreality of the world should be understood by us — so we are told by the Sage — by means of three analogies, namely the rope mistaken for a serpent, the waste land on which a mirage appears, and dreams. The Sage has told us that all the three analogies are necessary and should be taken together; for the truth we seek is transcendent and cannot be explained adequately by means of a single analogy.*

We have seen the use of the first analogy. But when a rope is first mistaken for a serpent, and then recognised to be a rope, the serpent *ceases* to appear. That does not seem to be the case with the world. Even when it is known that the world is only an appearance of the real Self, the world continues to appear. This is the objection raised by one that has heard the teaching and been more or less convinced. The correct explanation is that mere theoretical knowledge does not dissolve the world-appearance, but only the actual Experience of the Self. But this explanation may be premature at this stage. Hence the Sage seeks to convince us that a false appearance may continue to be seen even after it is known that the thing is false. This is illustrated by the analogy of the waste land on which a mirage is seen. The mirage is a false appearance, just like the snake. But it continues to be seen even after it is known that there is no water in the place. We thus see that the mere fact of an appearance persisting is no proof that

---

* It must be remembered that analogies are not proof, and no Sage thinks that he is proving anything by means of analogies. The teachings of the Sages are authoritative because they are Sages. Analogies are used by them as a means of helping us to understand the teaching.

it is real. But then a further doubt arises. The disciple says, the case of the mirage is distinguishable; the water of the mirage is conceded to be unreal, because even though it does not cease to appear after the truth of it becomes known, its unreality is proved by the water not being available for quenching thirst; the world is not so, because it continues to serve innumerable purposes. The Sage dispels this doubt by appealing to the experience of dreams. The things that are seen in dreams are useful; food eaten in a dream satisfies dream-hunger. In this respect the state of waking is in no way superior to the dream-state; the use of dream-objects seems as valid within the dream, as the use of waking-objects seems valid within the waking state. A man that has just eaten a full meal goes to sleep and dreams that he is hungry, just as a dreamer, having eaten a full dream-meal, wakes hungry. Both are proved false in sleep. This much we have seen from the dream-analogy, that a thing may seem to satisfy a need, and yet may be an illusion. The fact is, the need and its satisfaction are *both equally* unreal.

We thus understand that the world is not real as such, because it does not satisfy that test of reality given by the Sages.

There are a great many religions which do not accept this teaching, which is intended to lift the seeker of the Truth out of the morass of ignorance from which he wants to escape. Every one of these religions is based on a set of beliefs or creeds, in which more or less of the ignorance that sustains bondage is incorporated. For this reason the adherents of these religions are unable to accept this teaching. They seek to refute it. But in doing so, they are up against the standard of Reality that has been given to us by the Sages. They seek to overcome the difficulty in two ways. They deny the standard. All the same they feel that it is the right one, and seek to prove that the world is real according to that standard also. In doing so they are still uneasy, and relieve their consciences by inventing degrees of reality, a most unphilosophical device, condemned by all the Sages.

It may be here noted that a concession is made to human weakness by the Sages. The world is unreal from the point of view of the absolute Truth, but it is *as good as real* so long as ignorance retains its sway over our minds.*

Thus it happens that these believers have no real grievance against the Sages. The teaching does *not* mean that the world is not real for those that fully believe that the body or the mind is the self, — who do not feel that this is ignorance, and do not at all want to get rid of it. The ancient lore is twofold. One part of it is addressed to those who are not conscious of being in ignorance, and therefore have no use for a teaching intended to dispel that ignorance. The other part of the ancient lore is addressed to those that *are* conscious of the ignorance and are in earnest to escape from it. These two parts are quite distinct. But this feature of the ancient Revelation is not known to these believers. Besides they are offended by the inevitable corollary that theirs is a lower position; they also feel

---

* The Truth as taught by the Sages is *paramarthika*; the Truth as conceived in ignorance is *vyavaharika*; of course the latter is untruth as viewed in strict philosophy.

it a grievance that the world, which they believe to
be real, should be dismissed as unreal, and often want
to quarrel with us who are followers of the Sages; we
however have no quarrel with them, as the Sages have
pointed out, because we realise that for *them* it is all
right to believe as they do, and, so believing, to make
the best of the world while it lasts. They are like
dreamers who are persuaded that their dreams are
real, and do not want to awake. *We* have begun to see
that this worldly life is only a dream, because the
Sages tell us so; and we want to awake.

   That the world has no existence of its own is
stated by the Sage as follows: *The world and the mind
arise and set together as one; but of the two the world
owes its appearance to the mind alone; That alone is
real in which this (inseparable) pair, the world and
the mind, has risings and settings: that Reality is the
one infinite Consciousness, having neither rising nor
setting.**

   We are thus reminded of a fact not unknown to
us, but of which the importance has till now escaped
us. The world begins to appear just when the mind
comes into being, after remaining merged and lost in
sleep; it continues to appear only so long as the mind
continues to function; it disappears with the mind
when the latter is dissolved in sleep; it is seen again
only when the mind comes again into being on
waking. When the mind is lost in sleep, there is no
world-appearance. From this it follows that neither
the mind nor the world is real. This is so, not only
because they do not appear continuously, but also

---

* *Ulladu Narpadu* verse 7 (see appendix A, verse 12).

because they have no existence of their own, independently of the Reality, in which their risings and settings take place. Here also the standard of reality as defined by the older Sages is clearly accepted and applied.

It may perhaps be contended that the world does not appear only because there is no mind or senses to perceive it. The answer is very simple. It is true that in sleep there is no mind; but WE are there. And if the world were real, what is there to prevent its appearing to US? That there is no mind or sense-organs in sleep, is no reason for the world not being seen. The real Self does not need any medium to see whatever is real. The sacred lore tells us that the Self is the Eye of Consciousness[†], by which alone the mind and the senses are able to perceive; His power of being aware of reality, say all the Vedantas, is never lost. We do not see the world in sleep, because the world does not exist.

The Sage has also said the same thing in a different form. "The world is not other than the body, the body is not other than the mind; the mind is not other than the Primal Consciousness; the Primal Consciousness is not other than the Reality; That exists unchanging, in Peace."[*]

The question may be asked how we can be sure of the existence of the Reality, which is here said to be the Source from which mind and world arise, and into which they set. The answer is that this unreal

---

[†] This teaching is given later on in this chapter, where it is shown that forms are unreal.

[*] *Guru Vachaka Kovai* verse 99 (see appendix B, verse 19).

pair cannot appear and disappear without something real in which they can have their risings and settings.

Our chief difficulty in accepting this teaching is this. We have become accustomed to the thought that the world exists *outside* of us, and that we ourselves are the body, or that we are the mind, which is in the body. We have also assumed that the mind is an exceedingly small thing as compared with the world, and that makes it difficult for us to conceive how this wide world can be in the mind, or can be one with the mind. This difficulty is connected with another of our false assumptions, namely that time and space are real, because time and space are inseparable elements of the world-appearance. When the world appears, it does so with time and space, and when it vanishes in sleep or in the Egoless State, time and space do not remain.

The simple solution of the difficulty lies in this, that all these assumptions are out-growths of the primary ignorance, the ego-sense, and are therefore discredited.

Because of this notion, namely that the world is outside of us and consists of objects perceived through our sense-organs, the world is taken to be an *objective* reality, as opposed to mere thoughts, which are admitted to be subjective, and therefore unreal.

The Sages tell us that this objectivity is a gratuitous assumption — that in fact the world exists only in the mind. The Sage of Arunachala states the position thus: *"The world is nothing but the five sensations, namely sounds and the rest of its kind; thus the world consists of the objects of the five sense-organs, the one mind becomes aware of these five sensations through the five senses. That being the case,* *how can the world be other than the mind?"**

Here the Sage draws our attention to a fact upon which philosophers of all grades are now agreed — thanks to the elaborate demonstration by Immanuel Kant — namely that what all we perceive is not the world itself, whose reality is in question, but an ever-shifting mass of sensations, namely sounds, contacts, forms, tastes and smells. That these sensations are *not* outside — *if* there be any outside at all — but only inside, that is, in the mind, is undeniable: this is freely admitted, even by some scientists, who do not profess to be philosophers. They are thoughts arising in the mind. Along with these thoughts arises the thought that there is an outside in which things exist, which are the origin of these sensations; it may be noted that an exactly similar conviction arises during dreams also and persists in full force until the dreams come to an end. Those that maintain the objective reality of the world are bound to prove by unobjectionable evidence that these sensations are really caused by objects existing outside, because the burden of proof lies on them. The presumption is against their case, for the reason shown by the Sages.

The world, they say, is real; they contend that it does not become unreal simply because it does not appear to some who are unable to see it, being asleep. They allege that while some are asleep, others keep awake and see the world; so the world is being seen all the time by someone or other. They add up the waking states of all persons whom they suppose to exist as distinct individuals, and thus

---

* *Ulladu Narpadu* verse 6 (see appendix A, verse 11).

make out that there is a continuous world-
appearance. And this, they say, proves that the
world is real. If a person awaking from sleep
remembers that he did not see the world during
sleep and thus doubts whether the world existed
during the time he slept, he has only to ask someone
who remained awake and learn from him that the
world was seen by him during the interval.

The evidence is inconclusive; in fact it is not
evidence at all. Let us take the case of a sleeper who
on waking wants to ascertain by unimpeachable
evidence whether or not the world continued to exist
during the time he slept; let us even suppose that
this inquirer assumed that time existed when he slept,
and is therefore real. He is asked to accept the
evidence of those that did not sleep at the time. But
these 'witnesses' are themselves part of the world
whose reality is in question; the sleeper doubts the
reality of the world because it did not appear to him
in sleep, even though the world has begun to appear
again on his waking. Does not this doubt cover these
'witnesses' also? He was not aware of them in his
sleep, as the Sage pointed out to an objector. Therefore
their reality is as doubtful as the reality of the world
as a whole. How is that doubt to be dispelled? For the
awakened sleeper to admit them as witnesses, there
must be some *independent* evidence to prove that *they*
are real. No such evidence is offered. He is supposed
to accept their reality simply because he sees them;
that he had seen them before he slept does not make
any difference, because the same is the case of the
world. Thus the argument is simply a subtle way of
begging the question. The presumption that the world

is unreal is not only unaffected, but strengthened. It is as near conclusive proof as can be expected.

There is another argument for the objectivity of the world, namely, that it appears the same to all observers. It is questionable whether the world appears the same to all. It is common experience that there are wide differences among men in their views of the world. But let us suppose that there is substantial agreement among all observers. The Sage tells us that this argument is invalid, because it involves the false assumption that there are different observers. He explains the apparent 'agreement among observers' as being due to the fact that there is only *one* observer in all of them; hence the uniformity of the world-appearance is not due to the reality of the world; thus the argument fails.

The truth is this. The mind itself by its own power of self-deception creates hypothetical world corresponding to its sensations, along with the container of the world, an 'outside,' — and projects it into the 'outside'. This creation and projection are involuntary and unconscious processes, and hence the mind never questions the existence of an outside and of an objective world in this outside. If the mind consciously and deliberately created the world, it would be able to create a much pleasanter world; it is unable to do this, because the process of creation is not conscious. This we see in dreams; there the mind creates its own dream-world; but it is no pleasanter than this waking world; often it is worse, as in nightmares, which are like hell.

That the mind has this power of self-deception, itself creating a world and being deceived by it, is

what we see in actual experience. We have just now
seen that this power is the cause of dreams. The
dream-world appears real while the dream lasts; if
in the dream the dreamer doubts the reality of what
he sees and tries to find out the truth, he always
concludes, not that he is dreaming, but that he is
wide awake. In fact Nature never allows any one to
go on dreaming and at the same time know that he
is dreaming.

But this power can be seen at work in waking
too. By its power of abstraction, the mind can impart
to whatever it imagines a semblance of reality, by
which it is itself deceived for the time being, just as
in dreams. The sense of reality varies according to
the concentration of the mind and the consequent
vividness of the mental images created. When
witnessing a well-planned and well-acted play on a
stage, we are deceived into a belief, however short-
lived, that what we see is real. The same thing
happens when we are reading a novel written by a
great literary artist. In both these cases the characters
and events have no real existence. But they rouse
powerful emotions in us, because of the illusion of
reality created by the artist and assisted by our own
imagination. If the illusion be feeble, — as when the
skill of the artist is not up to the mark — the emotions
aroused — if any — are also feeble, and we are not
deceived. It is a fact that so far as unintentional
creation is concerned, all living beings are endowed
with a higher degree of artistic skill than any artist
that has ever existed.

We think that children have a much higher degree
of this power than adults. We fail to notice the same

power in ourselves, because our mental creations are
disciplined by the drill at school and in the drudgery
of life into a degree of uniformity with the creations of
other minds, whose very existence is itself a creation
of mind. We are aware of this self-deception in every
case in which it comes to an end, as on waking from a
dream, on laying down a book, or on the curtain falling
on a play. When however the illusion is not lifted,
naturally we are unable to see that we are being
deceived. The only way to end this self-deception is to
win the direct experience of the real Self. There is no
other way. We shall see later, when we discuss the
three states of our life in ignorance in contradistinction
from the Egoless State, that the Experience is the
waking from this dream of relativity and bondage.

The Sage has given us further proofs of the
untenability of the belief in the reality of the world
as such. Distinctions and variety are the very life and
soul of the world-appearance. All these are the
progeny, says the Sage, of the primal ignorance.
Among these distinctions we find time and space.

Have we any proof that time and space are objective
realities? If there be no proof to that effect, then it will
be ridiculous to contend that the world is real as such.

Philosophers of the West from the time of Kant*
have been familiar with the theory that space, time
and causality are the mind's creation.

Recent developments in physical science,
beginning with the theory of relativity enunciated by

---

* Kant may be said to have given a logical proof of the philosophical
principle of *relativity*. This principle is not new; it is the starting
point of Vedantic philosophy.

Einstein, make the case stronger still. But the strongest argument against the truth of time and space is that given to us by the Sage of Arunachala, which we shall study in due course.

According to Einstein time and space are not two distinct realities; there is only one thing that can be said to exist, namely space-time, not two things, space *and* time. But this 'space-time' is never directly experienced; it is just a hypothetical entity which is assumed by physicists in order to help them to understand — or think they understand — physical phenomena. No layman — no one who is not a mathematical physicist — can ever understand this 'space-time.' The world thus conceived is no longer an objective reality, but an abstraction represented by a mathematical equation.[†]

Thus the scientists have proved to us that time and space are illusions arising in a thing called space-time. But this new entity has not even the testimony of sense-experience in its favour.

We shall now see what we can learn from the Sage; he is emphatic that neither time nor space is real. He says: *Where are time and space apart from the sense of 'I'? If we were the same as bodies, then it could be said that we are in time and space. But are we bodies? We are the same at all times and in all*

---

† This is known as the theory of *Relativity*. This term, if it has any meaning, conveys the sense that neither time nor space has any existence of its own; each exists — or seems to exist — only in constant relation to and association with the other. The theory corroborates the advaitic teaching that time and space are mental.

places; hence we are that Reality which transcends time and space."

Time and space are mental forms, coming into existence subjectively *after* the ego-sense. In sleep there is neither time nor space. When we awake there sprouts up the ego, saying 'I am the body'; it thus creates time and space and locates therein the body and the world. When the ego sets in sleep, all these things cease also. Therefore it is said that *time and space have no existence apart from the ego*; and the ego and the mind are practically the same. Therefore they are mental. If it be objected that we have the experience of being bound and held in time and space, the Sage answers that this is an illusion, due to the notion 'I am the body'; the body alone is in time and space. What then are we? What is our true nature? The Sage tells us that we are neither the body nor the mind, but the eternal 'I am', which is unchangeable, and which runs like a thread through the succession of thoughts; in every thought there is this 'I am'. 'I am young', 'I am grown-up', 'I am old', 'I am a male', 'I am righteous', 'I am the sinner', — in all these thoughts the 'I am' is the constant factor. It never changes its nature; it only *seems* to do so, by the confusion of the real Self — who is this 'I am' — with the body; this confusion gives rise to the ego-sense. Time and place appear in and by this 'I am', but do not affect Him. This 'I am' is not a thought of the mind. It is the real Self, transcending time and space. We should reject the varying thoughts that

---

* *Ulladu Narpadu* verse 16 (see appendix A, verse 21).

pass, and isolate the pure 'I am', which is the Self. If
we do so, says the Sage, we shall find that He is
timeless and spaceless. And since these do not survive
the death of the ego, they are unreal. We may here
take this to heart: *Reality is that which exists in the
Egoless State.*

It is possible that some of us may be perplexed
rather than convinced by these considerations. But
only the most obtuse-minded can resist the conclusion
that there is *no* clear evidence to show that time and
space and the world that seems to fill them are
objective realities, existing independently of the mind
that imagines them.

The following consideration may be of some help.
Time and space are always imagined to be infinite.
We cannot help imagining so. But there is no proof
that they *are* infinite. When we dream we find both
time and space, and as our dream has a beginning,
we ought, if we are seeing reality, to be able to know,
then and there in the dream, that dream-time had a
beginning. But we are not able to do so. Only when
we awake do we find out that we were mistaken. There
is no substantial difference between dream-time and
waking-time in this respect.

Since time does not really exist, there is no past,
nor future, nor even the present; nor can there have
been anything like a creation of the world. Also all
things that presuppose time are unreal. So we had
no past births, nor shall have any in the future; nor
are we *now* embodied, nor can death be real. Neither
can there be actions done in the past, whose fruits we
would reap. Nor are we *now* doers of action, the fruits
of which would be reaped by us in future. This is the

absolute, undiluted truth, as experienced by all the Sages; this however does not affect the *relative* validity of the beliefs of the layman.

Since space is an illusion, the distinction between inside and outside — without which the world cannot be an objective reality — also becomes unreal. Thus all the multitudinous limitations which have always appeared to pertain to us are shown to be illusory.

Since there is no outside, there are not only no inanimate objects, but also no living persons, in that outside. We have seen already that many of the arguments for the world's reality took for granted the multiplicity of persons located in space. This idea is clearly an outgrowth of the ego-sense. The I-sense being limited to the *body* of the seer, he cannot help imagining that in every body that he sees there is a person. Thus the notions of 'you' and 'he' arise, and these are ignorance.

The Sage expresses this as follows: "*When the sense of 'I am the body' arises, then the notions of 'you' and 'he' also arise; but when, by the Quest of the Truth underlying the 'I', the I-sense is put an end to, then the notions of 'you' and 'he' also cease; that which then shines as the Sole Remainder is the true Self.*"*

The following episode taken from the *Vishnu Purana* — to which the writer's attention was drawn by the Sage — may help to a clearer understanding of the whole question. It tells how Sage Ribhu instructed his disciple Nidagha. The Sage went in disguise to the disciple and found him in his native town. The disciple failed to recognise the Sage; he

---

* *Ulladu Narpadu* verse 14 (see appendix A, verse 19).

took him for some rustic that had come sight-seeing;
just then a royal procession was going along, and the
Sage asked what it was; then the following dialogue
took place. Nidagha said: "The king of this place is
going in a procession." "Who is the king?" "The one
who is seated on the elephant." "Which is the elephant
and which the king?" "The one that is above is the
king, and the one that is below is the elephant." "I do
not understand your meaning; please explain it more
clearly." The disciple wondered at the profound
ignorance of the seeming rustic. To make him
understand, he got upon the shoulders of the Sage
and said: "Look here, I am above, like the king, and
you are below, like the elephant." The Sage said: "If
as you say you are above like the king, and I am below
like the elephant, then make me understand what
you mean by 'I' and 'you'." Then Nidagha jumped
down in haste and fell at Ribhu's feet and said: "Surely
thou art my holy Master Ribhu; for no one else has
such an unfailing awareness of the profound truth of
non-duality." Ribhu told him that that was the
teaching he needed, and went away. Thus it was that
Nidagha was instructed in the truth of the real Self.
He was led on step by step, and finally told that the
difference between one person and another is unreal,
and that there is only one real Self. Individuality and
the plurality of souls are illusions, the offspring of
the ignorance 'I am the body'. This very ignorance is
the sole root of *all* sense of difference. The notions of
above and below seemed to be true to the disciple in this
story, only because he identified himself with one body
and the Sage with another; the bodies were above and
below, not the Self. The Self transcends all differences.

The distinction of inside and outside is no more real than that of above and below. And without it there is no world.

It is also this very ignorance that makes us assume that the mind is insignificantly small, located in a corner of the body, the brain. This false belief makes it difficult for us to conceive how this vast universe can be *in* the mind; we even think it ridiculous. The Sage of Arunachala tells us that this notion of ours is an inversion of the truth. He says that it is the *mind* that is vast, not the world. *"The knower is ever greater than the known, and the seer than the seen." That which is known is in* the knower, and that which is seen is *in* the seer; the vast expanse of the sky is *in* the mind, not outside, because the mind is everywhere and there is no outside to it. The infinite universe, being contained in this seemingly external sky, is also in the mind; even the great Gods* whom the devotees adore and their respective heavens are in the mind alone.† That divinity which is conceived as different from the devotee is only relatively real; the true Divinity is the Reality, in which worshipper and worshipped are one, the mind

---

* 'Gods' — in the plural — means the diverse God-forms adored by different sects of devotees. All these forms are mental idols of the One, who is formless. When the word is written with a small 'g', it means the dwellers in heaven corresponding to the 'angels' of Christian theology. The heaven of these gods is different from those of the 'Gods'.

† यन्मनसा न मनुते येनाहुर्मनो मतम् ।
तदेव ब्रह्म त्वं विद्धि नेदं यदिदमुपासते ॥
— *Kena Upanishad*, 1.6.

that differentiates them having no place there. Thus
everything that the mind thinks of, or thinks it sees, —
the body, the objects of sense, the other bodies
supposed to be other persons, heaven, hell and other
regions or worlds — is inside and not outside. The
root of all these superstitions is the initial error of
taking it for granted that one single body is the Self,
and all the rest not-Self. And because of this ignorance
we do not even think of questioning the correctness
of this or any other belief that arises out of this
ignorance. Once we awake to the fact that we have
been deceiving ourselves as to the truth of the Self, —
in accepting as true the illusion that the body is the
Self — we shall have little difficulty in accepting at
least tentatively the teaching that the world is *not*
an objective reality.

We were told by the Sage that the world is unreal,
because it is nothing but the five kinds of sensations.
Among the five sensations there is one which merits
special consideration, namely *form*. Without the
sensation of forms we cannot become subject to the
primary ignorance, the ego-sense; the ego comes into
being by taking hold of a form — a body — confounding
that form with the real Self and thus limiting the real
Self. The question whether forms are real is therefore
separately dealt with by the Sage. He says: *"If the self
be with form, then the world and God would be so too.
But if the self be formless, then how and by whom are
forms to be seen? Is the spectacle ever otherwise than
as the seeing eye is? The real Eye is just the real Self; It
is infinite Consciousness, formless, and worldless."**

---

* *Ulladu Narpadu* verse 4 (see appendix A, verse 9).

The meaning was explained by the Sage himself as follows: "If the eye that sees be the eye of flesh, then gross forms are seen; if that eye be assisted by lenses, then even invisible things are seen to have form; if the mind be the eye, then subtle forms are seen; thus the seeing eye and the objects seen are of the same nature; *that is, if the eye be itself a form, it sees nothing but forms*. But neither the physical eye nor the mind has any power of vision of its own; the real Eye is the Self; as He is formless, being the pure and infinite Consciousness, the Reality, He does not see forms." *Forms are created by the very act of seeing.*

From this we learn that forms appear only because of the ego-sense, the primary ignorance.

For him that still seeks to evade the inevitable conclusion — namely that the world has no objective reality — the Sages appeal to our experience in dreams. We have already considered dreams as showing that *use* does not prove reality. We also need to see that the notion of externality and objectivity can be a delusion. And here dreams are helpful. When we dream we fully believe that we are seeing an external world composed of persons and things, extended in time and space, substantially similar to the waking world. This idea of externality is the cause of our taking the dream-world to be real; and this belief persists so long as we are dreaming. We have not the least doubt *at that time* that the dream-world is outside of us and real; if doubt arises, on account of something extraordinary, as when we find ourselves able to fly, or see a dead man come to life, and we begin to suspect that the whole might be a dream, the doubt is somehow overcome and the dream is taken as real until we awake. In fact, the continuance of the dream depends on our believing it to be real. This illusion of reality persists throughout the dream. It is only when we awake that we are able to see that it was only a dream — that there was no external world, but only a mental image which was so vivid as to create the illusion of externality and reality.

It may be objected that there is a difference; we awake from a dream and can thus realise its unreality; but our waking experience has no end; we do not have an opportunity to realise its falsity. But we are told by the Sages that there *is* a waking from this dream called waking, and that *then* the dream will come to an end; this aspect of the question will be discussed later, when we come to discuss the three states of personal experience. Here we are concerned only with the illusiveness of the sense of externality, which is the cause of the sense of reality. He that demurs to this conclusion must be able to tell us of some infallible device by which we can detect the dream-nature of dreams while we are dreaming. If there be such a device, it would be one that will enable us to discover the dream-nature of waking also. Whether in dream or in waking, if one turns aside from the world and tries to see him that sees that world, the world and its seer would vanish together, and the Self alone would remain.

These and other considerations must make it easy for us to entertain the view put forward by the Sages, that the world is not an objective reality, that it has no existence of its own. There is only one thing that has such existence, namely the real Self; this we shall see in a later chapter.

Since the world is nothing but mind, the truth of it depends on the truth of the mind. So we have now to see whether the mind, which is the creator of the world, both in waking and in dream, is itself real.

The Sage points out that the mind is discontinuous. It arises with a ready-made world and sets with it as we were told already. In dreamless sleep there is no mind, and no world. Judged by the standard of reality that the Sages have given us, the mind is unreal.

The mind, says the Sage of Arunachala, is nothing but the stream of thoughts that passes over Consciousness. Of all these thoughts, the first one is the thought 'I am this body'. This is a false thought; but because it is taken as true, it is possible for other thoughts to arise. So the mind is just an outgrowth of the primary ignorance, and is therefore unreal.

That we are not the mind, that the mind is not the Self, is clear from this. The mind does not exist in sleep, but *we* continue to exist in sleep. Besides, the Self exists in the state *beyond* the three states, namely waking, dream and sleep.

We have not exhausted all the possible objections that can be raised by an inveterate believer in the reality of the world. There is, of course, no end to the objections that the ego-mind will go on raising, if encouraged to do so. We have noticed already the reason why the mind is so tireless in raising difficulties. The Sage has shown us how to deal with the unruly mind when it proves troublesome in this or any other way.

The result of all this inquiry is this; to be able to recover our true nature as the real Self, we must free

ourselves from the superstition that the world is real.
Of course it is not necessary that we should bind
ourselves to the opposite belief, that the world is
unreal. But if it so happens that we cannot give up
our present belief in the reality of the world without
taking up the opposite belief, — namely that the world
is unreal, — we must take it up, even though it is not
strictly true, as explained before. The text-books of
the Advaitic lore ask us to steer a middle course, *if it
be possible*; they tell us to remember that the world is
'indefinable as true or untrue' — *anirvachaniya* —
and this is philosophically correct, as it is in accord
with the teaching of the Sages. We may put aside the
world and cease thinking about it, understanding that
the Truth can be realised only by the complete and
final extinction of the primary ignorance by the
Revelation of the real Self, which will come by
pursuing the Quest taught by the Sage. If we cannot
do this, we need to relax the grip of the ignorance by
reminding ourselves that in all probability the world
is just a fantasy of our own errant minds, somewhat
like the one depicted by Lewis Carroll in his 'Alice in
the Wonderland'; there the heroine takes the wonder-
world that she sees as quite real until the very end;
then she finds that that world was a false appearance
— that the men, women and animals she had been
seeing were only a pack of *cards*. So too the
emancipated one may find that this solid-seeming
world is only a pack of *thoughts*.

It may be useful to point out that the Sages do
not seek to impose a new faith of their own, but only
to *release* the disciple from the grip of those notions
that hinder the Quest.

The method that is being set forth in these chapters — namely, abstracting the mind from the world by tentatively accepting the view that it is only a pack of thoughts — has been called 'subjective idealism', because it resembles a somewhat similar view of the world taught by Berkeley. But our idealism, if it be so called, is an aid to the Quest of the Self. It is not recommended for acceptance by anyone who is not eager to obtain the direct Revelation of the authentic Self. It differs also from the *mere* idealism of Berkely, in that it is integrally related to the unique teaching of the Sages, that underlying the false appearance there is the transcendental real Self. It is not contended that for *all* aspirants this is the best of all possible methods. A method is better or worse than another only in relation to a particular person, not generally. It is also true that this is not the only method of escape from bondage; those whom this method does not suit can follow the path of devotion which is dealt with later. Such persons are told that the world is real, because the Reality — called God — is the material and efficient Cause of it. There is no inconsistency in this, because, as the Sage has often told us, the teaching must ever be suited to the taught.

Chapter 6

The Soul

WE HAVE THUS far discussed the nature of the sense-objects, together with the mind, in and by which they appear. There are two more subjects needing to be discussed, namely the individual soul and God. We shall first consider the former.

We have picked up in the course of life certain notions about the soul. We need to see how far these notions are based on evidence. Most of us believe that there *is* a soul, the perceiver of the sense-objects, which make up the outside world, and the thinker of the thoughts that arise in the mind. We also take it for granted that there is a distinct soul inhabiting every single body. It is this 'soul' that we regard as the self. And as this self is limited to a single body and the associated mind, we take it to be finite. When we say 'I' we mean this little self. We also believe that 'we' — namely these little selves — are in bondage, being subject to the laws of space, time and causality. Some of us believe also that this little self can become free, though we do not all mean the same thing by the word 'freedom'. Most of us believe that this self takes up a succession of bodies, not by its own will, but by the compulsion of the effects of actions. Further there is the almost universal dogma of the believers that the souls are distinct from God; a few believe that this distinction will vanish on the attainment of freedom; but all others believe that the distinction is eternal — that the soul will remain distinct from God for ever and ever. These believers do not question the reality of time and space and of this and other worlds.

All these believers assume that the mind is the self. But this assumption is often sub-conscious. Quite a large number of them profess to know that there is a self other than the mind; but subconsciously they believe that the self is a mind of some sort, attributing to their 'self' many of the properties of mind.

If these believers be substantially right, then it would follow that the self is a *person*, that is, an individual. All the questions that arise about the self are thus reducible to the one question, 'Is the self an individual or person?' If he be not a person, then there is *no* soul — no perceiver of the world, enjoying and suffering the consequences of actions.

Whether personality is real or not will appear from what the Sage tells us in his writings. It is as follows: "*The body, which by itself is inert, does not say 'I'; the real Consciousness has no rising nor setting. But between these two there arises a spurious being, an I, which assumes the size and shape of the body; this itself is the mind, (serving as) a knot between consciousness and the inert (body); this is conditioned existence, the ego, bondage and the subtle body; this is the real nature of the (so-called) soul.*"*

* *Ulladu Narpadu* verse 24 (see appendix A, verse 29).

The Sage tells us here that the real Consciousness is beyond time and therefore neither rises nor sets. It is like the sun, which — relative to the earth — does not move; the sunrise and sunset we speak of are due to the movements of the earth. So too the Reality shines constantly; the rising and setting of the ego are ascribed to it. The ego-sense is discontinuous; it rises and sets. Apart from the ego-sense there is no individual soul. It shines during waking and in dream, and sets in sleep. This little self is therefore not to be identified with the Reality. Nor can it be identified with the inert body. What then is this little self? The Sage tells us here that it is a hypothetical being, a chimera of the mind, compounded of the light of Consciousness and the body. These two utterly unlike things are confused together; the result is this incongruous being called the individual soul, which says, 'I am so-and-so'. Because of the light of Consciousness associated with it, it appears conscious; but at the same time it is indistinguishable from the body, which has no consciousness of its own. Because of the two incongruous elements of which it is composed, it is described as the *knot* between the Reality — the Self — and the body. That is why the little self is manifest as the ego-sense, which has the form of the thought 'I am this body'. The body thus identified as the self is not always the physical body; sometimes the mind, which is only a subtler kind of body, takes its place and then the sense of selfhood is restricted to the mind for a time.

Now, the thought 'I am this body' is the primary thought. It is like a thread on which all the other thoughts are strung. Hence the ego is indistinguishable from the mind. In fact the mind is but an expanded form of the ego. Hence the Sage tells us that the mind and the subtle body are the same as this hypothetical little self, which is no other than the ego. Conversely we can say that the little self is not other than these.

We thus learn that the so-called soul is nothing but the ego, which is due to a confusion of two elements which are distinct and can never mix, because one of them — the body — is non-existent, being a mere mental image. There can be a real mixture only if *both* the elements be real. The mixing up of the two, explains the Sage, is like a marriage contracted by a bachelor in a dream, where the bridegroom is real, but the bride is not; when the dreamer awakes, he finds himself as much a bachelor as before. Hence the real Self — who is the Reality — did not really become limited; He never really became the soul or little self; He was not really married to the body. Thus it is made clear that the individual soul has no real existence. All those questions that relate to that soul are meaningless, because they *assume* the existence of a soul. There is only one real Self, the Pure Consciousness, which is beyond time. We shall see later on why He is described as *Consciousness*, and not as conscious; we shall then see that there is a fundamental difference between the two descriptions.

Since the mind has no existence apart from this spurious entity, the ego, it follows that all the creations of the mind, including ignorance and bondage, and the consequent conditioned existence consisting of enjoyment and suffering — which we call 'life' — are outgrowths of the ego, and partake of its unreality. That ignorance is unreal will be seen later on.

That this teaching is correct will be clear to us if we look at the facts without bias. By the most careful analysis of the whole of our past experience we can find no proof of an individual soul other than the ego. The ego itself is just the primary ignorance, the recognition of which is the starting point of our inquiry. It is here shown that it is an imaginary entity being a compound of two uncompoundable elements. Thus the whole of this conditioned existence, which we call life, is founded on this lie, the individual soul. It is natural therefore that life should be full of lies, and therefore full of disappointments. This teaching may be difficult to grasp. But it is the fundamental truth as taught by the ancient lore.

There can be no correct understanding of the ancient lore, if this teaching be not accepted. So long as the notion of individuality is retained, all philosophical inquiries are bound to prove useless; for they cannot lead us out of the primary ignorance. This was clearly taught by the Sage Sankara as follows: "Only so long as there is an identification (effected by the mind) of the real Self with the intellect is there an appearance of individuality and of conditioned existence for that Self. But in reality there is no such being as the individual soul, other than the spurious entity imagined by the intellect. In the study of the Vedanta we do not find (support for the existence of) any conscious entity having an existence of its own, apart from the Supreme Being, who is ever-free and all-knowing; the sacred texts say: 'There is no seer, hearer, thinker or knower apart from this Being'; 'There is none but He, that sees, hears, thinks or knows'; 'Thou art That'; 'I am the Reality'; these and hundreds of other texts are our authorities."*

The ego is the only source of all our life-experiences; they are what they are because of the ego. We say, 'I am so-and-so', 'I am a doer of actions', 'I am happy', 'I am miserable', and so on. In every single thought we can find this 'I am'. It is in fact the common factor of all thoughts without exception. No thought can arise, which does not contain this 'I am'. But this 'I am' is not a property of the mind; so we learn from the Sage and from Upanishadic Lore. We are told that this 'I am' is the Light of the real Self. That Self being infinite and unqualified, this 'I am' is not really the little thing we take it to be. And we take it to be limited, imperfect and bound to the wheel of pleasure and pain, only because we do not discriminate and distinguish the element of reality in the ego from that which is false. Hence it ought to be clear to us that what obscures the real Self is simply the acceptance of this ego at its face-value, as our true Self, which it is not, as shown here.

---

* यावदेव चायं बुध्द्युपाधिसंबन्ध:, तावदेवास्य जीवत्वं संसारित्वं च। परमार्थतस्तु, न जीवो नाम, बध्द्युपाधिपरि- कल्पितस्वरुपव्यतिरेकेण, अस्ति । न हि नित्यमुक्तस्वरूपात् सर्वज्ञादीश्वरादन्यश्चेतनो धातुर्द्वितीयो वेदान्तार्थनिरूपणा- यामुपलभ्यते, 'नान्योऽतोस्ति द्रष्टा, श्रोता, मन्ता, विज्ञाता' 'तत्त्वमसी', 'अहं ब्रह्मास्मि' 'तत् सृष्ट्वा तदेवानुप्राविशत्' इत्यादिश्रुतिशतेभ्य: ॥

— Sutra-Bhashya, Chapter II, Pada iii, Sutra 30.

This was exactly the essence of the teaching of
the Sage known as Gautama Buddha.* He was once
asked by someone about the immortality of the soul.
The Sage replied: "That soul about whose survival
you are anxious does not exist even now; it is unreal."
What he meant was that the questioner was assuming
the existence of an individual soul, which does not
really exist, and hence the question was based on a
falsehood; Buddha did not mean to deny the existence
of the real Self. The questioner misunderstood the
answer; he thought that the Sage had told him that
there is no Self at all. He ought to have asked a further
question: 'Is there a real Self, and if there be one,
what is its real nature?' He did not do so, but went
away; and Buddha discovered that he had unsettled
the man's faith without enlightening him. The fact is
worthy of note that when questions are based on a
false assumption, it is not possible to answer them
by a simple 'yes' or 'no'; either answer would be wrong.

The individual soul being unreal, it follows that
there is no perceiver of the world. This may be
surprising; but it need not be so. The seer and his
spectacle are inseparable; they are like the two ends
of a single stick; as a stick will always have two ends,
so every perception involves the two, the seer and his
spectacle. The three, namely the seer, the spectacle
and the relation of seeing form a triad, of which the
essential element is the seeing, which becomes possible
by the light of Consciousness; by that light both the
seer and the seen are manifested. It is not possible to
attribute reality to the seer, while denying it to the

---

* The term 'Buddha' signifies 'a Sage.'

spectacle. If we accept the view that the spectacle, namely the world, is unreal in any sense, then we must also accept the view that the seer of the world is unreal in the same sense and to the same extent. The spectator is in fact an integral part of the world; both in waking and in dream the spectator and the spectacle form one single whole, appearing and vanishing together.

The Sage brings home to us the spurious nature of the ego — the individual soul — by means of a parable. On the occasion of a marriage an uninvited guest, an utter stranger to both the parties, came in pretending to be an intimate friend of the bridegroom. At first the hosts, namely the bride's party, believed him and honoured him accordingly. But after a time suspicions arose and inquiries began to be made as to who he was and what right he had to come in. The two parties met and began to question each other. The impostor saw that he was sure to be exposed and treated as he deserved if he remained; so he quietly disappeared. Just like the impostor in this parable is the ego. It is neither the real Self, nor the body; so long as no inquiry is made, the ego persists and enjoys the status of the real Self; but when an inquiry is made — when the quest of the real Self is begun and persisted in — it will vanish, leaving no trace. This is exactly what we are told by the Sage in the following passage:

*"This ego, which is but a ghost without a form of its own, comes into being by taking hold of a form; keeping hold of the form and enjoying sense-objects, it waxes greatly in strength: if the truth of it be sought, it will run away."**

---

* *Ulladu Narpadu* verse 25 (see appendix A, verse 30).

We need to study this teaching carefully. There
is no ego in sleep, but only in waking and dreaming.
In both these states the ego manifests by taking hold
of a body, saying 'I am this body.' That is, there is a
perception of the body, and at the same time there
arises the thought 'I am this body.' That body is taken
as the self, or as the abode of the self, and the other
bodies and objects that are seen at the same time are
taken as not-self. When again sleep comes on, both
the body and the ego disappear, and with them the
world also vanishes. Thus the ego is simply the
ignorance that limits the real Self to a single body
out of a multitude of bodies, all of which are its own
creation; this world which it creates is thus divided
by the ego into two parts, as self and not-self, the
former being a very small part, and the latter a very
large one. From this arise the twin notions of 'I' and
'mine', which are the substance of bondage.

Bondage is the outcome of the limitation of the
notion of the self to a single body. Hence it is evident
that but for the ego there can be no bondage. It thus
becomes easy to accept the teaching of the Sages, that
the real Self is ever free — never became bound or
subject to ignorance — and does not need to be made
free. The Sage, having no notion of being other than
the real Self in Its utter purity and perfection, is not
aware of bondage; he is not even aware of having been
bound at any time, because time itself has been
transcended by him. Bondage is just a thought like
any other thought, though it needs to be said that
the thought of bondage has its uses, in that it leads
wise people to this inquiry, which leads, through the
Quest of the Self, to the realisation that there is no

bondage. But since bondage is inherent in the ego-sense itself, it will not cease so long as the ego itself survives. Thus we have the curious result that the ego is itself bondage, as well as the sufferer from it. It follows from this that the ego is for ever debarred from the enjoyment of deliverance. How can *bondage* ever become free? Besides, in *that* state, only what is utterly real can survive, and the ego is not real. Those that nourish the hope of winning Deliverance without losing individuality are doomed to disappointment. In fact the blessed regions which they hope to win, and in which they are to retain their individuality, are as unreal as this world.

What has been said about bondage applies also to 'ignorance', because this also is identical with the ego, and has no existence apart from the ego.

We need to realise in all its implications the fact that the ego itself is the source of all the evil that besets life. But to most inquirers the ego is dear as life itself, because they think it is themselves, and do not want to lose it. They would rather suffer all the ills of life than be happy without it. Questions are framed, assuming the immortality of this non-existent soul and its survival in Deliverance. These will not arise if the teaching be understood.

One such question arises thus. There is the Vedantic teaching, 'Thou art That'. Formerly this teaching was kept secret and imparted only to well-tested disciples; thus the serious mischiefs arising from a misunderstanding of the teaching were prevented. But nowadays the sacred lore is accessible to all, and the consequences are far from desirable. For, the higher the teaching, the greater are the evils

due to its misapplication. Incompetent persons read
the books, and assume that the ego itself, with all its
vices, is infinite, all-powerful, and above the law of
right and wrong. And they cannot be set right. Even
the better sort of inquirer is puzzled by the teaching,
because he has not yet clearly understood the truth
that there is *no* individuality. He takes the sacred
text as meaning that the individual soul is God, or
whatever else there is that is infinitely great. But he
doubts the teaching, because, in the sense in which he
understands it, it is not only absurd, but blasphemous.
And he is right in this; he is certainly far more in the
right than those who *accept* the teaching, but in the
wrong sense. The better sort of student has an
instinctive sense that *something* is wrong. He is
assailed by doubts and he puts questions to get them
cleared.

Such a one asked the Sage: "If I am eternal and
perfect why am I ignorant?" The Sage replied as
follows: "*Who is* ignorant? The real Self does not
complain of ignorance. It is the ego in you that so
complains. It is that which also asks questions. The
Self does not ask any question. And this ego is
neither the body, nor the real Self, but something
arising between the two. In sleep there was no ego,
and you had no sense of imperfection or ignorance
then. Thus the ego is itself imperfection and
ignorance. If you seek the truth of the ego and thus
find the real Self, you will find that there is no
ignorance." What the Sage meant was that if the
real Self be found the ego would be extinguished,
and that the ignorance complained of will be
extinguished along with the ego.

The correct meaning of the sacred text, 'Thou art That', as given by the Sage, is recorded in the *Guru-Ramana-Vachana-Mala* as follows: "Thou art not the body, nor the senses, nor the mind, nor the vital force, nor the ego. Thou art That which will shine as the pure 'I AM' when, by the renunciation of the original sin* — which is just the notion of selfhood in these — and by the Quest of the real Self, the mind is utterly extinguished in the Heart and the world ceases to be seen."†

Incidentally it may be noted that the ego itself is the cause of all that vehemence of belief which engenders fanaticism and intolerance, and a taste for vain and even rancorous controversies. The religious man is ego-ridden, just like his more agreeable brother the sceptic. The latter is indifferent and therefore not disagreeable. But the religious man is rarely at ease, because he sees so many people believing differently from himself. He ardently looks forward to a time when all men shall be of one religion; but he cannot bear to think that that religion shall be in the least different from his own; he would rather that other people should be without any religion, than that they should cherish a religion not his own. Hence it happens that the more intensely religious a man is, the more unpleasant he is likely to be to those who differ from him in religion. If he obtains political power, he will persecute all that profess other religions. That is because religious belief is not inimical to egoism.

---

* We are told by the Sage that the 'original sin' which is referred to in Christian doctrine, is no other than the ego-sense (see p.221).
† *Guru Vachaka Kovai* vv. 671 & 673 (appendix B, vv. 153 & 154).

The religious man always thinks that his zeal for making converts is a virtue. It is not a virtue at all, but a vice, because this zeal is due to his egoism. He does not say to himself: "This faith seems to be true and good; so it shall be mine till I know better." On the contrary he says to himself: "This is *my* faith, and therefore it alone is true, and it is the duty of all men to accept it." Thus his attachment to his own faith is egoistic. That is why there is rancour in his condemnation of other faiths. The existence of those faiths is an insult to him. 'Orthodoxy is my doxy, and heterodoxy is the other man's doxy' — such is his mentality. Thus it happens that many a believer harbours a greater dislike for those that differ from him even slightly, than even for non-believers, or for believers in a totally different religion.

This is pointed out by the Sage in the following: *"He that has not attained the state of perfect identity with the Reality, — which is his Natural State, since that Reality is ever shining in the hearts of all creatures as the real Self — by seeking and becoming aware of It, engages in controversies, asserting 'There is something real,' 'No,' 'that something has form,' 'No,' 'It is one,' 'It is twofold,' 'It is neither.'"** *

From this we understand that the Sage has no creed of his own; and the reason is that he is egoless. The ego is itself the believer or unbeliever as the case may be. The ego-ridden ones are divided into two broad divisions, those that deny and those that assert the existence of a Reality underlying the changing phases of the world, including therein the threefold

---

* *Ulladu Narpadu* verse 34 (see appendix A, verse 39).

appearance, namely the soul, the sense-objects and God. The assertors again fall into numerous sub-divisions, because they differ as to the nature of that Reality. The main differences are mentioned here. In the first place there is conflict of beliefs about the reality of form: there are those who assert that the First Cause has form; naturally this is denied by some. Then there is the controversy about the unity or diversity of that Cause. Some assert that the First Cause is one, and that the universe is an appearance in it, so that It is both the material and the efficient cause. Others deny this and assert that First Cause is God, who is eternally distinct from the souls. There are still others who maintain that God and the souls are neither identical, nor distinct. Among these the believers in unity are also mentioned, because that teaching, though true enough, is not intended to be cherished as a mere dogma, but as an incentive to the attainment of actual Experience of the Reality; those that are averse to the Quest, by which the Experience is to be won, are therefore no better than the others; all are equally subject to the ego, and content to remain so. In truth, only *Experience* of the Self is real, not beliefs about Him, which imply that He can become an object of thought. Mere theoretical knowledge of the Self — even that derived from the sacred lore — is ignorance, just like the dogmas of the devotees.

What the Sage means is that the Reality transcends the mind, while creeds are purely mental. Therefore no creed can be a faithful description of the Reality. The Reality is neither in the creeds, nor in the books in which they are set forth. The believer is just the ego, whose nature is to hide or distort the truth. 'I believe' says the believer. To him the Sage says: "Find out the truth of this I, the 'believer'; then thou wilt know the Truth that transcends the mind, and therefore cannot be contained in a creed...."

We thus see that the ego is the primal seed of all this manifoldness — not only of the world of objects, but also of the world of ideas. This is a logical extension of the conclusion that we have arrived at in the last chapter, namely that the world is mental. Since the mind has no existence apart from the ego, it follows that the ego itself is both the mind and the world. This is just what the Sage says in the following: *"When the ego rises, then all the world comes into being; when the ego is not, then nothing exists; therefore the Quest of the Self by way of the question 'Who is this ego?' or 'Whence does he come into being?' is (the means of) getting rid of all the world."**

The teaching conveyed here should be considered along with that conveyed in another passage quoted in the last chapter. There the Sage told us that the plurality of selves appearing to us in ignorance is an illusion, and that this plurality would cease to be seen when the ego is extinguished by the Quest. Thus we get the result that in the State of Deliverance there is no world, whether of things and persons, or of thoughts — that the whole world is in the ego, and is nothing but the ego.

This is in perfect agreement with the teaching of ancient lore, which is clearly expressed in the *Mandukya Upanishad*, which says that "He is worldless, blissful,

---

* *Ulladu Narpadu* verse 26 (see appendix A, verse 31).

calm, without difference." There are other equally clear statements in the ancient lore, which assert the utter absence of difference in the Egoless State. "There is no manifoldness at all here."* And this is impressed by warnings to the seeker of the Truth, not to get entangled in the false belief that differences are real. We are told that whoever takes differences to be real shall die again and again.** He that imagines the least difference between himself and the Truth shall be the victim of fear.† Whatever is conceived by one as other than the Self has the power to deceive him.

That the world ceases to appear on the attainment of Deliverance is also asserted by the Sage in the following: *"I shall now state clearly the profound secret which is the supreme essence of all Vedanta: Understand that when the ego dies and the real Self is realised as the One reality, then there remains only that real Self, who is Pure Consciousness."*‡

This is also in accordance with the teaching of the *Gita* which tells us that even now the world does not really exist. "All the creatures are in Me; I am not

---

* नेह नानास्ति किंचन ॥
— *Katha Upanishad*, 2.1.11.

** मृत्योस्स मृत्युमाप्नोति य इह नानेव पश्यति ॥
— *Katha Upanishad*, 2.1.11.

† यदा ह्येवैष एतस्मिन्नुदरमन्तरं कुरुते । अथ तस्य भयं
भवति ॥
— *Taittiriya Upanishad*, 2.7.1

ब्रह्म तं परादाद्योऽन्यत्रात्मनो ब्रह्म वेद । .... सर्वं तं
परादाद्योऽन्यत्रात्मन: सर्वं वेद ॥
— *Brihad. Up.*, 4.5.7.

‡ *Ulladu Narpadu Anubandham* v.40 (see appendix B, v. 86).

in them; (*in truth*) they are not in Me; such is my divine Maya!"*

On the other hand, while the ego-sense survives, the world-appearance is inescapable. And conversely, so long as one sees the world, one cannot help confounding the body and the self, and assuming that the self is finite. And this is worse for those who cherish the false belief that the world is real as such. And in this there is no real difference between him that thinks that the body is the self and him that thinks that the mind is the self. The latter is always thinking of the body as the self — most of the time — just like the former. Thus it happens that people in the West speak of a dying man as 'giving up the ghost'; they do not say that he is giving up the body, which they would say if they were free from the delusion that the body is the self.

But though the ego is itself ignorance and the origin of all sin and suffering, this ego has very great importance in our inquiry, because it holds the clue to the finding of the real Self. This we shall see in the course of the description of the Quest of that Self. Besides, the ego is the proof of the real Self. These points are brought home to us by the Sage in the following: *"This insentient body does not say 'I'; no one ever says 'I did not exist in sleep'; but all this comes into being (only) after the rising of the ego; seek therefore the Source wherefrom the ego rises, by concentrating the mind on the Quest."***

---

* मत्स्थानि सर्वभूतानि न चाहं तेष्ववस्थित: ॥
न च मत्स्थानि भूतानि पश्य मे योगमैश्वरम् ।

— *Bhagavad Gita*, IX, 4 & 5.
** *Ulladu Narpadu* verse 23 (see appendix A, verse 28).

The first step in the Quest of the real Self is to understand that Self is *not* the body — physical or mental. The reason for this is two-fold. On the one hand the body is unconscious and hence cannot be the self, finite or otherwise. On the other hand we are sure that the Self — whatever it may be — can exist without a body. We know that this is so in sleep. Few people can even imagine the possibility of the Self ceasing to exist during sleep. Those that do so are the over sophisticated ones; their perplexity on this point is dealt with in a long talk given by the Sage to a doubter, which will be given later. Thus the ego itself is a proof that *we* exist. We are not the ego; we are That from which the ego takes its rise. That must be found by seeking the Source of the ego. Revelation tells us that if and when we find that Source, we shall find not only the Self, but also the Reality that underlies the world-appearance; and this will be the case, because the Self and the Reality are one and the same.

The ego is thus seen to be the arch-deceiver, the true Satan or *Ahriman*. He is the only enemy of God and man. He is the enemy of right knowledge. He is the inventor of murder and lying. He is the cosmic Macbeth, who is constantly murdering Peace, which is true Happiness. He is the impostor who has usurped the seat of the real Self. Therefore he is debarred from entrance into the State of Deliverance, the Kingdom of Heaven that is in us, taught by Jesus.

The Sage has told us that the ego is all the evil there is, while egolessness is all the good there is. From the ego, which is ignorance, proceed all the evils that beset life. All that is good and worthy of reverent cultivation belongs to egolessness.

Apart from the ego there is neither death nor rebirth. This vicious circle of deaths and rebirths is sustained only by the primary ignorance which is the ego. The ego itself is death, because he is the negation of the Truth, which is Life. He must not only be dethroned, but must be put to death. For there is no safety so long as he survives.

The ego must become considerably attenuated for the teaching of the Sages to be understood. This is clear from the following utterance of the Sage. He was explaining the true inwardness of the current notion that a disciple must, after finding a Guru, remain with him for a long time, serving him faithfully, and surrender himself utterly to the Guru, and that the latter would *then* teach him the great secret, 'Thou art That.' The Sage explained it as follows: "The true meaning of what is here called surrender is the complete wearing away of the ego-sense, which is individuality. And this is a necessary condition for the disciple being able to receive the teaching; for if there be no surrender in *this* sense, the teaching is *sure* to be misunderstood. Even with the limited egoism that now exists, man is liable to outbreaks of fury, to be tyrannical, fanatical and so on. What will he not do, if he be told that he himself is that Great Being? He would not understand that teaching in its true sense, but would take it to mean that his individual soul, the ego, is that Great Being. This is not at all the true sense of the teaching, because the ego is simply non-existent."

The true meaning of the teaching is that though the soul *as such* is a non-entity, there is in it an element of reality, namely the light of consciousness proceeding from the real Self, and experienced by us as 'I am'.

This light of consciousness does not belong to the soul; it belongs to the Self, the Reality, It must therefore be surrendered to Him. When that surrender is complete, then that Self alone will remain. And if individuality be *thus* lost, it is well lost. For this loss of individuality is not a loss. It is the loss of the greatest of all losses, the loss of the self; it is therefore the highest of all possible gains, the gain of the real Self. The effect of this surrender is thus described in the ancient lore: "As the rivers flowing into the ocean, and therein losing name and form, become one with the ocean, so does the Sage, losing name and form, become one with the Supreme Being, who is the transcendental Reality."*

Even leaving aside the truth that the ego is unreal, it has to be said that what the Sage has lost is just a mathematical zero, while what he has gained is the Infinite Reality. This is expressed by the Sage as follows — in one of his hymns to Arunachala: "What profit hast thou got, O Arunachala, taking me, — of no worth here and hereafter, — in exchange for Thyself, the greatest of all gains?"

This surrender to the real Self, to become final and perfect, needs to be effected by the Quest of the real Self in the manner taught in a later chapter. And since surrender is the culmination of devotion, the seeker of Deliverance needs to cherish devotion to the real Self. When this devotion becomes perfect, then it will be possible to enter on and persist in the Quest till success is won — till the real Self reveals Himself.

---

* यथा नद्यः स्यन्दमानाः समुद्रेऽस्तं गच्छन्ति नामरुपे विहाय ।
तथा विद्वान् नामरुपाद्विमुक्तः परात्परं पुरुषमुपैति दिव्यम् ॥
— *Mundaka Upanishad*, 3.2.8.

Chapter 7

God

WE HAVE COME to the conclusion that two out of the three subjects of our inquiry, namely the world and the soul, are unreal as such. We need to inquire now into the truth of the concept of God.

This part of the inquiry is very easy, because the conclusion is not in doubt. The three, namely the world, the soul and God, are one single indivisible whole, because each implies the other two. In fact the first member, the world, includes the second and third. The name 'world' means the totality of all distinct objects of thought. It implies and includes all inanimate objects, all sentient creatures, and the one cause of all these. The world of persons and things is an *effect*, the experience of which is inconceivable without the cause that permeates and sustains the effect, just as you cannot perceive a pot, without being aware of its cause or set of causes. Thus it happens that the three are practically one for this inquiry. We cannot regard one or two of these three as unreal, and the remainder as real. An ancient analogy is that of the hen, which has been given to us by the Sage Sankara. He points out that one cannot cut her into two, intending to cook and eat one part, and to reserve the other for laying eggs; he should forego one of these purposes, and be content with the other; that is, he must cook and eat the whole hen, or keep her alive for laying eggs. Just in the same way, we must reject the whole of this threefold entity as unreal — in the special sense of the word as used in Advaitic metaphysics, — or accept the whole of it as real in the sense in which materialists as well as theists call it real. There is no middle course.

The idea of God is relative to the ideas of the world and the soul. The world — restricting it to the totality of insentient objects — is the opposite of God, in that it is inert and without consciousness, whereas God is endowed with infinite consciousness. The soul is opposite to God, because it is finite, as compared to God, who is infinite. Thus God is a member of two pairs of opposites. And opposites have an existence only for the ego-mind. Therefore God is not an objective reality.

There is another consideration also. Considered as one of the three, — not as He really is — God is an object of thought. He is one of the triad of relation, namely the thinker, the object and the act of thinking. And *all* triads exist in the realm of ignorance, by virtue of the ego. Therefore God is not an objective reality.

This is clearly expressed by the Sage in the following: *"The triads all arise, depending on the ego-sense; so too arise the dyads (pairs of opposites); if one enters the Heart by the Quest of 'Who am I?' and sees the Truth of it (the real Self), all of them will vanish utterly; such a one is a Sage; he is not deluded by these."**

---

* *Ulladu Narpadu* verse 9 (see appendix A, verse 14).

If we can abstract from the world these dyads and triads, then nothing will be left of it, except perhaps space and time; and these two, we have seen, are not objective realities. What remains over on the extinction of the ego is the real Self alone, which is not divisible into parts.

Here we have one more proof of the unreality of God as such. It is asserted by the Sages that separate from the real Self there is no God in the Egoless State; and separateness is the very essence of the idea of God as God. In fact, where there is no separateness, there can be no ideas at all. God, as He really is, is not an object of thought.

The truth about God is that He is no other than the real Self, otherwise described as the Reality and as Pure Consciousness. As such He is *not* a Person, and is *not* related to the world of persons and things in any way. The relation of cause and effect, which is usually said to exist between the Reality and the world, is not real at all. If the Reality were related in any way to anything, it would *not* be the Reality, as defined by the Sages.

That God — as He really is — and the real Self are one and the same is the central theme of the Upanishads, as we have seen from the texts cited by Sankara. This identity is not merely stated as a fact; it is emphasised in all possible ways. Penalties are decreed for those that do not receive the teaching, and blessings are pronounced on those that accept the teaching and earnestly strive to realise the truth in their own experience.

"He that serves a separate deity, — thinking 'He is one, and I am another,' — is ignorant; he is like a quadruped for the gods in heaven."*

"When one becomes immoveably fixed in identity — without fear — with this invisible, unembodied, indefinable, placeless One, then he attains Fearlessness. When one makes the least division in this One, there is fear for him. That is the real (cause of) fear, in the case of him that wrongly knows (the Truth of the Self)."†

"He that sees as if there were difference here goes from death to death."**

God, as He really is, is therefore nameless, formless and without attributes of any kind. If He had attributes, He would be in relativity, and therefore unreal.

This is the ultimate truth about God as revealed by the Sages. Of course it gives rise to an apparent difficulty in giving an account of creation. The difficulty is got over by the Sage Sankara, by distinguishing between the Reality in Its true nature,

---

* योऽन्यां देवतामुपास्ते, अन्योऽसावन्योऽहमस्मीति, न स वेद ।
यथा पशुरेवं स देवानाम् ॥

— *Brihad. Up.*, 1.4.10.

† यदा ह्येवैष एतस्मिन्नदृश्येऽनात्म्येऽनिरुक्तेऽनिलयनेऽभयं
प्रतिष्ठां विन्दते । अथ सोऽभयं गतो भवति । यदा
ह्येवैष एतस्मिन्नुदरमन्तरं कुरुते । अथ तस्य भयं भवति ।
तत्त्वेव भयं विदुषोऽमन्वानस्य ॥

— *Taittiriya Upanishad*, 2.7.1.

** मृत्योस्स मृत्युमाप्नोति य इह नानेव पश्यति ॥

— *Katha Upanishad*, 2.1.11.

and the same conceived, for the purpose of teaching, as the origin of the world. The former is called *Para-Brahman*, and the latter *Apara-Brahman*. They are also called *Nirbija* and *Sabija*, *Nirguna* and *Saguna*.‡ The latter is also called *Isvara* or the Personal God.

There are those who confound the two and claim that He actually became all this multiplicity. They rely on texts of the ancient lore, which, literally understood, and without any reference to the *final* teaching as conveyed by other texts occurring later in the same books, — seem to be in their favour. The commentaries abound in arguments to show that a literal interpretation of these texts is improper. The question is set at rest for us by the clear utterances of the Sage of Arunachala.

One such pronouncement of the Sage is as follows: "*Even the statement that duality is real so long as one is striving to win the goal, but that in the goal there is no duality, is not at all correct. What else but the tenth man was the one in the parable, both when he himself was anxiously seeking the tenth man as one that was missing, and when he had found himself (to be the missing tenth man).*"*

Here the word 'even' signifies that a creed not mentioned is also wrong. That is, two different creeds are here condemned. One of them is implicitly condemned, and the other explicitly. The first one is that duality is true always, and persists even in the state of Deliverance. The second is that duality is true

---

‡ 'Nirbija' means 'seedless'; 'Sabija', 'with seed'; 'Nirguna', 'without
    attributes'; 'Saguna', 'with attributes'.
* *Ulladu Narpadu* verse 37 (see appendix A, verse 42).

for the present, and until non-duality is achieved by some method of spiritual endeavour. The former is the creed of the dualists. The passage cited above takes it as unquestionable that this creed is incorrect, having regard to the direct Experience of the Self in the Egoless State, which the Sages have. The latter is also incorrect, because of the peculiar definition of reality that the Sages have given.

If duality were real in the sense of the definition, it would endure for ever; there would be no possibility of non-duality realised or brought about by *any* means whatever. Besides, if non duality in the Egoless State be allowed to be an *effect* of the pursuit of the Quest or other means, then it would be unreal: having a beginning, it would have an end. An effect can endure only so long as it is sustained by its causative force. It is an axiom of the Upanishads that a finite cause — a course of activity — can never produce an infinite effect. The authors appeal to our common experience to prove this, if proof be needful. It is nobody's case that the state of Deliverance is other than endless. Even those who conceive of that State as becoming a denizen of a world of some sort do not allow that there is to be a return from it to a lower state of existence.

Those dualists that maintain the continuance of difference in Deliverance are at least logical in their claim. Of course they are unable to fit into their creed the testimony of the Sages. They achieve their object by rejecting that testimony.

Those dualists that seek to reconcile the experience of the Sages with their own creed are up against a dilemma. If they claim that difference is real while ignorance persists, they would have to say that

Deliverance has a beginning: but they are unwilling
to admit the inevitable consequence that it would also
have an end. If they admit that It is both beginningless
and endless, they would be logically driven to the
conclusion that difference is altogether an illusion, as
the Advaitists say.

The parable referred to is as follows. Ten men
from a village crossed a river, and then they counted
themselves to make sure that all had safely crossed
over. But as each man left himself out in the counting,
it seemed to them that they were only nine; so they
concluded that the tenth man was lost. While they
were bewailing the lost man, someone came up to
them, and inquired the cause of their sorrow. They
told him that there should be ten of them, but that
one was lost. The newcomer found that they were
mistaken; he counted exactly ten. And he saw also
how it was that they came to think they were only
nine: they had made a mistake in the counting. To
convince them that they were ten, he asked someone
to count the strokes he would deal on their backs.
The last stroke he reserved for the counter. When
the latter had counted nine strokes, the stranger dealt
one to him also, and thus ten strokes were counted,
showing that there were ten men in fact. If the counter
had counted right before, he would have found that
he himself was the tenth man; so he was the tenth
man all along, both before and after his discovery.
No new man was brought from elsewhere. He that
was the tenth at the time of his discovery, was the
tenth even before. So the real Self is the only Reality
all the time, both before and after the extinction of
the ignorance.

The truth is, ignorance is no more an existing thing than its products, the world, the soul and God. Ignorance does not exist for the real Self. It is a mere hypothesis, which is used as a means of conveying the teaching. We have seen that ignorance is no other than the ego, which has no existence at all. Hence ignorance, the origin of all creation, does not exist even now. The real Self is the One without a second all the time, — even now; that is, He is worldless. Therefore it is not open to us to entertain the belief that the Reality suffered a real change, — that It really became the three. If it could have suffered a change, It can never save *us* from the vicious circle of change, which we want to escape. Rightly was it said by Gautama Buddha that "if there be not an unchanging and unchangeable Reality, there can be no Deliverance for us from *samsara* (relative existence)." He declared that "there is an unchanging and unchangeable Reality, and that therefore we can obtain Deliverance." If we admit that the Reality is changeless, we must also admit that it is *not* the cause, material or efficient, of the world — that Its being undergoes no change of any sort.

This is the truth of God. God as conceived by the devotees is only relatively real, as we shall see in the chapter on Devotion.

We have seen before that he that looks upon God as a Person regards himself as a person. We have seen also that the personal God must have a form, gross or subtle, physical or mental.

Personality means existence in one's own right, as a being separate from all other beings. The claim to such existence is based on the ego-sense. The ego-mind is aware of itself as conscious and intelligent. This consciousness is not its own, but a minute fraction of the Consciousness which is the Self, just as the light of the image of the sun seen in a mirror is a minute fraction of the sun's own light. The notion that the mind or soul is a conscious entity is described in the sacred lore and by the Sage as an act of theft. This theft has to be undone by surrendering to the Reality the mind, with the ego reflected in it, by understanding that the Reality is the Self. This is the meaning we are told to find in the last line of the *Gita*-teaching (18.66).

सर्वधर्मान् परित्यज्य मामेकं शरणं व्रज ॥

This means: "Take refuge in Me, surrendering all (your) *dharmas*." Here 'dharma' is to be taken in a wider sense than usual. It does not mean duties or conduct; it means 'status' or 'attributes'. The soul is a bundle of attributes; the first and the foremost of these is *personality*. This has to be surrendered, says the Sage.

The manner of this surrender is the Quest of the Self.

Chapter 8

The Egoless State

THE WORLD OF RELATIVITY — comprising the three categories, namely the world, the soul and God — is seen to be a false appearance imposed by the ego-mind on the Reality. The latter is the *substratum*, the element of truth in the three. That Reality is obscured for us by the illusory appearance of these three. The origin of the illusion is the ego-sense. And so long as the ego-sense endures, there will be no end to ignorance and bondage. That is, we shall become free only by becoming egoless. This is what we learnt in the preceding pages.

The State of Deliverance is thus described as the Egoless State. This is also described in other ways, — as the State of Knowledge or Illumination, of Bliss, of Perfection, of Peace, and as the Natural State. These descriptions seem to convey some definite ideas about It; they do not do so, because, as we shall see later on, It is not within the scope of speech or thought.

Two questions arise in regard to that State, namely whether there *is* such a State, and whether It is desirable. The first question implies a doubt whether the State might prove to be one of utter nothingness — of the extinction of the self. The doubt is inspired by the deep-rooted belief that the ego is oneself. The answer to this is that there *is* a real Self, which is something other, and far greater, than the ego and that It survives the death of the ego, since it is real as defined by the Sages. The second question arises from the notion that happiness consists of pleasures, for which there is no scope in a State of worldlessness.

Neither of these doubts can assail the disciples of a living Sage. Those that have sat at the feet of the Sage of Arunachala are not troubled by them. The Sage himself is the best proof of the Egoless State. Those that have imbibed the mysterious influence that emanates from him do not need any evidence or argument to prove to them that the Egoless State is real and should be won at any cost. They know that It is the State of Completeness or Perfection, of eternal Happiness, undiminished by desires and unaffected by fear.

That these and similar doubts are not to be taken seriously is the teaching of the Sages. The Sage of Arunachala points out that the ego itself — the arch-enemy of Happiness — is the parent of all doubts. He is raising them as a means of postponing the day of his own extinction. To entertain these doubts and waste our time and energies in seeking solutions for them is to play into the hands of the enemy. The right thing to do, says the Sage, is not to go on framing questions and seeking answers — which are of little value, being merely intellectual — but to arrest the culprit — the ego —, put him in the dock, and dispose of him by the Quest of the real Self, which he pretends to be. In other words, one should discover the real

Self, who is the final answer to all questions. Every question that arises is vitiated by the ignorance which takes the ego at its face value, as the real Self. All questions are therefore reducible to one: "Who am I?" This question is the Quest of the Self, by which the Egoless State is won. In that State there is only the Self and nothing else, and hence there are no questions and no answers, but only Silence: so says the Sage.* The same sense is clearly conveyed by the Upanishadic lore. "When that Supreme Being is seen, then the knot (of desires) in the Heart is cut, *all doubts are dispelled*, and all the effects of actions are cancelled."† Thus we have clear warning that an endless raising of doubts is just a means of giving a new lease of life to the ego. It is a vice, perhaps more serious than those that are so called. It betokens a want of earnestness and a lurking love for bondage itself. But while an inveterate habit of raising doubt is discouraged, the well-meaning inquirer is helped to see for himself that there are answers to all possible questions — only that there must be a limit to questioning.

To the perfectly ripe disciple — that is, one who is in profound earnest to win the Revelation of the Self — these questions are of no importance. For he that is perfectly devoted to the real Self is also quite ready to renounce the prison-life that ego-ridden existence is. The Sage tells him that the real Self is the source of

---

* See *Guru Vachaka Kovai* verse 1181 (appendix B, verse 247-A).

† भिद्यते हृदयग्रन्थिश्छिद्यन्ते सर्वसंशया: ।
क्षीयन्ते चास्य कर्माणि तस्मिन् दृष्टे परावरे ॥
                                                    — *Mundaka Upanishad,* 2.2.8.

the ego, and should be sought and found, if he would have the fullness of Life. That is enough for him. He does not hesitate, allowing doubts to arise and hinder his Quest of the Self. We have seen in the first chapter that the Sage himself did not hesitate — was not held back by doubts or fears. It was as if he had concluded that *this* relative existence, shadowed by the ego, was of no value at all, and was prepared to lose the whole of it for finding that which is Real. We know also that he had not any of the advantages that are available to us in abundance — the sacred lore of the past and the teachings of the Sages.

We shall now see how these questions are answered by the Sages.

The state of egolessness is not nothingness; for the Self is there in His real Nature — as He really is, unlimited by the ego. We have the testimony of a long line of Sages to this effect. That real Self is the Life by which, even now, we are sustained — but for which our existence in relativity would be so intolerable that death would be preferred. "Who would go on living, but for this infinite Bliss?"* For even now, in this realm of ignorance, we are sustained by currents — however weak and fitful — of the Happiness of the real Self, trickling through the dense folds of ignorance and sin, in just sufficient amounts to keep us from despair and suicide. The ancient lore tells us also that "he that finds that

_____

* को ह्येवान्यात्, क: प्राण्यात् । यदेष आकाश आनन्दो
  न स्यात् ॥
                                    — *Taittiriya Upanishad*, 2.7.1.

Self — who is concealed in the Heart — shall enjoy that profound happiness, which is the *simultaneous* fulfilment of all desires."[†]

There is a special significance in the word 'simultaneous' in the last-cited passage. The happiness following the fulfilment of any desire is not only temporary, but even while it lasts it is discounted by the ghosts of other unfulfilled desires. Such is *not* the case with the bliss of the Self enjoyed by the Sage; this is explained by a later passage in the Upanishad, where it is shown that in the Self is the fullness of Bliss, where desire cannot possibly arise.[*] The Sage explains to us that the unalloyed, complete and timeless bliss of the Egoless State is due to the fact that the ego — itself the root of discontent, desire, and the fever of activity — is dead once for all, so that it can no more raise its ugly head. "As a small animal cannot raise its head when the ocean overflows, so this little ego cannot raise its head in the State of Illumination (by the pure Consciousness)."[**]

Both the ancient lore and the Sages appeal to reason also, to confirm this teaching. The older

---

[†] सत्यं ज्ञानमनन्तं ब्रह्म । यो वेद निहितं गुहायां परमे
व्योमन् । सोऽश्नुते । सर्वान् कामान् सह । ब्रह्मणा
विपश्चितेति ।
— *Taittiriya Upanishad*, 2.1.1.

[*] The reference here is to the eighth Anuvaka of the Brahmananda Valli of the *Taittiriya Upanishad*.

[**] *Guru Vachaka Kovai* verse 1142 (see appendix B, verse 231).

Revelation, for example, is often at pains to show that out of nothing, nothing can arise. कथमसतः सज्जायेत?[†] How can the world come to birth from a mere nothing? The Sage also tells us that because we have the conviction that the things seen by us exist, therefore there *must* exist a Consciousness, the element of reality in the world-appearance.[‡]

From this we learn that the Infinite Consciousness is the underlying reality, not only of the world of things, but also of the world of persons.

We are aware of a self. We have seen, however, that we are mistaking the ego for the Self. But since there can be no idea of a self, without there being a real self of some sort, we must perforce believe that there *is* a real Self. The *Truth* about that Self can however be gathered only from the Sages. From them we learn that it is the pure and infinite Consciousness that dwells in the Egoless State.

Common experience also, as pointed out by the Sages, confirms the teaching. The Sage tells us that no one can deny his own existence. Whatever else he may deny, he must admit that he himself exists. For the very nature of the Self is that It is an indubitable reality. If it be found that the particular, finite self imagined by us does not exist, it only means we have ascribed selfhood to the wrong thing — *not* that there is no Self at all.

The real Self is not experienced in *His purity* in any of the three states known to us, namely waking,

---

[†] *Chandogya Upanishad*, 6.2.2.
[‡] See *Ulladu Narpadu* benedictory verse 1 (appendix A, v. 4).

dream and deep sleep. There is, of course, the experience of 'I am'; but this awareness of the real Self is reduced to a mere atom by the limitation imposed by the ego and its creations. As pointed out by Sage Sankara — in verse 365 of *Vivekachudamani** — the light of the Self is hopelessly blurred by the medium of the mind, — that He shines as He really is only in the Egoless State, which is the negation of all these three states. But even before we attain that State, we can find traces of the Self in the state of deep sleep, which are sufficient proof of His reality for the present, — until we win for ourselves the *full* Revelation of that Self by transcending the three states.

In deep sleep there is no body, nor mind, nor ego. But we are as sure as we can possibly be, that we ourselves survive in sleep. It is by this survival that the continuity of selfhood — which no one can deny — is maintained, as we shall see later on. But before we discuss this in detail we need to make a study of the three states in comparison with the Egoless State, in the light of the teachings of the Sages.

The waking state is the one in which we see this world. It is supposed that in this world there is a multitude of finite selves, to all of whom this world is common. We suppose also that this world is an objective reality, with which we come into contact through the gateways, our senses. These are open only in this waking state. In seeking to persuade ourselves that the world is real, we forget that the body and the senses are part of the world-appearance; so forgetting, we assume that these are real in the first place.

---

* This has been cited already on page 54.

Having thus surreptitiously assumed what is unproved, we naturally find it very easy to prove the truth of the rest of the world by the interested testimony of the senses. The judge who gives a decision on this point, namely the intellect, is incompetent, being the offspring of the ego, the father of lies.

The ancient Revelation tells us that the waking self is not really a finite being, as the intellect makes him out to be. He is not restricted to a particular body. His body is the whole universe — the whole of creation. He is called Vaisvanara or Visva — the All-Man. Our own Sage tells us that this world of waking is one indivisible whole, so that we should either take the whole as ourselves — if we can — or renounce the whole as an illusion. This is what he says: *"Since every single body in the world is made up of five sheaths, all the five sheaths together answer to the name of 'body'. Such being the case, how can the world exist apart from the body? Is the world ever seen by anyone without a body?"**

Here the Sage reminds us of a fact that we as a rule ignore. But it is a fact that we cannot deny. When one sees the world, he sees also a body of his own. This is the case both in waking and in dream. The body and the world are inseparable co-appearances. When there is no world-appearance, neither is there a body. The Sage asks us here, "If the world were something having a distinct existence apart from the body, why does not the world appear to us in sleep, when we are bodiless?"

---

* *Ulladu Narpadu* verse 5 (see appendix A, verse 10).

The question is unanswerable. The fact is that the world has no existence apart from the body. So the whole world is our body — a creation and projection of the ego-mind — just as it is in dreams.

The objection may be raised that being bodiless in dreams, we still see a world of some sort. The dreamer's body lies inert on his bed; but still there appears to him a world of variety, similar to the waking world. Also when one 'dies' and goes away, leaving his physical body to be burnt or buried, he is bodiless, but is able to travel to another world and dwell there for some time, before taking birth in this world again; while he dwells in that other world he must be seeing that world. To this the answer is that the word 'body' does not mean only this body of flesh, but also others of a finer texture. This is the teaching of the sacred lore; which the Sage accepts and gives as the answer to these questions. There are five bodies, or rather five *sheaths*, covering the indwelling Self and concealing him. All these put together make up the body; and hence so long as one or more of these sheaths are left, the self is not bodiless, and hence can see a world corresponding to the remaining sheaths. When one dreams, the subtle or mental body is left to the ego; and it is this subtle body that expands and becomes the dream world. Similar is the case with the passenger to another world; he travels in his subtle body, which enables him to hold commerce with that other world; of course that world is the creation of his mind. Hence in every case, where a world is seen, there is also a body for the ego. Thus it has been rightly said that body and world are always seen together. That they are one single, indivisible appearance, as stated above, is unquestionably true.

We have already seen that the waking world is substantially similar to the worlds seen in dreams. That the latter are unreal, few would deny. Those that deny this need not be taken seriously; they are driven to this absurd position by the exigencies of a defective creed. We came to the conclusion that both waking and dream are dreams. What we call waking is not true waking. The true waking is the Egoless State, which is the waking from the sleep of ignorance, in which this dream called waking takes place. In *that* waking no falsehoods can appear.

Now we shall take up the question of the continuity of the Self. The question relates to the state of deep sleep, since it is only in relation to it that a doubt may be raised at all, there being no body, nor mind, nor ego in dreamless sleep.

The common man does not question the continuity of the self through sleep, on to the next waking. Of course he is unaware that the sleeping self is not the finite, ego-wrapped self of waking and dream. As the Sage has remarked, "No man says 'I did not exist in sleep'." It is sophisticated humanity alone that is troubled by doubts about the continuity of self-existence. But all the Sages are emphatic that the Self underlies all the three states, and give reasons to help us to understand it.

In the first place, we are mistaken in our supposition that dreamless sleep is empty of all consciousness. When this question was raised by someone, the Sage said: "You say so *after* waking from sleep. You do not do so in sleep itself. That in you which *now* says that sleep is unconsciousness is your mind. But it was not present in your sleep, so it is natural for the mind to be ignorant of the consciousness there is in sleep. Not having experienced sleep, it is unable to remember what it was like, and makes mistakes about it. The state of deep sleep is beyond the mind." This shows that it is unfair for us to judge of any one state, with the mind of another state. The waking mind cannot judge of sleep, for the reason given by the Sage. A correct valuation of the three states is possible only to the Sage, who has transcended all of them.

In the second place, there is sufficient proof of the survival of the self in deep sleep; this we can understand from the following dialogue, in which the Sage answered a series of questions. A Western visitor asked a very wide question — concerning the practical utility of the Egoless State, and in the course of the talk that ensued he raised the question of the reality of the world; when he was told that the world appears discontinuously, he sought to meet it by the argument that the world *does* appear all the time to someone or other, who is awake at the time; the Sage showed that the argument is inconclusive, as shown already. Then the Sage proceeded as follows: "You take the world to be real, because it is a creation of your own mind, as in your dream. You do not see it in sleep because then it is wound up and merged in the Self, together with the ego and the mind, and exists in seed-form in your sleep. On waking the ego arises, identifying itself with a body and at the same time sees the world. Your waking world is a creation of your mind, just like your dream-world. There must be someone that

sees the world, both in waking and in dream. Who is
he? Is he the body?" "No", "Is he the mind?" "It must
be so." "But you cannot be the mind, since you exist
in sleep, when there is no mind." "I do not know that.
Perhaps I cease to exist then." "If so, then how do you
recollect what was experienced yesterday? Do you
seriously contend that there was a break of continuity
of your self?" "It is possible." "If so, then Johnson going
to sleep may awake as Benson. But this does not
happen. How do you explain your sense of the
persistence of your identity? You say 'I slept' and 'I
woke', implying that you are the same as the one that
lay down to sleep." The questioner had no answer to
make. The Sage continued: "When you awake from
sleep you say *'I slept happily and feel refreshed.'* So
sleep was *your* experience. He that remembers the
happiness of sleep — saying 'I slept happily' — cannot
be other than the one that experienced that happiness.
The two are one and the same."* The questioner
agreed that it must be so.

------

* The remainder of this instructive dialogue is as follows: The Sage
continued: "If as you say the world existed in your sleep, did it tell
you so then?" "No; but it tells me now. I get proof of the existence of
the world when I knock my foot against a stone in my path; the hurt
proves the stone and the world of which it is a part." "Does the foot
say that there is the stone?" "No; *I* say so." "Who is this I? It cannot
be the body; nor can it be the mind. It is just the witness of the
three states — waking, dream and sleep. They do not affect the I.
The three states come and go; but the I remains constant and
unmoved. He is the real Self, ever happy and perfect. The Experience
of this Self is the cure of all discontent and the realisation of
happiness and perfection." "It would be selfishness for anyone to
remain in that State, enjoying happiness, especially if he did nothing
to contribute to the happiness of the world." "You are told about
this State so that you may win that State and thereby realise the
truth that the world has no existence apart from your Self. When

Thus we have ample proof that there is a continuing self of some sort in sleep. That that self is not the soul, but the real Self of the Upanishads, is what we learn from the Sages. From our experience of sleep we learn also that the true Self can exist without the body and the mind; there being no body of any kind in sleep, there is no ego-sense in it.

Sleep is in fact very similar to the Egoless State. We shall see later that there is an important distinction. But here we need to notice only that the absence of individuality and of the mind in sleep is not inimical to happiness being enjoyed in it and remembered on waking. According to Revelation, the happiness of sleep is due just to its egolessness, imperfect as it is.

The three states are kept distinct from the Egoless one by the persistence of bodies or sheaths veiling the Self and limiting It. Three bodies are spoken of, and five sheaths. The physical or gross body corresponds to the state of waking. The mental or subtle body is related to dreams; it is also the body by which one goes to and dwells in other worlds, such as

---

you realize this, the word 'selfishness' will have no meaning, since the world will be merged in the Self." "Does the Sage know that there are wars and suffering in the world? If he does, how can he be happy?" "If a picture of a flood or a fire passes over a cinema screen, does it affect the screen? The real Self is just like this screen. He is unaffected by the events of the world. *Suffering is possible only while there is distinction between subject and object.* This distinction does not exist in the Egoless State. There the Self alone is. The Sage in that State is that Self. He is pure Spirit, the Holy Ghost. For him this world is the Kingdom of Heaven. And that Kingdom is within you." The Sage here refers to the teaching of Jesus. The Kingdom of Heaven that he taught is the Egoless State, where the Self is all there is; questions about the world — such as how to reform it — do not arise there.

heaven or hell. There is another body, *called* the causal body, which is the only body that is left over in sleep. This body is nothing but ignorance, the ego and mind in seed-form. The five sheaths are the same as these three bodies, as shown below.

The gross body is the same as the *Annamaya* sheath.

The subtle body is made up of: the *Pranamaya* sheath, the *Manomaya* sheath, the *Vijnanamaya* sheath.

The causal body is the same as the *Anandamaya* sheath.

The three sheaths comprised in the subtle body are named as above, according to their functions. The *Pranamaya* has the function of life, the *Manomaya*, of sensations and thoughts, and the *Vijnanamaya*, of intellection and making decisions.

The *Anandamaya* is not to be confounded with *Ananda*, which is the real Self in the Egoless State, *not* veiled by bodies or sheaths. The Sage tells us that the last sheath is only hypothetical, invented for the purposes of teaching. Anyhow that sheath is of no use for the seeker of the Self; it has to be jumped, as we shall see later.

The sheaths or bodies are of course not to be taken as real. The Experience of the Self, which is usually termed 'Right Knowledge', is just the realisation of the non-existence of all the things that are non-existent, but which seem to be existing by virtue of the ego-sense. Hence 'Right Knowledge' is nothing but the falling off of these sheaths. What remains over afterwards is that which is real, the pure, unvariegated, infinite Consciousness, namely the Self.

We shall now see what we can learn about that Self from the Sage's Revelation.

The real Self in the Egoless State is none other than the Reality, called 'Sat' — that which *is*. This *Sat* is also *Chit*, Consciousness. For nothing is real that does not exist in its own right. Whatever has no consciousness can exist only by consciousness. That is why the Sages say that the world is mental. The Self, we have seen, is the one indubitable Reality. And when the sheaths fall away, It remains as *pure* Consciousness, beyond the three states.

We shall now see why the Self is said to be consciousness, instead of saying that It is conscious. The explanation is very simple, though of very great importance. The mind is conscious, but poorly and fitfully so. Its consciousness fails utterly in sleep. There must be some Source, wherefrom the mind receives consciousness, as was pointed out before. This Source is therefore the Original Consciousness, which shines constantly, unlike the mind. Because Its Consciousness never fails, therefore Consciousness is Its very nature. And this meaning is expressed by saying that the Self — the Source here meant — is Consciousness. We find the teaching in the ancient lore also. The real Self is described in one of the Upanishads as 'endless Consciousness' — ज्ञानमनन्तम्. The purpose of this description is, says Sage Sankara, to differentiate It from the fitful awareness of objects that goes by the name of knowledge among men.

Consciousness, therefore, is not to be understood as a mere attribute of the real Self, but as Its very essence. This Consciousness is manifest as the 'I am', the common factor of all thoughts and of all perceptions. This truth is clearly expressed in the *Aitareya Upanishad** where the Self is called *Prajnanam* (प्रज्ञानम्), which means Consciousness. In its purity — uncontaminated by mixing up with the unreal sheaths, or with their changing states — it is the real Self. The common notion that knowledge or awareness is an attribute or quality, is just the reverse of the above teaching. Consciousness is not a quality; It is the very substance of Reality, and Reality is real solely because It is Consciousness. Consciousness alone exists; there is nothing else. It is often styled the supreme Consciousness, to differentiate It from the mind and intellect.

This Supreme Consciousness, say the Upanishads, existed alone in the beginning — when all this universe did not exist. It created out of itself the bodies of creatures, and Itself entered into them *as soul*. This becoming or creation is not to be taken as an event that happened actually; we shall see that presently. The purpose of these stories of creation in the ancient lore is to convey in a graphic manner the teaching, that the Self in us is just the Reality — that there is *no* individual soul.

If creation actually took place, it would follow that the Reality was broken into parts. That is absurd, as we have seen before. This is what the Sage tells us: "The Reality is neither broken into parts, nor does It suffer limitation. It only *seems* to be so. The mind it is that causes the appearance of parts, by falsely identifying It with bodies of sheaths and thus limiting It. The mind imagines the Reality as finite, thinking itself to be finite. These limitations and divisions are

---

* *Aitareya Upanishad*, 3.1.2 and 3.1.3.

in the mind alone. But the mind has no existence apart from the Self. A jewel made of gold is not *quite* the same as gold, because it is gold with a name and a form super-added. But it is not other than gold. Mind is just a mysterious power of the Self, by which the One Self appears as many. Only when the mind rises, do the three — God, the soul and the world — appear. In sleep the three are not seen nor thought of."

This is just what is known in Advaitic metaphysics as the *Truth of Non-becoming* — *Ajati-Siddhanta* — which is found definitely and categorically stated by Gaudapada, the author of the *Mandukya Karikas*, on which Sage Sankara has written a lucid commentary. Sankara's own writings are in perfect agreement with it. And our Sage has made it his own. It is said of him by a disciple: "Though the Holy One has given out truths modified according to the bias of questioners, yet he teaches the Truth of Non-becoming as verified by his own experience of the Self."* Also in the same work we find the clear enunciation of the Truth of Non-becoming, as follows: "There is no creation, nor destruction; there is no one that is bound; nor is there one that strives for Liberation, nor anyone that has attained that State. There is no mind, nor body, nor world, nor anyone called the 'soul'; One alone exists, the pure, calm, unchanging Reality which has no second, and no becoming."†

The ego-ridden person sees the variety and is curious to know how it came about. He is told that God made it all, and also that He made it all out of Himself. By thinking on this he comes to see that all

---

* *Guru Vachaka Kovai* verse 100 (see appendix B, verse 22).
† See Appendix B, verses 20, 21.

this multiplicity is a unity in something, which is called
God. He next wants to know about God. He is
persuaded that God must be a person, like himself,
though different in size, power and qualities. In the
beginning, therefore, he has to be allowed to go his
own way. But there comes a time when he can bear
to be told that God is not a person at all. Then the
Sage tells him, that God is egoless. The meaning is
that He is the One Reality that is the Self in all.

The description that God is egoless may seem to
be a poor one. It conveys no sense to the ego-ridden
mind. People want to be told that God dwells
somewhere in the sky, in a world of great splendour,
surrounded by wonderful beings, called gods or
angels. Even to understand that God dwells in their
own hearts men take time. Even there they want to
make a distinction between Him and the Self. It seems
to them a blasphemy to think of God as the Self.

Egolessness is impersonality. Now we shall ask
ourselves the question: Which is greater, personality
or impersonality? Personality seems to be something,
and impersonality nothing. But that is because we
do not easily see that personality is limitation to a
body, while impersonality is just the absence of all
limitation. In both there is the same Consciousness.
Personality is consciousness cabined, cribbed and
confined, and Impersonality is Consciousness as It
really is, unconfined, infinite and pure.

We see thus that impersonality and personality
are opposed like light and darkness, like freedom and
bondage, like knowledge and ignorance, or like the
mathematical signs, plus and minus. Which is plus
and which is minus? After what we have heard from

the Sages we cannot be in doubt about the answer.
Impersonality — egolessness — is plus. Personality
is minus.

Impersonality is Consciousness undiminished.
It is Existence in its entirety, — Existence as pure
Consciousness. This Existence is made into the three
by the mind. The Sage explained it as follows:
"Existence plus variety is the world. Existence plus
individuality is the soul. Existence plus the idea of
the all is God. In all the three, Existence is the sole
element of reality. Variety, individuality and all-ness
are unreal. They are created and imposed on
Existence by the mind. Existence transcends all
concepts, including that of God. Inasmuch as the
name 'God' is used, the concept of God cannot be
true. The truth about God is most faithfully
expressed as *I AM*. The Hebrew name of God,
'Jehovah,' — which means 'I AM' — expresses the
truth of God perfectly."

The Sage also drew pointed attention to the
mystery-sentence that occurs in the *Bible*, which is
said to have been uttered by God Himself. The story
there is about the vision of a Light that appeared to
Moses. Out of that Light a Voice speaks to him,
instructing him to lead his people out of Egypt. Moses
desires to know who it is that speaks to him; so he
begs to be told, so that he may tell his people. The
Voice tells him 'I AM THAT I AM'; this is the only
sentence in the whole book, the whole of which is
printed in capital letters, as the Sage pointed out. It
must be of great significance. The Sage tells us that
in this sentence God has given out the secret of His
own Nature — that He is just the 'I AM' which is the

ever-shining Light of Consciousness in our hearts. In other words, He is the Self.

That the One Self alone is true, and all else is superimposed on It by ignorance, has been clearly stated by the Sage in many ways, and on many occasions.

The Self is the Real Consciousness, and the persons and things of the world appear by the ascription of names and forms to It. This is expressed in the following: *"The Self who is Consciousness is alone real, and nothing else. All so-called knowledge, which is manifold, is only ignorance. This ignorance is unreal, since it has no existence of its own, apart from the Consciousness which is the Self, just as the unreal jewels made of gold have no existence apart from the real gold."**

What is here referred to as 'knowledge' is the world itself. The world, we have seen, is not other than the thoughts that arise and pass in the mind. These thoughts are described as knowledge by the ignorant, because they think that there is an outside world which the mind knows through the senses. The totality of this knowledge is not only ignorance, but also non-existent; this we can now understand, because the ego-sense is the origin of it all. Besides, 'ignorance' is a negation, and negations do not exist by themselves. This ignorance, consisting of views about a non-existent world, is nothing but the Consciousness that is the Self, plus the names and forms created by the mind. These names and forms,

---

* *Ulladu Narpadu* verse 13 (see appendix A, verse 18).

says the Sage, are unreal, like the names and forms imposed on gold, calling it 'jewels', when in fact it is gold all the time. It is to be noted that the Sage *purposely* employs the word 'unreal' and 'real' to qualify 'jewels' and 'gold'. Jewels are not commonly thought of as unreal. But here the purpose is to illustrate the unreality of the manifold knowledge, which is the world. The words are put in here, to make the parallelism complete and accurate. If these words were not there, some misguided disciple would twist the meaning and make it out that the Sage teaches the reality of names and forms. The same teaching is conveyed in the following: "The Reality is like the lighted screen, on which move the pictures (in a cinema-show); the soul, the world and God are like the pictures that move; the Infinite alone (like the lighted screen) is real. It is pure, without difference. Though these (pictures) are unreal, they are not different from the Reality. But the Reality is different from them, because it exists without them in Its state of Unity (in the Egoless State). He that sees the unreal appearances does not see the Reality; he that sees the Reality does not see the unreal appearances. The mind becomes deluded, because it loses hold of the immovable Self, who is like the unmoving screen, and sees one of the moving pictures as itself, and the other pictures as the other souls and the world."*

It will appear from this, that the 'soul', the seer of the world, is inseparable from the world, which is his spectacle; the whole is a creation of the ego.

---

* *Guru Vachaka Kovai* vv. 1216 to 1219 (see appendix B, vv. 289 to 292).

The whole of this teaching was given by the Sage to an American disciple as follows: "*Only one Consciousness, equally distributed everywhere. You through illusion give It unequal distribution. No distribution, no everywhere.*" In this instance the Sage spoke in English, and the above are the very words spoken by him. Here, in the first sentence, the ideas of 'distribution' and 'everywhere' had to be admitted. But in the third sentence the Sage makes it clear that they too are illusions, because they are the creations of the ego-mind.

The Self of the Egoless State is often called the great Self (परमात्मा) thereby distinguishing It from the pitiful little self (जीवात्मा) that appears in the three states. But the Sage tells us that the true distinction, thus expressed, is not between 'great' and 'little', but between 'real' and 'false'. The great Self is the real Self; the other self does not really exist. This self is displaced by the real One when the ego dies, because it is false.

The Sage is often loosely described as 'one that knows the Self'. But this is not intended to be taken in a literal sense. It is a tentative description, intended for those that believe ignorance to be something that exists; they are told that this ignorance is to be got rid of by winning 'Knowledge of the Self'. There are two misconceptions in this. One is that the Self is an object of knowledge. The other is that the Self is unknown, and needs to be known. The Self being the sole Reality, He cannot become an object of knowledge. Also being the Self, He is never unknown. The ancient lore tells us that He is neither known nor unknown, and the Sage confirms it.

How can this be? The Self is the pure 'I AM', the only thing that is self-manifest; by Its light all the world is lighted up. But It seems to be unknown, and to need to be known, because It is obscured by the world and the ego. What is needed is to remove these. The Sage explains this by the analogy of a room that is encumbered with unwanted lumber. If space be wanted, all that is needful is to clear out the lumber; no space has to be brought in from outside. So too, the ego-mind and its creations have to be emptied out, and then the Self alone would remain, shining without hindrance. What is loosely called 'knowing the Self' is really being egoless, and the Self. Thus the Sage does not *know* the Self; he *is* the Self.

This Upanishadic truth — that the Self is the deathless, self-existent Reality — is also proved, — so we are told by the Sage — by a fact of common experience, which however has been described as something anomalous. We all know that death is certain. But we ignore it and act always as if there were no death. And this is accounted a strange thing.* But if we take into account the teaching of the Sage, namely that we as the real Self are deathless in fact, what is there strange in this? This is an indication that the Self never really became bound or confined — never really lost His nature as the Reality.

The real Self is therefore neither non-existence nor unconsciousness. It is Existence and Consciousness.

---

* अहन्यहनि भूतानि प्रविशन्ति यमालयम् ।
शेषाः स्थावरमिच्छन्ति किमाश्चर्यमितः परम् ॥

— *Mahabharatam.*

It is also defined as Happiness. or Bliss. Here again we have to beware of notions that belong to the world of the ego. The Self is impersonal, and therefore it is Happiness; and not someone that is happy. He that is happy is not so at all times. Sometimes he is miserable. And he is more happy at one time than at another. This we have seen in the second chapter. The real Self in the Egoless State is not at all like this 'happy man'. Happiness is of the *essence* of His nature, like Existence and Consciousness. Just as the Self is the original of all existence and of all consciousness, wherever manifest, so He is the original of all the happiness — chiefly in the form of pleasure — that is experienced by ego-minds.

Another clear proof of the reality of the Self in the Natural State is given by the Sage, quoting the *Yoga Vasishtham*: *"Just as in spring-time there comes to trees an increase of beauty and other qualities, so to the Seer of the real Self, who is contented in the enjoyment of the Bliss of the Self, there comes surely an increase of Light, Power and Intelligence."** These manifestations are a proof to those who are inclined towards doubt, that there is Something behind the new blossoming of excellences. That Something is the Fullness of power and of knowledge.

This is most evident in deep sleep. It cannot be doubted that the Self himself is the source of the happiness that prevails in that state, and is remembered afterwards. We have taken note, already, of the truth that even the pleasures that come to us

---

* *Ulladu Narpadu Anubandham* v. 29 (see appendix A, v. 75).

in waking, and which we suppose to be *caused* by the contact with sense-objects, come from the Self alone. They are just droplets of the Happiness that is the Self. This natural Happiness is as a rule dammed up — so to say — by the primary ignorance and its progeny, the desires and discontents, and fears and worries that go to make up the thing called mind. The mind, functioning as a distinct entity, almost completely effaces the happiness that is ours by nature, as the Self. But sometimes the mind ceases to obstruct, more or less, and then what seems to us an abundant measure of happiness comes to us. What happens is that the mind for a brief space becomes one with the Self — as in deep sleep — and then we are filled with happiness, as it were. This occasional union with the Self occurs whenever the mind's unrest abates, by the fulfilment of some ardent desire, or the removal of some fear. This happiness is transitory, because there are other unsatisfied desires, which soon become active, and then the mind loses its hold on the Self. The Sage tells us that unhappiness is no other than this separation of the mind from the Self, and that happiness is just the return of the mind to its Source, the Self. The mind is active as mind when it is separate from the Self. To become aware of anything is to disconnect the mind from the Self, and that is unhappiness. Not to be aware of things or thoughts is happiness. For then we are the Self.

This is graphically expressed in the ancient lore as follows: "As one that is locked in embrace with his beloved wife knows not anything outside or inside, so the person who is locked in the embrace of

the real Self knows not anything outside or inside."*
That this is not unconsciousness is pointed out in a
later passage. "Seeing, He sees not. Certainly the
Seer's sight never fails, because it is indestructible.
But there is no second object, separate from Him,
for Him to see."†

Thus both the questions propounded about the
Egoless State are answered. There *is* a real Self
underlying the three states, who is by nature immortal
and would survive the reduction to nothingness of the
unreal, the ego. Happiness is the very nature of that
Self, and hence the Egoless State is the one thing
that is desirable, beyond all comparison with anything
that there is in relativity.

The one great difficulty that the intellect finds
in accepting this teaching is this. The intellect
demands a rational link between the world it knows
and the Self or Reality it is told about. It wants a
bridge over which it can pass and re-pass between
the two. Such a bridge does not exist, and cannot
possibly be built by anyone — even by a Sage. The
reason is extremely simple, namely the fact that *the*

---

* तद्यथा प्रियया स्त्रिया संपरिष्वक्तेन किंचन बाह्यं वेद,
  नान्तरं, एवमेवायं पुरुष: प्राज्ञेनात्मना संपरिष्वक्तो न
  किंचन ब्राह्यंवेद, नान्तरम्

                                          — *Brihad. Up.*, 4.3.21.

† यद्वै तन्न पश्यति, पश्यन् वै तन्न पश्यति । न हि
  द्रष्टुर्दृष्टेर्विपरिलोपो विघतेऽविनाशित्वात् । न तु तद्वि
  तीयमस्ति ततोऽन्यद्विभक्तं यत् पश्येत्

                                          — *ibid.*, 4.3.23.

world and the Reality are negations of each other. We
have seen before that what appears as the world is
just the Reality. And this was made intelligible to us
by the analogy of the snake seen in a rope. So too the
world and the Reality are negations of each other.
They cannot be seen simultaneously. The rope is
unrelated to the snake; it did not give birth to the
snake. So too the world and the Reality are negations
of each other, in the sense that he that sees one of
them does not and cannot at the same time see the
other. The two cannot be experienced simultaneously.
He that sees the world sees not the Self, the Reality;
on the other hand he that sees the Self does not see
the world. So one of them alone can be real — not
both. Hence there is no real relation between them.

The world did *not* come into existence from the
Reality. The latter is wholly unrelated to the former.
Therefore it is clear that the bridge that the intellect
demands does not exist and cannot be built.

Questions that are raised, assuming that there
is such a bridge and wanting to know all about it, are
therefore meaningless and deserve no direct answer.
One such question we have noticed before; it was
about the origin of ignorance. The same question was
put to the Sage in a more general way, as follows:
"How can the State of Deliverance be harmonised with
the world?" The Sage answered: "That harmony is in
Deliverance itself." The Sage who is in that State is
not aware of any disharmony; on the contrary there
is perfect harmony there, because the Self alone is
there, — worldless. But the intellect cannot know that
harmony, because it can never get there — because,
if it gets there, it will cease to be. This is the meaning

of the statement, many times reiterated in the ancient lore, that the State of Deliverance, — that is, the real Self that is in that State, — is beyond the intellect.

As this State is beyond the intellect, so it is also beyond speech. Attempts to give a faithful description of the State in words are bound to fail. That is, any description making a *positive* statement about It will be inevitably false in one or more particulars. Many such statements, that are found in the ancient lore, are corrected by fresh statements, and these again by others, until the disciple is ripe for being told that It cannot be objectified by the intellect without falsification, and that direct Experience is the *only* means of knowing It aright, or rather of ceasing to know It wrongly.

The consequence is that we can only know what the Self is *not*, never what the Self *is*. In the final teaching, no attempt is made to tell us anything about the positive content of the State. In the ancient lore we are told that we should understand the Self as *Neti, Neti,* — 'not this', 'not this'. Its language is Silence, not words. This truth is brought home to us by the story of the instruction by Silence, that was vouchsafed by God Himself — appearing as Dakshinamurti — to four Sages, named Sanaka, Sanandana, Sanatana and Sanatkumara. The disciples understood that they had to become silent in speech and thought, in order to find the Truth which is beyond both. They did so and found it. "Silence," says the Sage, "is the language of the Self, and it is the most perfect teaching. Language is like the glow of the filament in the electric lamp; but Silence is like the current in the wire."

Thus we are not to expect any *positive* description of the Egoless State, or of the Self that is in that State. Even the Sage cannot tell us anything positive about that State. All that he can do is to remove our misconceptions about It. He tells us what It is *not* or rather how it differs from the states known to us in relativity. And the only one who could tell us anything at all about that State is the Sage. There is a saying current among the people, to the effect that *"he that speaks about It has not seen It; he that has seen It does not speak."*

It may be said that there *are* positive descriptions about It in the ancient lore, namely that It is Reality, Consciousness and Happiness — *Sat, Chit* and *Ananda.* The answer is that these descriptions are positive only in form; they are negative in meaning, being intended only to dispel misconceptions. It is called Reality, to dispel the notion that It is non-existence. It is called Consciousness, to show that It is neither insentient like inert objects, nor fitfully conscious like the mind. And It is called Happiness to show that in It we transcend this relativity which is essentially unhappy.

One thing that is clear about the State is that It is not a world or place of abode, to which the liberated ones are to go either now or after death. Very queer beliefs are being cherished and taught by different kinds of believers. Some say that when Deliverance comes to one, he is *bodily* taken up into the sky. Others say that the body simply vanishes, being miraculously transformed into something invisible; according to these persons, if there be a dead body left, there has been no deliverance. Most people believe that

Deliverance means going or being taken to some kind
of heavenly world. We are told in the *Yoga
Vasishtham*: "Deliverance is not in the top of the sky,
nor deep inside the earth, nor on the earth; It is just
the extinction of the mind, with all its desires."* The
meaning is that the Egoless State is not in relativity.
And It cannot be in it, because It is the utter negation
of it. The same is the teaching of the ancient lore,
which says: "When all the desires infesting the Heart
become extinct, then the mortal becomes immortal;
just here he becomes Brahman."†

But there is a statement about the Self which
might seem to conflict with this. Both the ancient lore
and the Sage tell us that the Reality dwells in the
Heart. The Sage also tells us that Jesus meant the
same thing when he said: "The kingdom of Heaven is
within you." This at the first thought seems to imply
that the real Self is in relativity, and is even of atomic
size, being confined within a space no bigger than a
man's thumb. But this is not intended to be taken in
a literal sense. For we are told also that the infinite
sky, together with all the worlds, is *inside* that small
space. The purpose of the teaching is that the Self
must be sought and found by turning *inwards*, away
from the world; this we shall see in the next chapter.
We are told by the Sage — quoting from the *Yoga*

---

* न मोक्षो नभस: पृष्टे न पाताले न भूतले ।
सर्वाशासंक्षये चेत:क्षयो मोक्ष इतीर्यते ॥

† यदा सर्वे प्रमुच्यन्ते कामा येऽस्य हृदि श्रिता: ।
अथ मर्त्योऽमृतो भवत्यत्र ब्रह्म समश्नुते ॥

— *Katha Upanishad*, 2.3.14.

Vasishtham — that the Heart meant is not the lump of flesh called by that name, but the real Self, the original Consciousness. It is called the Heart, because It is the Source of intelligence from which the mind takes its rise and expands into the world. To that Source it must return, so that relativity may be wound up and may cease. When the mind, with life, returns to the Heart and stays there in unity with It, then it can no more project on the Self the world-appearance which conceals it. From this it follows that the Sage does not see the world, though he rarely says so, having regard to the weaknesses of questioners; this we shall see later, when discussing the questions that concern the Sage.

The Self is therefore *in a sense* the All. It is spoken of as the Totality, of which the worlds and creatures are fractions, though in *absolute* truth it has no fractions. Thus to gain the Self is to gain the All. The sacred lore tells us: "That which is infinite is Happiness; in the finite there is no happiness."* The Sage tells us: "The Self alone is great; all else is infinitesimally small. We do not see anything whatever, other than the Self, for which we may sell the Self."† We are here reminded of the saying of Jesus: "What does it profit a man, if he gains the whole world, yet loses his own self?" For a very very small price, — the surrender of the ego — this infinitely great One, the Self, is to be had. But this small price has to be paid.

---

* यो वै भूमा, तत् सुखम् नाल्पे सुखमस्ति ॥
— *Chandogya Upanishad*, 7.23.1.

† *Guru Vachaka Kovai* verse 1060 (see appendix B, verse 300).

And yet it happens that men are *afraid* of this
State. They are not afraid of the ego-ridden existence,
which is the source of all their fears, because they
believe the ego to be themselves, and know not the
real Self. They are afraid that if they lose the ego,
they themselves shall cease to be. They are afraid
and unafraid of the wrong things. They are afraid of
Fearlessness, which is egolessness, and unafraid of
Fear, which is the ego.* That the loss of the ego is no
loss ought to be clear to them from their experience
of the happiness of sleep. No one is afraid to go to
sleep, says the Sage, though it is egoless. So why
should one be afraid to lose the ego — the cause of all
Fear — once for all, and thereby win Fearlessness?

This Natural State needs to be distinguished
from the Yogi's trance, which is called *Samadhi*. This
we are told by the Sage of Arunachala. There are
various kinds of trance and the highest is called the
Trance without thought — *Nirvikalpa Samadhi*. The
description 'without thought' applies also to the
Natural State. The Yogic trance is called the *Kevala
Nirvikalpa Samadhi*. The Natural State is called the
Sahaja Nirvikalpa Samadhi. 'Sahaja' means
'Natural'. This alone is the State of Deliverance —
not the other. The distinction is brought out by the
Sage's answer to a question. A disciple asked him: "I
am convinced that one that is in the *Nirvikalpa
Samadhi* remains unmoved by any activity of the body
or the mind. I base my opinion on my observation of
your State. Someone else maintains that *Samadhi*

---

* योगिनो बिभ्यति ह्यस्मादभये भयदर्शिन: ॥

— *Mandukya Karika*, 3.39.

and bodily activity are mutually incompatible and cannot co-exist. Which of these views is correct?" The Sage answered: "Both of you are right. There are two *Nirvikalpa Samadhis*; one is called the Natural State or *Sahaja Nirvikalpa Samadhi,* or simply the *Sahaja.* The other is called *Kevala Nirvikalpa Samadhi.* Your view concerns the former; the other view concerns the latter. The difference between them is this. In the former the mind is dissolved and lost in the Self; and being so lost, it cannot revive, and hence there is an end of bondage. In the latter case, the mind is not dissolved and lost in the Self; it is immersed in the Light of the Consciousness, which is the Self; while it is so immersed, the Yogi who is in that *Samadhi* enjoys great happiness; but since the mind remains distinct from the Self, it can and does become active again, and the Yogi becomes subject to ignorance and bondage. He that has won the Natural State is the Sage; he is free once for all, and cannot become bound again. The difference is illustrated thus. The mind of the Sage that has attained the Natural State is like a river that has joined the ocean and becomes one with it; it does not return. The mind of the Yogi that is in the Yogic *Samadhi* is like a bucket let down by a rope into a well, where it remains submerged in the water; by the rope it can be pulled up again; so the mind of the Yogi can go back to the world; he is not free; thus he is very much like common men. The Yogi's mind in *Samadhi* is like the mind of a sleeper in sleep, with this difference, that while the sleeper's mind is immersed in darkness, that of the Yogi is immersed in the Light of the Self. The Sage, that is, the one whose mind has become dissolved into the Self, is not

affected by the world in any way, though to all
outward appearance he — that is, his body and mind
— may be active in the world. His activities are like
the eating of a meal by a somnolent child, who is being
fed by the mother, or like the movements of a carriage
in which the driver is asleep." We shall come to this
point later on.

It is thus clear that only the one that has won
the Natural State, — that is, the one that has become
egoless — can become a Teacher of the Truth about
the Self to others — not the mere Yogi who has won
the *Kevala Nirvikalpa*. That the attainment of the
latter does not make one free is illustrated by the
Sage, by the instance of a Yogi who had attained this
Samadhi and was able to plunge into it by effort and
remain in it years at a time. Once he came out of
Samadhi and felt thirsty. His disciple being near, he
told him to fetch water. But the disciple was long in
bringing the water. Meanwhile the Yogi dived into
Samadhi again. Centuries passed, during which the
sovereignty of the land passed from the Hindus to
the Muslims, and from them to the British. At last
the Yogi awoke and his first thought was that his
disciple would have brought the water; so he just
called out 'Have you brought me the water?' Here
clearly the mind was surviving in latency during the
Samadhi and resumed its activity just from where it
left off. While the mind survives, there is no
Deliverance.

It seems likely that the Natural State may come
after repeated experience of the other state for some
months or years; the mind might get worn away little
by little in this way, just as a doll of sugar immersed

again and again in a sea of sugarcane-juice might get worn away until nothing is left of it.

We are now able to answer a question which was raised and answered long ago — in the ancient lore. This question might have occurred to the reader also. The State of Deliverance is egoless. So is deep sleep. So it would seem as if one can become free by merely going to sleep. But it is not so. No one becomes free by going to sleep. When he awakes he finds himself as much in bondage as ever before. We have seen that even the Yogi, when he comes out of his trance, called *Samadhi*, is in the same predicament. The question is: "Why does not the sleeper, who becomes egoless in sleep, stay egoless? Why does the ego revive again on waking?"

Before we consider the answer, we may notice another feature of sleep, which we find from Revelation. Not only is sleep not the gateway to Deliverance; it is also an obstacle to It. We shall see later on that if the seeker of the Self falls asleep while engaged in the Quest, he has to begin over again on waking. Only if he keeps wide awake all the time, and persists actively in the Quest till the Revelation of the Self takes place, does he become free from bondage. We find this indicated in the third part of the *Taittiriya Upanishad*, where we are told that Bhrigu, who received his teaching from his father, Varuna, obtained Experience of the real Self, — therein named Bliss, *Ananda*, — straightaway from the sheath of the intellect; he did not shed that sheath and become lost in the sheath of bliss — the *Anandamaya* — which would have meant falling asleep. This last sheath — the causal body — is not

separately transcended, but only along with the
sheath of intelligence.

When this question was put to the Sage, he
referred to the Upanishadic lore, where the question
is answered. There is a vital difference between the
two states. The Sage enters the Egoless State by the
utter and final extinction of the ego, which is the
primary ignorance. In the language of relativity he
is said to lose contact with the subtle and gross bodies
by the dissolution of the causal body, — otherwise
called the sheath of happiness — which is just this
primary ignorance. He passes straightaway from
the waking state — by the extinction of the ego —
to the Egoless State, which is beyond relativity.
Hence it is clear that the Sage becomes free from
the causal body. But for this body, there is no sort
of connection between the Real Self — which the
Sage is — and the other bodies. Therefore he is
bodiless and mindless.

The case of the common man going to sleep is
quite different. His causal body — the primary
ignorance — is not dissolved. Into it the ego and mind
are merged and remain there in seed-form until the
time of waking. The mind having become quiescent,
there is happiness in sleep; but this happiness bears
no comparison whatever with that of the Egoless
State. The Sage tells us: "The happiness of sleep is
like the meagre light of the moon that passes through
the thick foliage of a tree and lights up the ground
beneath; but the happiness of the Sage is like the
unobstructed moonlight that falls on open ground."[*]

_____

* See Appendix B, Verse 310.

This vital difference between the sleeper and the Sage is illustrated in the ancient lore by the analogy of an ordeal by fire, in which an accused person took hold of a red-hot axe, making protestation of his innocence. If he was burnt he was adjudged guilty and punished. If he was not burnt he was declared innocent and set free. Here the guilty man got burnt, because he covered himself with a lie when he grasped the burning iron. The innocent one was not burnt, because he covered himself with the truth, which protected him from being burnt. In the same way the common man goes into union with the Reality in sleep, covering himself with the false knowledge 'I am the body.' Thereby he is a liar, and by that lie he is thrown out and returns to bondage. The Sage becomes one with the Reality, covering himself with Right Knowledge — that is, giving up the ego-sense — and is not thrown out.

The Egoless State is therefore something unique. It does not belong to the world-order at all, to which the three states belong. We have seen already that there is a profounder sleep, the sleep of ignorance, by which the real Self is veiled, so that it is possible to take the ego at its face value, as the real Self. The Egoless State is the State of unclouded Reality, where It shines as the pure 'I AM.' This is called the Fourth State, to distinguish It from the three. But this is just a tentative description. The *Mandukya Upanishad* is careful to say: "They regard It as a Fourth State."[†] The Sage tells us: "*The peaceful and*

[†] चतुर्थं मन्यन्ते ॥

— *Mandukya Upanishad*, 7.

*timeless state of the Sage, called Waking-Sleep, which
to those that live in (the vicious circle of the three states
namely) waking, dream and sleep, is said to be the
Fourth State, is alone real; the other three are merely
false appearances; therefore the Wise Ones call that
State — which is Pure Consciousness — the
Transcendental State."*[†] Thus it is clear that there are
not four states, but only one, which is the Natural
State of the Self as the sole Reality.

The description of the Natural State as Waking
Sleep is very instructive. It tells us that It is the true
Waking, but that It resembles sleep. This is clearly
brought out in the *Gita*, which says: "The Sage is
awake to That, which is (as good as) Night to all
creatures; all that to which the creatures are awake
is night to the wide-awake Sage."[‡] The meaning is
that the Sage who abides in the Egoless State is awake
to That which alone is true, namely the Self; the world
is Night to him, because being unreal it is not seen
by him at all. Thus Day and Night are distributed
between the Sage and the ignorant. What is Day to
the Sage is Night to the ignorant, and what is Night
to him is Day to them. We have seen already that
this Day of the Sage is beginningless, as well as
endless, because time is unreal.

Since true waking is this Egoless State and not
the dream miscalled waking by the ignorant, it follows
that the believers in heavens of sorts, where the ego

[†] *Ulladu Narpadu Anubandham* v. 32 (see appendix A, v. 78).

[‡]   या निशा सर्वभूतानां तस्यां जागर्ति संयमी ।
      यस्यां जाग्रतिं भूतानि सा निशा पश्यतो मुने: ॥

is to endure for ever, do not want to awake, but only to dream in a pleasanter fashion. This is clearly due to their invincible attachment to ego-ridden existence. Because of this attachment, the loss of the ego appears to them as the worst of deaths. Really, as the Sages testify, this ego-ridden existence is death — the only death there is, — because it keeps us in perpetual exile from our true Life, namely the real Self; having lost That, we have lost all. In fact, as the Sage has clearly pointed out, birth is not birth, because we are born only to die; and death is not death, because we die only to be born again. On the other hand the attaining of the Natural State is true Birth, because then death is dead once for all. Of the Sage in that State Sri Ramana says: *"That man of elevated mind is alone really born, who has been born in the Source of his being, the Supreme Reality, through the Quest 'Whence am I?'; he is born once for all, (never to die any more); that Lord of the wise is ever new."** Being the Reality beyond time, he is ever new, ever fresh, unaffected by the passing of time.

We may repeat here what we have noticed before, namely that the Sage himself is the most convincing proof of the Natural State. By coming into direct contact with a living Sage, we can sense, though somewhat dimly, yet in a way that will change our lives, the greatness and glory of the real Self. In him the Self will appear to us as It really is, the greatest of all gains. We shall then see that the Self is the fulfilment of all desires and the annulment of all fear. We shall see that what the sacred lore tells us about

---

* *Ulladu Narpadu Anubandham* v. 11 (see appendix A, v. 57).

the Self is far from exaggerated — that in fact that
lore has not told us a millionth part of His greatness.

It has to be said that this Self, which we are
always, — even now, in spite of ignorance, — seems
to be a good deal too great for the many clever but
little minds that set up to be religious. The sacred
lore that tells them about the Natural State does not
appeal to them at all. They are after the winning of
powers, which they shall possess and enjoy. Winning
these powers — called 'Siddhis' — they hope to enjoy
a much more glorious status in the universe. These
siddhis are to be won by various occult practices. Some
even propose to win them through what they call
'Knowledge of the Self', though how they could win
right Knowledge, while cherishing these selfish
ambitions, is difficult to understand. Physical
immortality, and even sovereignty over all creation,
are aspired to by some. These men seem to feel that
God has not proved a success as the governor of the
universe, and that they themselves can do the work
far better, after winning the necessary equality with
God, and then superseding Him. They promise the
world at large that if and when their turn should
come, they would establish a Heaven on earth. The
Sage has repeatedly told us that the care of the world
is not *our* business, but God's.

There would be no need to take any notice of
these false teachers, but for the fact that many really
good people are led astray by their teaching, which
is superficially attractive. So that his own disciples
at least may not go astray, the Sage tells us that
these *siddhis* are in the realm of the ignorance, and
hence unreal. This is what he says: *"True* SIDDHI

*is one's own Natural State, in which one is the real
Self, and which is won by becoming aware of that
Self, which we already are; the other* siddhis *are like
those that are won in a dream. Does anything gained
in a dream remain true on waking? Can the Sage
that has cast off falsehood, by becoming fixed in the
Real, be deluded by them?"** Here it is made clear
that these *siddhis* are false; we know the reason,
namely that they are the creations of the ego. He
that wins these *siddhis* sinks deeper into the
ignorance that is bondage. To the genuine seeker of
the Self they sometimes come unsought, before he
attains egolessness; in that case they are to him a
snare; he must renounce them, and after they pass
from him, must begin over again. If they come after
the Natural State is won, he would not be aware of
them and would not be affected by them.

We may here take special note of the statement
that there is no need to *become* the Self, or *win* the
Self. The ideas of becoming or winning the Self are
on the face of them absurd. We are the Self always.
We are never other than He. If He were something to
be won, He might be lost again. As He is the Self, He
can never be lost. The *siddhis*, on the other hand, are
not *naturally* our own; therefore they will not be ours
for ever, but will be lost in due course.

There is another contrast between the true
Siddhi — the Natural State — and the false ones.
The Self is One. The *siddhis* are many. Manifoldness
is a mark of unreality. Unity is a sign of reality.

All this is in keeping with the main teaching

---

* *Ulladu Narpadu* verse 35 (see appendix A, verse 40).

of Revelation, both old and new, that the real Self
is the One Reality that transcends time and space,
and that all else is unreal. Hence it follows that
the Natural State is not in time. Hence it can never
have a beginning, nor an end; for beginning and
end are in time, which is unreal. The real Self is
One, and Its oneness too has no beginning, because
manifoldness is always unreal, as we saw in the
last chapter. Therefore it is that the Sage is not
aware of having *become* free. Once he was asked
when he became free. He replied: "Nothing has
happened to Me; I am as I have always been". This
means that bondage and freedom are *both* in
relativity, and are both unreal. This is what the
Sage tells us in the following: *"If the thought 'I am
bound' arises, then will arise also the thought of
deliverance. When by the Quest of 'Who am I that is
bound?' the ever-free real Self alone remains, ageless
and deathless, then how can the thought of bondage
arise? If that thought does not arise, then how can
the thought of Deliverance arise to him that has
done with actions?**

As this State is not in time, so too It is not in
space. We do not need to go somewhere — to some
distant world — to be free and happy always. This we
have seen already. Deliverance is here and now — if
only we lose the ego. Ignorance, bondage and the
incidents of bondage, namely all this multiplicity and
difference, do not exist even now. Therefore it follows
that the Sage who is egoless does not see all this,
which seems so real to us. For him this cinema-show

---

* *Ulladu Narpadu* verse 39 (see appendix A, verse 44).

of the world and its seer, the ego, have ceased; so he does not recognise its having been seen before. For him the screen alone remains, the Light of Consciousness; the moving pictures have vanished. That screen, we know now, is the pure "I AM", on which is imposed by ignorance the whole of this false appearance. Therefore said the Sage: *"Since we see the world, it follows that there is One Supreme Being, of whose power of illusion all this is a becoming; this cannot be disputed. All the four things, namely the pictures consisting of names and forms, their supporting screen, the light, and the seer, are not different from Him, the real Self in the Heart."*[†] The true Self, it is here expressly pointed out, is not Itself the cause of this variety. It has no becoming, as shown before. What becomes the universe is *Maya*, the mysterious power that has to be assumed as belonging to the Self, to account for the world-appearance. This *Maya* is the same as mind, which is the ego. Out of this *Maya* come forth the four, of which the individual soul is one, that is why he is unreal. Therefore it follows that this false appearance will persist only so long as the ego-sense continues, not after the extinction of the ego. Therefore we have to understand that to the Sage the world does not appear, though it may appear to others that the Sage sees the world, and though the Sage himself does not always deny seeing the world.

There are certain other details about this State, which can conveniently be studied in a later chapter,

---

[†] *Ulladu Narpadu* verse 1 (see appendix A, verse 6).

where we shall seek to understand something about the Sage, whose State It is.

This transcendent State, which alone is true, is obscured by the ego and its creations, the mind, the body and the world, just as the rope is obscured by the snake. Therefore they are declared to be unreal as such, — that the element of reality in them is the Self. Those that want to realise for themselves the reality of the Real have to turn aside from the world, by accepting the teaching that it is unreal, and seek the Truth within, in the Heart, in the manner shown by the Sage of Arunachala and described in the next chapter.

Chapter 9

The Quest

A CLEAR SUMMARY of the preceding chapters, together with an introduction to this one, is given by the Sage in the following: *"Where the ego rises not, there we are That. But how can that per Egolessness be attained, if the mind dives not i Source? And if the ego dies not, how can our State be won, wherein we are That?"** The the mind, that from which the mind tak which is here indicated, is the Heart, have seen before, is to be tentatively r Own Abode of the Self. Of course the is that the Self is Itself the real He refers to the Egoless State as because there we are what we Pure Consciousness.

That the ego must be g on which, as the Sage tells They differ only in regar of Deliverance. Once a "Which of the two vi says that God and

---

* *Ulladu Narpadu* verse

one?" The Sage said: "Get to business on the agreed
point, namely that the ego must be got rid of." Hence
the essential teaching is that which tells us how to
get rid of the ego; all else is of less importance. For
what we shall do to win Egolessness is far more
important than the beliefs, if any, we shall cherish
about It, or about the world that keeps us from It.[†]

The methods inculcated by the diverse religions
for Deliverance are all of them right in a way. But
the direct method is the one taught by the Sage. The
other methods just prepare the mind for the right
method. They can do no more. The Sage explained it
thus: "The ego cannot be subjugated by one that takes
it to be real. It is just like one's own shadow. Imagine
a man who does not know the truth of his shadow.
He sees it following him persistently, and wants to
get rid of it. He tries to run away from it, but it still
follows him. He digs a deep pit and tries to bury it,
filling up the pit; but the shadow comes to the top
and again follows him. He can get rid of it only by
looking away from it, at himself, the original of the
shadow. Then the shadow will not worry him. The
seekers of Deliverance are like the man in this
parable. They fail to see that the ego is but a shadow

---

ama once spoke a parable, in order to discourage
he origin of bondage; he said: "Here you are, bound
desire and fear, and here is the straight path to
sk questions about how you came to be bound.
You should be content to know how you can
ct like the man who died because he raised
insisted on getting answers. He was going
emy who was waiting for him in an
poisoned arrow. Accidentally the wounded

of the Self. What they have to do is to turn away from it, towards the Self, of which it is the shadow."

The first thing to do before beginning the Quest is to analyse the ego-sense and separate the real from the unreal part of it. We have seen already that the ego has an element of reality mixed up in it, namely the light of Consciousness, manifest as 'I am'. This 'I am', we know, is real, because it is the part that is constant and unchanging. We need to reject the unreal part, the sheaths or bodies, and take the remainder, the pure 'I am'. This 'I am' is a clue to the finding of the real Self. By holding on to this clue, the Sage tells us, we can surely find the Self. He once compared the seeker of the Self to a dog seeking his master, from whom he had been parted. The dog has something to guide him, namely the master's scent. By following the scent, leaving everything else, he ultimately finds his master. The 'I am' in the ego-sense is just like the master's scent for the dog. It is the only clue the seeker has for finding the Self. But it is an infallible clue. He must get and keep hold of it, fix his mind on it to the exclusion of all other things.

---

man was seen by a friend, who went and spread the news. Soon his kinsmen came to him with all necessary appliances. They wanted to pull out the arrow and apply antidotes, to save his life. But the wounded man prevented them, saying 'You must first inquire and find out all possible details about the enemy, — whether he is of high or low caste, tall or short, fair or dark and so on — and about the arrow and him that made it.' The kinsmen tried their best to convince him that these questions could wait, and that it was urgently necessary to save his life first by applying the remedies. But the man was obstinate, and precious time was wasted. So he died. Be not like this man. Cease questioning; hear the Way to Deliverance, and follow it."

It will then surely take his mind to the Self, the source of the 'I am'.

The analysis is like the following. "I am not the gross body, because when I dream, another body takes its place. Neither am I the mind, because in deep sleep I continue to exist, though the mind ceases to be, and I remember, on waking, the two features of sleep — namely the positive one of pure happiness, and the negative one of not seeing the world. As mind and body appear fitfully, they are unreal. As I exist continuously, I am real, as the pure 'I am'. I can reject these as not myself, because they are objects seen by me. I cannot reject this 'I am', because it is that from which body and mind are rejected. Hence the 'I am' is the truth of Me. All else is not I."

We do *not* thus arrive at the practical experience of the 'I am'. What we gain by this analysis is just an intellectual grasp of the truth of the Self. The Self thus known is a mere mental abstraction. What we need to experience is the *concrete* presence of the Self. We have seen in the last chapter that to do this we need to break the vicious circle of the three states. The method by which this vicious circle can be broken is the Quest of the Self taught by the Sage.

We may presume that this was the method followed by the Sages of the past. In one place in the Upanishadic lore we are told that '*the Self must be sought*'. It appears that the method followed by Gautama Buddha was this. But somehow the secret of this method seems to have been lost. For what we find in the books is not this method, but something else, which we shall call the traditional method. We shall first study this latter.

This method is as follows. First the seeker learns the truth of the Self as given out in the ancient lore, called the Upanishads; these and other books take the disciple through the philosophical inquiry set forth in the foregoing chapters; the Self is shown to be 'not this' and 'not this' and so on — eliminating at each step some one thing that has been taken to be the Self; in this way the gross body, the vital principle, the mind and the ego are rejected; or we are taken through the three states of being and the selves that are experienced in them are shown to be not the Self in his natural greatness; what remains over after all these are rejected, we are told, is the real Self, as well as the Supreme Being, the hypothetical cause and sustenance of all the worlds; we are further told that this Great Being is really unrelated, absolute, formless, nameless, timeless, spaceless, alone without a second, unchanging and unchangeable, perfect, the principle of happiness. which filters down into this world and is the cause of all the enjoyment in it.

The next step is for the disciple to reflect on this teaching, especially on the identity of the real Self and the Great Being spoken of — to consider the evidence for and against it; in doing so he is to remember that the sacred lore is the *only* evidence he can have of the truth of the real Self, which is supersensual and therefore beyond the intellect; the sacred lore is, of course, authoritative, because it embodies the testimony of Sages that have found the Truth; he is told to employ logic, not for discrediting that testimony, but for accepting it; for logic is by itself barren and can be used either way, according to the predilections of its user; it can lead to no final conclusion of its own. By this reflection he is to arrive at the conclusion that the sacred teaching is correct — that really the Supreme Being is his innermost real Self; and he is to repeat this process until he gets firmly convinced that the truth of the Self is expressed in the sentence 'I am That'.

The third and last stage of the method is meditation on this teaching; he is to fix his mind on the thought 'I am That', to the exclusion of all other thoughts, until he attains perfect concentration on that thought and his mind begins to flow in a steady current of meditation on that thought. The books tell us that if and when this happens the real Self will reveal Itself and ignorance and bondage will cease once for all. This is the threefold method as taught in the text-books.

The Sage of Arunachala allows that this threefold method has its use; he says it is a good method for purifying and strengthening the mind, so that it may become a fit instrument for the Quest that is taught by himself; for the strength of the mind consists in its freedom from distraction by the multiplicity of thoughts that usually arise and dissipate its energies; and it is unquestionable that only a strong mind can reach the goal, never a weak one; so says the ancient lore, as well as the Sage of Arunachala.

He says: "*The direct method of winning the real Self is diving into the Heart, seeking the Source of the 'I am'; the meditation, 'I am not this, I am That,' is of course helpful; but it is not itself the method of finding the Self.*"* Speaking to a visitor he said: "You are told that the ego is not your real Self; if you accept it, then

you have only to search for and find that which is
your real Self, the real being of which the ego is a
false appearance. Why then do you meditate 'I am
That'? That only gives a fresh lease of life to the ego.
It is like some one trying to avoid 'thinking of the
monkey when taking medicine'; by the very act of
trying he admits the thought. The source or truth of
the ego must be traced and found. Meditating 'I am
That' is of no use; for meditation is by the mind, and
the Self is beyond the mind. In the Quest of its own
reality the ego perishes of itself; hence this is the
direct method; in all else the ego is retained and hence
so many doubts arise and the eternal question
remains to be faced; until that question is faced there
will be no end to the ego. Then why not face that
question at once, without going through those other
methods?" Whatever assumes the reality of the ego,
whether explicitly or by implication, would even take
us further away from the goal, the Egoless State, if
we do not beware.

The Sage criticises this method as follows: *"If one
goes on meditating 'I am not this, I am That,' —
instead of winning the Natural State, which is
indicated by the Upanishadic text 'Thou art That,' by
pursuing, with one-pointed mind, the Quest "Who am
I?' — it is due to mere weakness of the mind; for that
Reality is ever shining as the Self."*[†] Here it is pointed
out that the Upanishadic text, 'Thou art That', tells
us the fact that the Self experienced in the Egoless
State is the Supreme Reality. It therefore means that

---

* *Ulladu Narpadu* verse 29 (see appendix A, verse 34).
† *Ulladu Narpadu* verse 32 (see appendix A. verse 37).

we should win the Egoless State, by the proper
method. It does not tell us to meditate 'I am That'.
From the text we must understand that by a single
effort we shall win two seemingly different things,
namely the Self and the Supreme Being, because both
are one and the same.

The Quest of the real Self consists in gathering
together all the energies of body and mind by
banishing all alien thoughts, and then directing all
those energies into a single current, namely the
resolve to find the answer to the question 'Who am I?'.
The question may also take the form of 'Whence am
I?'. 'Who am I?' means 'What is the *Truth* of me?';
'Whence am I?' means 'What is the *Source* of the sense
of self in the ego?' The Source in this Quest is to be
understood not as some remote ancestor or progenitor
in evolution, nor as some being existing before the
birth of the body, but as a *present* Source. Someone,
who seemed to think that it was important to know
about his own previous births, asked the Sage how
he could get to know of them; the Sage answered:
"Why bother about previous births? Find out first if
now you have been born." In this as in other idle
questions the ego lurks and manages to side-step the
search for the Truth; really the Self was never born,
so the Source is to be sought, not in the past, but in
the present.

This Quest is the one sure method of breaking
the vicious circle of the three states; for it not only
quietens the thinking mind, but prevents it from
falling asleep and thereby losing all consciousness;
therefore it has been described as 'sleeping
watchfully'. Neither in ordinary waking — when the

mind wanders from thought to thought — nor in sleep — when even the basic consciousness of 'I am' is submerged — can that vicious circle be over-passed; but for an instant of time in the passage of the mind from the vagrancy of waking to the utter stillness of sleep, the consciousness attains its purity as the formless 'I am'; by the force of the resolve in this Quest the consciousness is reduced to and kept steadily in this formless state, and by this the vicious circle is broken and the Egoless State is won.

The Sage describes the method of the Quest in the following: "*Just as one dives into a lake, seeking a thing that has fallen in, so should the seeker dive into the Heart, resolved to find wherefrom rises the ego-sense, restraining speech and the vital breath.*"* This brings out the devotional aspect of the Quest; as the diver devotes himself to his purpose — the recovery of the lost article — by restraining the breath and diving with all his weight, so too the seeker must be devoted to the finding of the real Self — the source of the 'I am' in the ego — by the ingathering of all the vital and mental energies and directing them Heartwards. The resolve to find the Self is the dynamic element in the Quest, without which there can be no diving into the Heart; the question 'Who am I?', or 'Whence am I?', implies this resolve. To him that so dives, says the Sage, success is assured; for then, says he, some mysterious force arises from within and takes possession of his mind and takes it straight to the Heart; if the seeker be pure of mind

---

* *Ulladu Narpadu* verse 28 (see appendix A, verse 33).

and free from love of individuality he would yield
himself unreservedly to this force and get the highest
of all rewards; for whatever a man is devoted to, that
he gets, and there is nothing higher than the real
Self. He that has not this perfect devotion will need
to practise the Quest repeatedly till the mind becomes
pure and strong, or to practise some kind of meditation
or devotion to God.

Devotion implies renunciation, which means non-
attachment to the unreal; so we are taught by the
Sages; he that is greatly devoted to any one thing is
so far indifferent to other things; he that is devoted
to the Self that is inside is so far indifferent to the
world that is outside. Devotion and renunciation are
like the two sides of a single medal; they are
inseparable. Renunciation strengthens the mind and
ensures success in the Quest; this we know from
common worldly experience; whoever is devoted to
any worldly end renounces of his own accord whatever
stands in the way, and gains his end; naturally
renunciation is equally necessary for the winning of
the greatest of all gains, the Egoless State. But we
must see to it that we understand renunciation aright;
it is a purification of the mind, a harmonious and
concentrated direction of the mind to the goal — not
simply the observance of external forms of self-denial.

We were told that speech and the vital breath
should be restrained; but the Sage explains that the
breath does not need to be actively restrained, if the
resolve be keen and persistent; for then the breath
would automatically be suspended, and the energies
hitherto operating the body indrawn and reunited to
the mind, thus enabling it to dive into the Heart. This

ingathering of the vital energies is essential; for so long as these energies are united to the body, the mind cannot turn away from the body and the world and dive into the Heart; when the breathing ceases by the force of the resolve, the mind is no longer aware of the body or the world; the body then becomes almost a corpse.

If the seeker has not the needful strength of devotion, so that the breathing does not stop of itself, he is advised to bring about suspension of the breath by the simple method of *watching the breathing process*; when this watch is steadily kept up, the breath slows down and finally stops; then the mind becomes quiet — free from distracting thoughts, — and can be then devoted to the Quest.

As in meditation of any sort, so in the pursuit of this Quest, thoughts of surprising variety may arise and distract the mind, and a sense of defeat and discouragement may be felt. The Sage tells us that these thoughts arise only to be quelled, and hence there is no need for the seeker of the Self to be disheartened — to accept defeat; if it seems that success cannot come in the near future — that it could come only after long delay — he should meet the thought by remembering that time itself is not real and that the Self is not in time. In a book of great antiquity it is stated that the seeker of the real Self must have as much perseverance and patience as is involved in attempting to dry up the ocean by removing water from it drop by drop. In another book there is a parable of a pair of sparrows whose eggs were washed away by the sea: the birds determined to recover the eggs, and punish the sea

at the same time, by drying it up; this they proceeded
to do by repeatedly plunging into the waters and
shedding the clinging drops on the shore; the fable
says that finally the gods intervened and the eggs
were restored.

Every alien thought that arises in the Quest and
is quelled adds to the mind's strength, says the Sage,
and thus takes the seeker one step nearer to his goal.

When the seeker has persisted long enough in
the Quest, and the power from within has arisen and
taken possession of the mind, the Heart is quickly
reached; that is to say, the mind becomes reduced to
the state of pure Consciousness and begins to shine
steadily in its pure form, as the formless 'I'; the Sage
calls this formless Consciousness the 'I am I' to
distinguish it from the ego-sense which has the form
of 'I am this (body)'; that implies the cessation of the
ego-form; the finite ego is swallowed up by the infinite
Self; with the finite ego are lost all the imperfections
and limitations which beset life; desire and fear are
at an end, as well as sin and accountability. The real
Self was never subject to these; they belonged to the
ego and they do not survive the ego. In the Egoless
State the Self abides in Its own glory; the Sage that
has thus found the Self, having shed the ego, is not
an individual, though he may appear as such to
immature disciples and to the rest of the world.

The Sage recommends also meditation of the pure
'I am' or 'I' — 'Aham' — as an equivalent of the Quest.
He says: "Since His Name is 'I', the *sadhaka* that

---

* *Guru Vachaka Kovai* verse 716 (see appendix B, verse 108).

meditates on the 'I' is taken to the Heart, the World of the real Self."*

How to reconcile devotion to the Self with the daily routine of work that the world demands? This question was put to the Sage by one who had come from a distant place by rail; the Sage replied as follows; "Why do you think you are active? Take the case of your coming here. You left home in a cart, took your seat in a train, alighted at the (Tiruvannamalai) station, again got into a cart and found yourself here. When asked, you say that *you* came here from your town. Is it true? As a matter of fact you remained as you were; only the conveyances moved; just as these movements are taken as yours, so also are the other activities. They are not yours; they are God's activities." The questioner objected that such an attitude will simply lead to blankness of mind and work will come to a standstill. The Sage told him: "Go up to that blankness and then tell me." From this we may understand, that to the extent we realise that the Self is not the doer, it is not necessary for the earnest seeker to retire from his worldly activities — to become a recluse or hermit — in order to prosecute this Quest: he may just allow the mind and the senses to do their work automatically, remembering that he himself is not the doer; all the time he may be active in the Quest, or in meditation, just as one thinks while walking.

Not only is it unnecessary to renounce one's everyday activities — to become a recluse or hermit — in order to take up this Quest, but it would appear from what the Sage has actually said that it may be desirable for most of us to continue to be active in order to prepare for the Quest. The Sage tells us that dissolution of the mind in the Self is accomplished by steadily cultivating the knowledge that the mind is but a phantom of the Self, and that this can be done while going through one's everyday activities. These activities can thus be utilised as a preparation for the Quest. When this knowledge — that the mind is but a phantom of the real Self — is firmly established, then it will be easy to take to the Quest and persist in it watchfully to the very end.

Many times the question was raised before the Sage, whether or not it is necessary to renounce house and family-ties and fare forth as a mendicant ascetic. The Sage has said that if one be fated to become an ascetic the question will not arise, but that as a rule it is not necessary. On one occasion there was a short dialogue. A visitor asked: "Should I leave home, or may I remain there?" The Sage said: "Are you in the house, or is the house in you? You should remain just Where you are even now; you cannot go away from That." "So I may remain at home." "I did not say so; listen; you should remain steadfast just in that Place which is naturally yours always." The questioner put the question assuming that he was in the house; but the truth is that the whole world is in him as the real Self; So he was told to remain in the Self, that is, to cease to think that the world is real. On another occasion the Sage said: "A householder who does not think 'I am a householder' is a true ascetic, while an ascetic who thinks 'I am an ascetic' is not; the Self is neither an ascetic nor a householder."

It may be remarked that the assumption of an ascetic mode of life is a serious affair; the Sage points out that in any case it is the *mind* that has to be harmonised to the Quest, and if it cannot be done at home, it would be equally difficult elsewhere.

A great power for good, which the disciple must utilise wherever possible, is the society of Sages. The sacred lore seems to use even the language of hyperbole in recommending this. The Sage cites these texts freely. The extent to which one would be benefited depends on one's understanding of, and devotion to, the Sage as Guru. Such devotion is of great importance, as we shall see in a later chapter.

An important caution to the disciple is given in a minor work attributed to the Sage Sankara, and this is adopted by the Sage. *"One should inwardly reflect on the truth of Non-Duality always, but should not seek to apply the teaching in his actions. Meditation on Non-Duality is proper in respect of all the three worlds. But understand that it should not be done in respect of the Guru."** It may be difficult to make out the reason for these injunctions. But if we remember the power of the ego to pervert and frustrate even honest efforts to realise the Truth — which would mean its own death — we need not be puzzled. Reflection on the truth of Advaita tends to dissolve the ego and develop devotion to the Truth. But action from the Advaitic standpoint is suicidal, because *the enemy would be in charge of such action.* While ignorance is alive, duality persists in appearing as real, because of the ego-sense, and truly Advaitic

---

* भावाद्वैतं सदा कुर्यात् क्रियाद्वैतं न कर्हिचित् ।
  अद्वैतं त्रिषु लोकेषु नाद्वैतं गुरुणा सह ॥
  — *Tattvopadesa* v.87 (see *Ulladu Narpadu Anubandham* v.39).

action is impossible. The Sage alone can put Advaita
into action, because he is egoless. Hence the sacred
lore and also the Sage advise us to restrict our
activities and not to extend them, so as to give as
little scope as possible for the ego to frustrate our
efforts.* Herein it will be useful to remember that a
theoretical knowledge of the Self does not destroy the
ego, the enemy within us.

   Devotion to the Guru as God incarnate is proper
and necessary, as we shall see later. Until one
becomes egoless, therefore, it would be unwise to try
to look upon the Guru as oneself, because the actual
result will be something quite different. It will result
in believing oneself to be the equal of the Guru. To be
really one with the Guru is to be egoless. Hence the
caution, not to imagine non-difference with the Guru.

   The following cautions and instructions are from
the *Guru Ramana Vachana Mala, Sadhakachara
prakarana.*†

   "Forgetting (the Self) is verily Death; therefore
for him that is out to conquer Death by the Quest,
the one rule to fulfil is not to forget."

   "Since even one's own activities are a cause of
forgetting (the Self), is it necessary to say that he

---

* Superficial students of Advaitic Vedanta — who have not sat at the
feet of the Sage or any Sage — do not know of this rule of caution,
and hence think it proper to apply the teaching in action. They as a
rule apply it fractionally. The worst mistake they make is in regard
to what is called equality; their ideas on this subject are due to a
misunderstanding of the teaching. This will be discussed in the next
chapter, where it will be shown that true equality is something that
the Sage alone can practise.

† See Appendix B, verses 170, 172, 176, 178, 182, 185, 187, 188, 193,
196, 199, 201 to 208 and 214.

that is engaged in the Quest of the Self should not engage in the work of other people?"

"Though there are numerous observances, the rule of regulated eating is alone sufficient for the *sadhaka* (seeker), because it augments the *Sattva* quality."*

"The rule of food-regulation is that one should allow time for the stomach's rest, and when hungry, eat a limited amount of *Satvika* food."

"Until the ego dies finally, humility alone is good for the *sadhaka*; he should never *accept* homage done to him by others."

"The pot sinks, because it takes in water. Timber floats, because it does not. He that is attached becomes bound. He that is not, is not bound, even if he is in the house."

"One should overcome misfortunes with faith, courage and serenity, remembering that they come by God's grace, in order to give strength."

"For one that is devoted to the Highest, it is better to be in a worldly condition to be pitied by men, than in one that would cause envy."

"Indifference all round, with the mind serene, without desire and without hate, is the beautiful way of life for *sadhakas*."

"What is called fate is nothing but actions done by oneself before. Hence fate can be wiped off by suitable effort."

"What is done with peaceful and pure mind is

---

* There are three main qualities or moods of the mind, *Sattva*, *Rajas* and *Tamas*. Of these the first is the state of clarity and calm. The second of restlessness and action, the third of darkness and indolence. The first one is to be cultivated and other two to be outgrown.

righteous action; whatever is done with the mind agitated and from desire is wrong action."

"To be unattached and at peace, resigning all burden to God the Almighty, is the highest *tapas*."

"As the grains that remain at the base of the pivot in a handmill are not crushed, so those that have taken refuge in God are unaffected even by great misfortunes."

"As the magnetic needle swerves not from the north, so those that have their minds devoted to God do not swerve from the right path through illusion."

"Never give way to anxiety, thinking 'When shall I attain this State?' It is beyond space and time, and therefore is neither far nor near."

"Pervading everything by Its own nature, the Self is ever free. How can It be bound by *Maya*? So do not give way to despair."

"The notion 'I am an unstable soul' has arisen by letting go one's immovable Nature. The *sadhaka* should cast off this notion and rest in the Supreme Silence."

"This is the device for overcoming the capricious nature of the mind. Look upon all that is perceived and on the perceiver as the real Self."

"As a thorn that is used for taking out a thorn, should be **thrown** aside, so a good thought, that is useful for **driving** out an evil thought, should also be given up."

"As one dives into the sea with a (heavy) stone and takes out pearls, so one should dive with non-attachment into the Heart and gain the Self."

The Quest of the real Self is fundamentally different from all the methods of winning Deliverance which are in vogue. These are known as Yogas. Four of them are generally known, namely, the Yogas of action, of devotion, of mind-control and of right understanding. The Sage compares these four with the Quest in the following: *"The Quest, 'Who is he, to whom belong actions, separateness (from God), ignorance or separateness (from the Reality)?', is itself the Yogas of action, of devotion, of right understanding and of mind-control. That is the True State (of the Self) — the untainted and blissful Experience of one's own Self — where, the seeker, the 'I', being extinct, these eight have no place."* Here is made clear that in the four Yogas the follower takes the ego to be himself, and thus attributes to the Self some one or other of the defects that appear in himself because of the conclusion. The Yogi of action takes it that the Self is the doer of actions and is thus bound to suffer their effects; he wants to neutralise these actions by other actions. The Yogi of devotion is persuaded that he is other than God and needs to become united to Him by devotion. The Yogi of right understanding thinks that the Self is in ignorance and wants to remove that ignorance. The Yogi of mind-control thinks that the Self is separated from the Reality and seeks reunion by mind-control. These are wrong assumptions, because there is no individual soul — because the whole world-order is an illusion. When the real Self is sought and found, it will be found that that Self was never bound, but is ever perfect. The seeker of the Self starts with this knowledge. When by the Quest the ego dies, it will be seen that

---

* *Ulladu Narpadu Anubandham* v. 14 (see appendix A, v. 60).

neither these four defects, nor the four remedies for them, have any place in the Egoless State, which alone is real. The Sage once told this writer that the Quest is the Great Yoga — Maha Yoga — and the reason is that, as shown here, all the Yogas are included in the Quest.

Chapter 10

The Sage

PERHAPS THE MOST difficult subject in this inquiry is the Sage. He is both beyond and — though only seemingly — within relativity at the same time. He is thus in two mutually contradictory states at the same time; for relativity and the Real are negations of each other. This is the root of the perplexity that besets the ideas of disciples on this subject.

The text-books mention two kinds of Deliverance; the living Sage is said to have one kind of Deliverance; when his body dies there is another kind of it. The former is called Jivan-Mukti, Deliverance in life; the Sage that has it is called a Jivan-Mukta. The latter is called Videha-Mukti, bodiless Deliverance. The Sage tells us that there is only *one* kind of Deliverance, namely Egolessness. Since the world has no existence without the ego, it follows that the Sage is bodiless in fact, whatever he may seem to be. Even those that think that the Sage has a body and mind, and are unable to realise that they are unreal, can understand this much, that his causal body, — which is the primary ignorance — has been dissolved, and that therefore the Sage — who is just the real Self and nothing else — is in no way connected with the

surviving, subtle and gross bodies, as the ignorant
one thinks himself to be. For the Sage, therefore,
nothing exists except the Self; there is neither body,
nor mind, nor world, nor other persons. In speaking
of the Sage, therefore, we need to keep distinct the
two points of view, the point of view of the semi-
ignorant disciple, and that of the Sage himself. The
Sage himself has repeatedly emphasised that for him
there is no problem at all — no need of reconciling
inconsistencies. From *his* point of view *all* the three
bodies are non-existent. Not only that, he does not
even recognise that they existed before. Hence it is
only as a concession to the semi-ignorant disciple that
the distinction is mentioned in the books. The absolute
truth of Deliverance is that It is bodiless and worldless,
because *Deliverance is the state where the Truth alone
shines.*

The Jivan-Mukta is therefore not a person. But
because of the dual role stated before, personality is
attributed to him. In the Upanishadic lore this point
of view is tolerated, and it is said that his body will
be subject to the law of causality while it survives.
By the force of this law his body will be affected by
the reactions — pleasant or unpleasant — of previous
actions, which are called karmas. These are divided
into three parts or lots. There is the particular lot of
karmas which came to fruition at birth — which gave
the Sage the present body, and will go on regulating
what happens to it till it dies. This karma is called
prarabdha, because it has *begun* to yield fruit. There
is another lot of karma called *agami*, 'actions to come.'
The remainder is called *sanchita*, the reserve; this is
an enormous lot, because of the great number of the

past lives that have been lived. It is said that the first lot alone retains its power, but that the second and third lots become liquidated when one becomes a Sage — when individuality is 'lost'. The Sage will have no more rebirths. Nor will he go to other worlds. But he will reap the fruits of the *prarabdha* or current karma; so says the ancient lore in some places. We shall see that this is not strictly correct.

We have seen before that the Sage is in the Natural State — in *Sahaja Samadhi* — always. This is not, as we have seen, the *Kevala Nirvikalpa Samadhi* of the Yogi, which is inconstant. This Natural State is not inimical to the automatic bodily activities which are attributed to the Sage. So it may be said *in a sense*, that the Sage is awake to the Self and to the world also. He seems to eat, sleep and live like other persons. Because he is in the *Sahaja* he is able to hear and answer questions. The Yogi that is sometimes in trance and sometimes awake cannot give us any such teaching, because he himself is still in bondage and ignorance. If there were no *Sahaja* State, then it would happen that whoever obtains direct and perfect Experience of the Self would at once cease to appear with a body in this world; and thus there would never be anyone who could impart *authentic* teaching about the Self and the method of finding Him. But the *Sahaja* State exists and is attained by some rare seeker now and then. Thus the teaching of the sacred lore is confirmed and corrected, added to where necessary, and made intelligible to qualified disciples by an unbroken line of Sages. Within historical times there were the Sages Gautama and Sankara. How many others there were we do not know. This office is *now* fulfilled by the Sage Ramana.

Those that have not heard and understood the
truth of the Natural State — namely that it is not
inimical, like the *Kevala, to bodily activity*, — raise a
question about the Sage, the answer to which is not
easy to understand for all; even among the Sage's
disciples, there are some who cannot understand the
answer; but that is so because they are believers in a
fascinating, but complicated creed, in which the chief
tenet is that the world is real as such; it is therefore
quite natural that they should refuse to understand
the Sage's teachings, of which the essential part is
that the world is not real as such. They are dualists
in fact, and as such violent haters of Advaitic teaching.

In this connection we may take note of the
tenderness the Sage shows for the weaknesses of
believers. The Sage observes the rule enunciated in
the *Gita* (3.26) that no one's faith should be disturbed.
Therefore when ardent dualists are present, the Sage
is very careful in what he says. He does not, while
they are present, give out clear Advaitic teaching. But
as soon as the dualists go out, he turns round to the
Advaitis that remain, and apologetically explains to
them that he had to water down the teaching to suit
the dualists. He thus treats the latter as immature
ones, and the Advaitis as adults who can understand
that allowances have to be made to the immature.
But he leaves us in no doubt at all, that the Advaitic
teaching is the highest there can be.*

---

* On many occasions the Sage has clearly testified to this. One such occasion
was this. Somebody had written in a book, that the Truth would be
whole only if the world be real as such — with all its variety — not else.
When this writer was reading this, the Sage exclaimed: "As if the Truth
would be mutilated otherwise."

We have two kinds of views about the Sage. First there is the view that is held by those who claim to be Advaitis, but who have not sat at the feet of the Sage. Then there is the view held by disciples of the Sage, who are hostile to his Advaitic teaching.

The former class of people argue thus: "The person called Ramana Maharshi lives in the world very much like other people. He eats, sleeps, acts, talks and does other things. He remembers the past and answers questions about it; therefore he has both ego and mind. Also, he says 'I', 'you' and 'he', just as we do. Therefore he is not a Jivan-Mukta, though we are willing to allow that he is a holy person." We need have no quarrel with these people. It is clear that they imagine the *Kevala Nirvikalpa* to be the final state. Hence they are unable to understand how a Sage can live among men as a Light from the real Self.

To be able to recognise a Sage one must be a genuine devotee of the real Self. This implies a refinement of understanding, a humbleness of spirit and other virtues. For such a one the Sage has a real and abiding attraction. On the other hand those that are in love with bondage — even though they are learned in the sacred lore — are not so attracted; they are prosperous in a worldly sense and think themselves happy; and they are perhaps afraid that if they go to the Sage, he might effect a change in their outlook, of the consequences of which they are sincerely afraid; being so afraid, they keep at a safe distance from the Sage.

But those that have been attracted to the Sage, having felt keenly the need of a competent Guru, are able to see that he is something unique. They may take time to understand that he is a Sage. That is because they need first to understand what a Sage is, and what are the unfailing marks of one. The one unfailing mark is the *non-perception of difference.*

Now we shall consider the other view — that which is upheld by certain sectarian devotees of the Sage. They say that he is a Sage. But they also maintain that he is a person. They say that he is an exalted 'Person'. They hold it as an article of belief that personality is real, and that it persists in Deliverance, though, inconsistently enough, they admit that the ego is lost in Deliverance. The Sage, they say, has a mind, and therefore has a distinct existence. They say that in Deliverance the mind is changed into something wonderful and becomes endowed with divine powers of *'siddhis'.* To these powers they attach a profound importance. They seem to think that it is these powers that prove him to be a Sage.

We have seen in the chapter on God that the essential teaching of the Sage is the Truth of Non-Becoming, which means that the Reality never actually became the three, these being merely creations of the ego-mind, which is itself unreal. In other words the Sage is at one with the Sage Sankara, in saying that this is all Maya. He explains that Deliverance consists in the reduction to nothingness of what is always nothing; the threefold false appearance is unreal even now, but appears as real through ignorance. That appearance will cease in such a way that it could not even be said that it appeared before and ceased to appear later.

This is made clear by the following utterance of the Sage, which tells us what is accomplished by the Guru's grace: "Reducing the unreal to unreality, and causing the one real Self to shine, the Guru puts a final end to the unreal soul."* The sectarian views under discussion are certainly not reconcilable with these teachings.

We have seen that the *Siddhis*, which loom large in the eyes of these disciples, are unreal, being part of the world-illusion, which is the substance of bondage. It is therefore ridiculous, as the Sage points out, to seek to appraise the greatness of a Sage by the *siddhis* that seem to be manifested in his presence.†

The rejection of the Truth of Non-Becoming has led these disciples to misunderstand the Sage. One such misunderstanding is pointed out and corrected by the Sage in the following: "Ignorant people say, 'The Sage sees differences, but enjoys non-difference in them.' "

This non-perception of differences is twofold, as non-perception of difference between oneself and others and non-perception of difference among others. The former is manifested by the Sage's indifference to praise and censure. The latter is seen in what is termed the 'equal eye' which is referred to in the famous but much-misunderstood verse of the *Gita*,

---

* *Guru Vachaka Kovai* verse 281 (see appendix B, verse 132).

† Intellectual appraisement of any kind is open to the same objection, since the intellect, which looms large in the estimation of some critics, is as much a part of the world-illusion as *siddhis* are. In fact, the very idea of appraising anything involves relativity and is a contradiction of pure *advaita*.

where it is said that Sages look with equal eye on all creatures.‡

The former quality is, as we have seen in the first chapter, peculiar to the Sage; no one that is not perfectly egoless is *naturally* unaffected by praise and censure, as is indicated by the verse, तृणतुलिताखिलजगतां cited on page seventeen. There is a historical anecdote connected with this verse, which is told of a Sage of the recent past: and we must presume that the incident took place before he attained sagehood. The holy one had renounced the world at an early age, and was wandering in the forests, practising *samadhi* for the sake of Deliverance. Once a co-pupil of his met him somewhere and warmly praised him to his face. The holy one was visibly elated, and this was noticed by the other; it was a surprise to him that such a holy one could be moved by praise. He at once expressed what he thought. The holy one replied by uttering the verse cited above. The meaning of it is this: "It is next to impossible for one to cast off subjection to the harlot, Praise, even though he has renounced the world as trash, and mastered the secrets of the sacred lore." While even a trace of egoism remains, the hearing of praise or censure will automatically cause a sense of pleasure or pain. The egoless one is not moved by these; he does not feel pleasure or pain from praise or blame, as is expressed by the Sage in the following: *"To one who is firmly*

---

‡ विद्याविनयसंपन्ने ब्राह्मणे गवि हस्तिनि ।
  शुनि चैव श्वपाके च पण्डिता: समदर्शिन: ॥

                                                            — *Gita*, 5.18.

established in the blissful Natural State beyond change, and therefore is not aware of difference — who does not think 'I am one, and he is another' — who is there, other than the Self? If anyone says anything about him, what matters it? For him it is just the same as if it was said by himself."

Non-perception of difference among others, which is called equality of vision, is equally a peculiar feature of the Sage. We have noticed that the Sage does not recognise distinctions, whether natural or man-made. This is what the Sage says about it: *"The equal vision of the Sage is just the recognition that the One Self, who is Consciousness, is present in all that appears."†* In other words it is egolessness. The same is the meaning of the grossly misunderstood and mis-applied text of the *Gita*, where it is said that the Sage looks with equal eye on all creatures. This equal eye is not for the ego-ridden ones, because they do not see the real Self in all. Equal vision does *not* consist in acting as if all human beings are equal, *as such*. Not equality, but unity, is the teaching, and that can be realised only by oneself becoming egoless. In this connection we may remember the caution against applying the teaching of Non-difference in action.

This truth about the Sage, namely his non-perception of difference, is sometimes erroneously described as 'perception of non-difference in difference.' This description is favoured by some of his sectarian disciples. They say that the Sage sees

---

* *Ulladu Narpadu Anubandham* v. 38 (see appendix A, v. 84).
† *Guru Vachaka Kovai* verse 1250 (see appendix B, verse 343).

difference in non-difference, and enjoys non-
difference in difference. This description is
picturesque, but contrary to the Truth of Non-
Becoming, which has been set forth before. On this
point the Sage says: "It is wrongly said by the ignorant
that the Sage sees difference, but enjoys non-
difference in them. The truth is that he does not see
difference at all."†

Besides, the primary difference is that between
subject and object, and in the State of Non-difference,
namely the Egoless State, this difference does not
survive. Hence perception is impossible in that State.
It is therefore absurd to describe the Sage as
perceiving non-difference. He can be rightly described
only as not perceiving difference. Perhaps what these
sectarians mean is that the Sage knows the
underlying Unity while seeing the differences. If so,
then we have to ask whether this 'Knowledge of the
Unity' is experiential or merely inferential. This
Revelation makes it clear to us that so long as
differences are being perceived — that is so long as
the ego survives — only inferential or theoretical
knowledge of the Unity is possible, not Experience.
This means that the Sage has no Experience of the
Unity, which is absurd.

An argument advanced by these sectarians is that
there must be something to maintain the distinction
between one Sage and another. They here take it for
granted there is a distinction, and to account for it
they claim that each Sage has a subtle body of his
own. We have seen that the subtle body is not other

---

† *Guru Vachaka Kovai* verse 931 (see appendix B, verse 338).

than the ego, and that the latter is just a hyphen joining two mutually negatory things, the real Self and the body. It logically follows from this that there is no distinction between Sage and Sage and this is true because the Sage is not the knower or enjoyer of the Self, but utterly identical with the Self. This is what Sage Sri Ramana says on this point: "It is from ignorance that you say, 'I have seen this Sage; I shall see that other Sage also.' If you know by experience the Sage that is *within* you, then all Sages will be seen to be one."*

It may be said that we do see a body and mind belonging to the Sage. But so do we see other bodies and minds, and the teaching is that they are unreal. The truth is that it is our mind that creates the Sage's mind and body, just as it creates the whole world, including God. We see the Sage as a person in our dream of relativity, occurring in the sleep of ignorance. In the *Guru Ramana Vachana Mala* we are told: "The body or mind that appears as pertaining to the Sage, — who is, in truth, intangible like the sky, — is just a reflection of the body or mind of him that sees it. It is not real."† Whatever may be the case of other men, *disciples* ought not, we are told, to entertain the notion that the Sage is embodied. In the same book it is said: "Understand that he that regards as really embodied, the Sage, his Guru, — who appears like a human being, but who is really Infinite Consciousness — is sinful and of impure mind."‡

---

* *Guru Vachaka Kovai* verse 121 (see appendix B, verse 131).
† *Guru Vachaka Kovai* verse 119 (see appendix B, verse 130).
‡ *Guru Vachaka Kovai* verse 274 (see appendix B, verse 128).

The immature disciple cannot help making the mistake here pointed out. And there is some excuse for him, because he may plausibly argue that only the causal body of the Sage is dissolved, but that the other two bodies survive. But he must outgrow this tentative point of view. How can he himself attain absolute bodilessness, as pure Spirit, if he regards his Guru as not having attained that State?

We have to recognise, therefore, that though the Sage appears to us behaving like a person in the world, he is in fact the pure Consciousness, which cannot even be described as the Witness of the activities of the mind and the body. A question was put to the Sage: "Does the Sage see the world as others do?" The Sage replied: "The question does not arise for the Sage, but only for the ignorant. He puts the question because of his ego. To him the answer is. 'Find out the Truth of him to whom the question occurs.' You ask the question because you see the Sage active like other men. The fact is, the Sage does not see the world as others do. Take for an illustration, the cinema. There are pictures moving on the screen. If one goes up to them and tries to seize them, he seizes only the screen. And when the pictures disappear, the screen alone remains. Such is the case with the Sage." The same question is answered by the Sage also as follows: *"The world is real, both to the ignorant and to the Sage. The ignorant one believes the Real to be co-extensive with the world. To the Sage the Real is the formless One, the basic Substance on which the world appears. Thus great indeed is the difference between the Sage and the ignorant one."** Here the Sage

---

* *Ulladu Narpadu* verse 18 (see appendix A, verse 23).

begins by saying that, superficially considered, the ignorant one and the Sage are alike. For they both say that the world is real. But it is here pointed out that what the Sage means by the words is quite the opposite of what the other means. The ignorant man takes the world to be real as such, with all its variety of name and form and, has no idea of the basic Reality which, as shown before, is like gold to the jewels made of it — is the Substance that is real as opposed to the forms that are unreal. The Sage rejects the unreal part of the world and takes as real only the Substratum, the formless Pure Consciousness, the Self, which is unaffected by the false appearances. "The Self is real," says the Sage, "not the world, because He exists alone in His State of Purity as the Pure Consciousness, without the world. The world cannot exist without the Self."

Thus we have to conclude that the Sage does not see the world and has no part or lot in it. What seem to us to be his activities are not therefore really his. Being egoless and mindless, he does not *will* those actions. The self-same power, by which the activities of *all* creatures are prompted and sustained, is behind those of the Sage also, with this difference, that while the ignorant think they themselves are the doers, the Sage does not think so. He acts automatically as a sleepy child eats, when roused and fed by his mother. If agency has to be ascribed to somebody, let it rather be ascribed to God, than to the Sage, because while God is in one point of view the regulator of the world, the Sage has nothing to do with the world. In truth, that is, in the Egoless State, both are identical; neither is an agent, because neither is other than the real Self, which is One.

The real Self is never an agent. Agency is ascribed to him only through ignorance. The Sage, we saw, is the Self in his utter purity, as unvariegated Consciousness. Hence he is never an agent. This is brought out in the following: *"If the Self were ever himself the doer than He himself would reap the fruits of actions. But since the sense of doership is lost on the Experience of the Infinite Self, by the Quest 'Who am I that is a doer?', with it will be lost the three kinds of actions. The wise know this state as timeless Deliverance."**

From this, incidentally, we learn that Deliverance is perfect and absolute, not qualified, as might appear from some of the Upanishadic texts. These tell us that a portion of the *karma* of him who has attained sage-hood remains unaffected, and will be exhausted only when his body dies. This *karma* is the *prarabdha* or current *karma*, that which came to fruition at birth, which gave him the body, and will regulate all that happens to it till its death. We are to understand that the liability to reap the fruits of this *karma* is only apparent, not real. The Sage emphasises this in the following: *"What is said in the books, namely that the actions of the future and those of the reserve, belonging to the Sage, are certainly lost, but that the current* karma *is not lost, is intended for the ignorant. (But) just as one wife out of many cannot remain* sumangali *(non-widow) on the death of the husband, so all the three divisions of* karma *are lost, when the doer, the ego, is lost."†* 'I am doer' is a thought; it cannot survive the ego.

---

* *Ulladu Narpadu* verse 38 (see appendix A, verse 43).
† *Ulladu Narpadu Anubandham* v. 33 (see appendix A, v. 79).

That the Sage is in his real nature mindless, and does not *will* the actions he seems to do, will be seen from the following: Once the Sage was going about somewhere on the Arunachala Hill, when he accidentally disturbed the hive of a community of wasps, hidden by the dense foliage of a shrub. The wasps got angry and settled upon the offending leg and went on stinging. The Sage stayed there motionless till the wasps were satisfied, saying to the leg: "Take the consequences of your action." This incident was narrated by the Sage to many disciples, and so it was known to all. Long afterwards a disciple-devotee put him the following question: "Since the disturbance of the wasp-hive was accidental, why should it be regretted and atoned for, as if it had been done intentionally?" The Sage replied: "If in fact the regretting and atoning is not *his* act, what must be the true nature of his mind?"* Here the Sage met the question by another question. The disciple knew his Guru to be a Sage. But it seems that at the time he was not fully aware of the truth that a Sage is one who is a native of the Egoless State and is therefore mindless. Hence he assumed that the act in question was done by the Sage, and based his question on that assumption. The Sage graciously pointed out that the assumption was wrong, and indicated that the so-called mind of a Sage is not really mind, but Pure

---

* The following is a Sanskrit rendering of the above answer of the Sage:

भृंगदंशसहनं बभूव यत् भृंगनीडनिचयेखिलीकृते ।
तत्कृतं न तदिति स्थिति सति कीदृशं भवति तन्मनो वद ॥

Consciousness; the Sage has confirmed this teaching many times, saying that the mind of a Sage is not mind, but the Supreme Reality.

Since the Sage is mindless, he is in no way related to the world and its affairs. That is the essence of his being free. He does not feel *obliged* to do certain things or not to do certain other things. Whatever he does, he does spontaneously and automatically, without forethought, as one would do that has no mind. The ancient lore tells us that the Sage is not assailed by regrets, 'I have done wrong,' or 'I have not done right.' The Sage expresses the same truth as follows: *Can the Sage that dwells in the State of Unity with the Truth, which arises by consuming the ego, and is calm, happy and beyond relativity and is therefore wantless, be bound to do anything whatever in the world? Since he is unaware of anything other than the Self, how can his State — which is mindless — be conceived by the mind?*[†] Thus we have to conclude that for him the words 'duty' and its correlative 'right' are meaningless.

Of course, having a divine mission to fulfil — to illumine and uplift those that are ripe for Deliverance — he is not inactive. But he does not will the actions he does. In fact his activity is far more efficient because of his egolessness than it would be if he willed them. The sacred lore and the Sage tell us that the Sage is a non-doer and great doer at the same time. There is no contradiction in this, because he is not a doer in truth, but appears to be greatly active to those who see him. He cannot be really active, because if he were, he would be aware of persons different from the Self; we have

---

[†] *Ulladu Narpadu* verse 31 (see appendix A, verse 36).

been clearly told this is not the case. Actions are willed out of desire; he is desireless, *Aptakama*, because he is happy in the Self, *Atmarama*.

On one occasion the Sage was asked whether it was not his duty to preach the Truth to all the people and thus make them free. He answered: "If a man awakes from a dream, does he ask: 'Have those men, that I saw in the dream, awakened?' Just so the Sage is not concerned about the people of the world." Referring to the notion — now fashionable — that it would be selfish to attain freedom for oneself, leaving all the world in bondage, he said: "This is like a dreamer saying: 'I shall not awake till all these dream-men awake'."

A cryptic saying of the Sage is as follows: "The Egoless State is not one of indolence, but of the intensest activity." This seems to be in conflict with another description by the Sage himself where it is said that It is the Sleep of Bliss. We may remember that in a passage cited before, the Sage describes the State as Waking-Sleep. This means that both the above descriptions are true, and mean the same thing. The sleep-aspect concerns the world of illusion. To that the Sage is asleep. This is brought out in the following: *"Just as, to one that is asleep in a carriage, its three states, namely its movement, its standing still and its being left with the horses unyoked, are all alike, so to the Sage that is in the Sleep of Self-Awareness in the carriage, the body, the three states of it, namely bodily activity,* samadhi *and sleep, are alike."** Here the parallels between the Sage and the sleeper should be

---

* *Ulladu Narpadu Anubandham* v. 31 (see appendix A, v. 77).

noted. The body is compared to the carriage and the
sense-organs to the horses. Hence waking activities
are like the movements of the carriage. The states of
samadhi and sleep are both states of rest. But the
former is compared to the standing still of the carriage
with the horses still yoked, because in *samadhi* the
senses are not detached; hence says the Sage, in
samadhi the head does not bend, but remains upright.
In sleep the senses are detached and hence the head
bends — if the sleeper is sitting. Thus *outwardly* there
are differences. But inwardly there is no difference.
The above comparison to the sleeper in a carriage is
given only to show that the changes of bodily condition,
and hence of the world as a whole, do not affect the Sage.
It is not to be assumed that the Sage is in unconsciousness,
as in sleep. This we shall see presently. The truth of
the Sage's condition is brought out in the *Gita* verse
cited on p. 107, where it is contrasted with that of the
man in ignorance — where it is said that what is Night
to all creatures is Day to the Sage, while what is Day to
them is Night to the Sage, who however is wide-awake.
The cryptic saying of the Sage — that the State is one of
intense activity — will now become intelligible. The
Sage is awake in and as the real Self, who is
Consciousness. But Consciousness can never become
unconscious. Hence he can *never* sleep. That is his
activity. And that is all the activity there is. All else is
maya. That the Sage is not asleep, — even when the
body sleeps — may be inferred from the observed fact,
that the Sage is always alert, ready for any kind of
activity. This is because the Sage is ever in the Natural
State, which is neither trance, nor the waking state of
the ignorant.

We have seen already that only a Sage can be a Guru, because he alone can work both from within and from without. The true Guru, it is said, pushes the disciple's mind inside from without, and pulls it in from within, and thus gives him that Experience of the Self, which will make him free. For this work of grace to be accomplished, the disciple must practice devotion to the Sage as God. It is said: "He that meditates on the True Nature of the Sage, who dwells (in the Heart) mindless as the Blessed One, the Self of all, obtains the Experience of the Self."*

---

* *Guru Vachaka Kovai* verse 1126 (see appendix B, verse 347).

Chapter II

Devotion

WE HAVE THUS far studied the testimony of the Sages. From them we understand that the direct and immediate means of winning Deliverance is the Quest of the real Self, by turning the mind away from the world — that is, from everything that can be objectified — towards the Self in the Heart. But we find that this is not easy, because in the mind there are attachments to objects, gross or subtle, and habits of thought, which are mostly latent, but spring into feverish activity one after another, and pull the mind back to the world. These are mental taints, which are called *vasanas*, because they have been acquired by intimate contact with objects, and linger in the mind, like the smell of the contents that lingers in a pot after it is emptied. Because these 'smells' of things are more in some than in others, there is a great difference between one disciple and another. The Sage tells us that disciples are of four grades, comparable to gun-powder, dry charcoal, ordinary fuel, and wet fuel. The first kind of disciple needs only a word, like a spark, to consume his ignorance at once. The second kind needs some teaching and personal effort. The third kind needs a long course of teaching, training and practice. The fourth kind needs to be made fit for discipleship by practices suitable to his condition. Hence most disciples would need to persevere in the Quest for a long time, before they could become confident of winning ultimate success. Many might become discouraged at the want of success, and be inclined to give up the enterprise. What are these disciples to do, so that they may be able to make some steady progress towards the goal? The answer is, they must practise devotion to God.

Now we come to the testimony of the saints. We have already seen that these, as a class, are much safer guides than the yogis. What we learn from the saints is not the pure Truth, but truth in relativity. But because the way followed by the saints leads ultimately to Egolessness, therefore the Sages freely approve of that way, though they do not approve of the narrowness and crudity of the utterances of many of the saints. It is a fact that few saints rise above sect. Sectarianism is a drag on progress. Hence the disciples of the Sage must, in following the path of devotion, discriminate between saint and saint, and beware of becoming entangled in sectarian beliefs. As a disciple of the Sage he must know that beliefs are to be held tentatively — not bigotedly — because all beliefs will one day be consumed in the Fire of Experience of the Self. He must take only what the most sagelike saints say, and leave out all the rest. And he must understand the teaching in the light of the Advaitic teaching of the Sages.

The Sage himself gives us the essence of the teaching of the saints. He tells us that to attribute name and form to the Reality, thereby adding personality to It and making It into what we call God

— is quite proper and necessary as a means of mental
purification. But he says also that *any* name and *any*
form may be so attributed — that it is narrowness to
claim that a particular form is alone holy. And he
reconciles this devotion with the foregoing teaching
about the Quest and the Egoless State, by telling us
that the goal of the devotee is the same as that of the
seeker.

It is said of devotion — in the *Gita*, chapter IX —
that even men of evil life are benefited by it; they
become good very soon and finally reach the State of
unending Peace, the Egoless State.* But as a general
rule only men of pure mind and good conduct are
drawn in devotion to God, because a certain degree
of egolessness is implicit in devotion, and character
is proportional to the degree of one's egolessness.
Hence one should devote some attention to the
improvement of character. This, of course, is necessary
for all — for seekers of the Self, as well as for devotees.

As a man is, so he acts; conversely as a man acts,
so he will become in time. The human personality
attains impersonality through self-regulated
expression in conduct. Hence regulation of conduct
is necessary for him that aspires to the highest good.
In the ancient lore we are told that *he that would
find the Truth must have eschewed wrong-doing,
subdued his passions and attained mental harmony.*

---

* अपि चेत् सुदुराचरो भजते मामनन्यभाक् ।

साधुरेव स मन्तव्य: सम्यग्व्यवसितो हि स: ॥

क्षिप्रं भवति धर्मात्मा शश्वच्छान्तिं निगच्छति ।

30.31.

Truth and goodness are essentially the same. The
sacred book known as the *Gita*, also lays great stress
on this condition; the seeker must have what it calls
the 'godly endowment' in order to reach the goal; this
includes 'fearlessness, clear thinking, meditativeness,
readiness to give, control of mind and body, reverence
to whatever is holy, love of truth, straightforwardness,
non-injury, forbearance, not telling tales, compassion,
freedom from greed, gentleness, shrinking from
wrong-doing, not being capricious.' All this may be
summed up as good character; they are the aroma of
the real Self that dwells in our hearts; therefore they
make for impersonality; to them belong the persons,
not they to the persons for *goodness is not a possession;
it is the possessor.*

Rightly do all the religions emphasise goodness; a
man of bad character may become a good mathematician
or scientist; but only a good and pure-minded man
can cherish devotion to things that transcend the
world. Wrong-doing is because of the ego-sense; and
since egolessness is our goal in fact — whatever
believers may think — the itch to do wrong must be
conquered, no matter how. The Buddhists have their
'eightfold noble path' and the Christians have the
'sermon on the mount'; humble righteousness is nine-
tenths of the Egoless State.

Devotion is already there in all men; it only needs
to be refined and directed to proper objects; when
directed to ignoble objects it is called attachment; but
when it is diverted from them and fixed on holy objects
or ends it is called devotion. It is natural for the
common man to feel devotion to a person; it becomes
finer if it be directed to a person of great excellence.

Taking advantage of this fact, the Sages and Saints
present to us a person of exceptional and inimitable
excellence, namely God, and whoever comes into some
kind of contact with Him becomes His devotee.

The quality of devotion is not strained; it is
effortless, natural. God does not command us to love
Him. We love Him because we cannot help it. If we
are so fortunate as to be drawn to Him in love, let us
yield ourselves freely to that impulse, the more freely
because we have submitted a good deal too freely to
impulses of a different order. A legendary devotee
named Prahlada, we are told, prayed thus: "May I
ever bear unto Thee that love which the ignorant bear
to the means of pleasure they find in the world." And
not only should there be devotion to God, but it should
be also pure — free from bargaining. *Devotion should
not be conceived as a means to some end*; otherwise it
would not be devotion to God.

Here an objection may arise, which maybe stated
thus: 'Since God, the soul and the world are a triad,
and since the whole triad is unreal as shown before,
there is no God, and hence there is no scope for
devotion.' The answer is implied in the very argument
by which the unreality of God was proved. There we
saw that there are only two alternatives: Either all
the members of the triad are unreal, or all are real.
This was illustrated by the analogy of the hen. So for
one that accepts the teaching that the world and the
soul are unreal, the whole triad is unreal; this was the
argument there. But for one that does not accept — or
is unable to assimilate — this teaching about the
world and the soul, the position is quite different. The
same argument and the same analogy will lead him

to the conclusion that God is real as God, and hence there is scope for devotion, until he loses the ego. Besides we were not taught that God is altogether unreal, but only that in His real Nature He is not God — a person — but the real Self in the Heart.

The following utterance of the Sage will make this clear: "So long as there is division (*vibhakti*) there must be devotion (*bhakti*); so long as there is separation (*viyoga*) there must be a method of reunion (*yoga*). So long as there is duality there will also be God and devotee. In the Quest of the Truth also there is duality till the Source is reached. So too it is in devotion. When God is won there is no more duality; nor is He different even now; for God is thought in and by the Self, which proves that He is really one with the Self. If one that is told to have devotion to God straightaway does so without further question, it is all right; he will automatically become one with God in due course; such a one is the ripe one.* But there is another kind of man who turns round and says: 'There are two, God and I; before knowing God who is far off, let me know the closer one, myself '; for him the Quest is prescribed. Really devotion and the Quest are the same." On another occasion the Sage said to someone: "God is as real as you are."

There is therefore no real inconsistency between the truth of God as revealed by the Sages — which is the absolute truth of His being — and the personality of God for the purposes of devotion; for the devotee

---

* We may have to distinguish such a one from the dogmatist who has an elaborate system of beliefs regarding God, insisting on His eternal separateness from the self.

dwells — at least in the beginning — in the region of relativity.

However, because God is really the indwelling real Self of the devotee, therefore He is the source of what is called 'Grace'; and this is so both for those that know that He is the real Self and for those that know it not. The practical implications of 'Grace' are very important; therefore almost all the religions lay great stress on it; if there be no such thing as Grace, then deliverance would never be possible; for the utmost efforts of finite beings can never produce an infinite result; the devotee calls it Grace, while the philosopher — disciple of a Sage calls it the Power of the Truth that vanquishes untruth.

It may be mentioned that one who, not believing in God, goes through the philosophical inquiry outlined in the foregoing chapters and is thereby convinced that the Egoless State of the Sages is worth attaining, but finds that he is severely handicapped by mental discords or weakness, *may* afterwards come to accept belief in God and begin to practise devotion to Him, so that through His grace he may win the Egoless State. The point is that when one thinks one is not equal to the enterprise of finding the Self it is an enormous advantage to one if one believes in God and becomes inspired with devotion to Him; we shall understand this better when we study that stage of devotion which is called self-surrender.

Devotion, at least to begin with, is with difference; the devotee regards God as a Person, distinct from himself. For this reason many *Advaitis* regard it as something beneath themselves. The Sages do not approve of this. Someone put the Sage the following question: "I am unable to meditate on God as formless. Meditation on God with form is inferior. What am I to do?" The Sage answered: "Who told you to distinguish between higher and lower methods? If you meditate on God with form, as a Person, that will surely take you to the goal." We know already that personality means the same as having form.

So, a theoretical knowledge of the Truth of Non-duality, far from being a bar to devotion, is actually a great aid to it. Convinced Non-dualists have been sincere and ardent devotees. Great Saints have had the Experience of the Unity of God and the Self, and that has not destroyed their devotion; on the contrary their devotion has been intensified, because, whereas formerly their love was divided between two, namely their own self and God, now there remains only One, on whom all their love is lavished. Sages have composed hymns to God, as if He were a Person, and these hymns are intensely devotional, though they also give expression in the hymns to the Truth of Unity, thereby showing that there is no *practical* incompatibility between that Truth and devotion. In fact the Unity is in the transcendental State, while devotion is in relativity.

The *advaiti* or Non-dualist gives to God the whole of his love, whereas the *Dvaiti* (or Dualist) gives Him only a part. The self is the dearest of all things, as the Upanishads say, because whatever is dear to us is so for the sake of the Self, not for its own sake. When the two are taken as two, then love is necessarily divided. When the two are one, the love is undivided. Hence the Sage and the *Gita* tell us that Sages are the best of devotees. In fact the highest praise of God —

the most pleasing to Him, if we may say so — is *not*
that He is the supreme Lord of all creation, but that
He is the most beloved of all, as the Self in the Heart. The
greatness of God as God is in relativity — in *Maya* — but
the Nature of God as the Self is the Absolute Truth,
beyond *Maya*.

The devotee that has the Advaitic faith regards
God as the Consumer of the ego. This is expressed by
the Sage in one of his hymns as follows: "Oh men
that are ready to give up the body, having lost all
desire to live, there is, even here, a Medicine without
equal, which will surely kill the false little self without
taking life, if it be meditated upon even once. That,
you should understand, is the immortal Arunachala,
which is the blissful Real Consciousness."*

We shall now make a detailed study of devotion
as we find it in practice.

Devotion consists in the spontaneous turning of the
mind to God; this can be only when one finds happiness
in thoughts of God; this happiness sometimes takes
the form of ecstasy, the memory of which deepens
devotion and binds the heart to the object of devotion;
he that has once felt the ecstasy of devotion becomes
thereafter a Saint and his mind gets steadily weaned
from the sense-objects which are the means of
pleasure to common men; when thus one becomes

---

* The above meaning is rendered into Sanskrit as follows:

मुक्तास्था इह जीवने बत वपुस्त्यागाय सज्जा नरा:
अस्त्येकं भुवि भेषजं निरुपमं यद् ध्यानमात्रात्सकृत् ।
प्राणानामवियोजनेन नियतं हन्यान्मृषाजीवकं
तज्जानीह्यरुणाचलाख्यममृतं सच्चित्स्वरुपं शिवम् ॥

sainted one prays to God for more and more of devotion, as did Prahlada; indeed the Saints regard devotion as an end in itself; they say it is so precious that God would freely grant Deliverance itself, but not devotion, except to those who are the objects of His especial grace.

Devotion therefore is a form of emotion, a mode of feeling; it has different levels — depressions and elations. The heart of a Saint — said a great Saint-sage — is like the river Yamuna which flows unevenly, while that of a Sage is like the river Ganga (Ganges) which flows serenely and majestically. Therefore the Saints as a class are poets; and the poetry that the Saints of all ages have bequeathed to us is immense; and as poetry is infectious, many become devotees by the taste of such poetry, and ever after they are mad with devotion, as poets alone can be; such poetry becomes their food and drink. Sometimes they become drunk with ecstasy by the mere chanting of His names.

Of course not all devotion is equally efficacious; a verse ascribed to a great Saint, Sri Krishna Chaitanya, tells us: "Lowlier than the humble blade of grass, more patient than the tree, never claiming honour from others, but freely giving honour to all — such a one should take the name of God always."

Being essentially a poet, the devotee has all the weakness and all the strength of that tribe; he is often guilty of extravagances, but he is also susceptible to inspiration: in this way he tends to become wonderfully wise; for the truth is, the devotee is in some mysterious way much nearer the real Self and much more amenable to Its teaching than his less

fortunate brother, the philosopher. Of course there is
in this a difference between the beginner in devotion
and the advanced one; the latter as a rule outgrows
the crudities and narrowness that often mar the
utterances of devotees of the former kind; but it so
happens that the believers cannot pick and choose
between these; the result is that the religions of
devotion are made up chiefly of the mistakes of the
raw devotees; the fanatic usually manages to explain
away the wiser intuitions of the ripe devotee; and that
is how religions are distorted and tend to divide
instead of uniting men. And this brings us to the chief
distinction between a Saint and a Sage; the former
has yet some ego to lose; the Sage has none; therefore
the Saint has a mind, and holds to a creed; the Sage
is mindless and creedless; the Saint may become a
persecutor for his religion, the Sage never. It is also
possible for a Saint to suffer a fall from grace which
would postpone his winning of Deliverance. Of course
the Sage may also be a Saint, and there have been,
and may be, Saints who are sagelike in their catholicity
and freedom from fanatic zeal.

The fact is, the devotee does not *need* to have a
clear-cut creed; it would be good for all concerned if
the devotee did not *bind* himself to definite beliefs;
for beliefs must change from time to time as the mind
becomes more refined; an elastic creed would be
harmless; but such a creed cannot be devised by
devotees; they must go to a Sage for that. The reason
is that devotion is poetic and blunders disastrously
when it sets its hand to prose.

The Sage can be a Saint, but it is hard for the
Saint to be also a Sage; for in the Egoless State is the

potentiality of all that is good and great, and he that still retains the ego is necessarily imperfect.

Devotion in some cases matures into the mystic mood of love, which is little distinguishable from the Egoless State. We can learn a good deal on this subject from the literature of Sri Ramakrishna, as also from the poetry of devotion that has come down to us. The Sage of Arunachala hints at the very slight difference there is between the ripe Saint and the Sage; he says: *"That which dwells in the hearts of one and all as Pure Awareness is the Oneself; so when the heart melts in love and the Cave of the Heart where He shines is reached, then the Eye of Awareness opens and He is realised as the real Self"*; when love is perfect then the Saint becomes a Sage.

Devotion must differ in its modes according to the mental level of the devotees. Two distinct grades of devotion are mentioned by the Sage of Arunachala and in the ancient lore. Crude minds cannot grasp even theoretically the teaching that ultimately God is to be realised as the real Self; they have devotion to God with a sense of being different from God and subject to Him; for them God is the universal Master whom they are to serve faithfully and thereby win His Grace. Their idea of God being anthropomorphic, they think of Him as a very superior kind of man; they try to practise all the virtues — to be good to other beings — because they think that God expects it of them as the common Master of all. Naturally this devotion is selfish; the devotee looks forward to a personal reward; the eternal continuance of his individuality he takes for granted; this kind of devotion gives a fresh lease of life to the ego.

The ripe devotee somehow comes to see that this is anthropomorphism and cannot be the truth; he learns to think of God as somehow not different from himself, as only apparently different; even this apparent difference, he knows, would melt away by the unfailing power of His Grace; and he is not in the least afraid of this; for he has ceased to be anxious to retain his individuality; he is fast approaching Egolessness. Naturally the flow of Grace is in his case more abundant; for the ego is the one thing that shuts off or curtails that flow.

The aim of the devotee is to establish a personal relation with God — to see Him in visions, to speak to and be spoken to by Him, and so on; and sometimes he gets his wish and is thereby much elated; but the visions fade away and then he is much depressed. The Sage of Arunachala tells us that the forms of God seen in these visions are purely mental, not real; therefore they do not last; he says that so long as even a trace of egoism is left there can be no seeing of God as He really is; seeing Him as He really is, is no other than abiding in the Egoless State, which the devotee ultimately wins through God's Grace. There is therefore not the least difference in respect of the final goal between the devotee and the seeker of the real Self. The call of the real Self comes to the lover of the Truth in one form and to the lover of God the devotee, in another form; that is all the difference. This is denied by those philosophers who want to retain their individuality for ever; that they are mistaken will be seen from what the Sage of Arunachala said regarding what is true surrender of the self to God; this will be quoted in its place later on.

The goal that is attained by the seeker through the Quest is attained by the devotee through self-surrender; this comes through the understanding which comes by the working of what is called Grace, — the power by which God draws the souls unto Himself. The devotee realises more and more that the 'soul' is a mere nothing and that God alone exists; he sees also that God alone is worth the winning and that the whole world would be well lost for His sake; that leads to the mood of self-surrender.

'Grace' is, of course, a rather unphilosophical word; but it is a name for something that is real and effective; it consists in the truth that God is even now the real Self; that truth fulfils itself in some mysterious way; but the devotee can give it no other name than 'Grace.'

Grace, we learn, has three states; in the first stage the ultimate Truth appears as God, who is far away and unapproachable; by devotion to God the second stage is reached, when God comes near as *Guru* — the Sage that tells of the real Self — and then devotion to *him* takes the place of devotion to God; this devotion leads up to the manifestation of the highest Grace, the Experience of the real Self in the Egoless State, — the third and last stage.

Self-surrender is the condition of the perfect working of Grace. It may be partial or complete; but in any case it tends towards Egolessness, and anticipates in some measure all the good that there is in Egolessness. The surrenderer, says the Sage, need not worry about his own good and evil actions of the past; their reactions would not work to his disadvantage; for Grace would dispose of them so as to turn them to his advantage. The whole function of Grace is the elimination of the sheaths, after which the real Self alone will remain.

Grace is not something special; it is really universal; it is the only power for good there is, and all alike participate in its goodness; but the ego interferes and discounts its work; by self surrender this interference is made less and less, and the work of Grace becomes more and more effective.

In the practice of nature-cure one proceeds on the conviction that mind, life and body are entirely amenable to divine grace and that they work to the best ends if there be complete self-surrender; interference by means of drugs or otherwise is condemned as more or less certain to interfere with the natural process of self-cure; the prevalence of this method of curing diseases is *prima facie* evidence that there is an impersonal but gracious power working from within.

The Sage was asked by someone what he should do to *deserve* Grace; the Sage answered: "Are you asking this question without Grace? Grace is in the beginning, the middle and the end; for Grace is the Self; but because of ignorance of the Self it is expected to come from somewhere outside of you."

What is true self-surrender is explained by the Sage as follows:

"All that one needs to do is to surrender oneself to the Source of oneself. There is no need to get confused by calling that Source God and assuming that it is somewhere outside. One's Source is *within* oneself. To that Source the surrender should be made; that is, *one should seek that Source and by the very*

force of that search merge into It. The question 'Where
is the Source?' can arise only if it be thought that the
Self is different from the Source. If the ego becomes
merged into its Source, then there is no ego, no
individual soul; that is, the seeker becomes one with
the Source. That being the case, where is
surrendering? Who is to surrender and to whom? And
what is there to be surrendered? This loss of
individuality — which even now does not really exist —
is devotion, wisdom and the Quest.

"The Vaishnava Saint Nammazhvar sang as
follows: 'Not knowing the truth of myself I was
deluded by the ideas *'I'* and *'mine'*; but when I came
to know myself I knew also that Thou art both *I* and
mine.' So true devotion is to know oneself aright; and
this is consistent with the creed of the Vaishnavas.
But their traditional belief is expressed as follows:
The souls are the bodies of God; these must become
pure and then must surrender themselves to Him;
then they go to His heaven and there enjoy Him! They
contend that if the soul becomes God there will be no
enjoyment, just as one cannot taste sugar if he himself
becomes sugar; therefore they want to be separate
from God and enjoy Him. But what they mean by
purification is extinction of egoism. Is God inert like
sugar?* If the surrender be real and complete, how
can there be *any* separateness?

"Not only that, they believe that, remaining
separate in His Heaven, they are to serve Him and
adore Him. Is God deceived by this talk of service?

---

* The sugar-simile of the Vaishnavas is thus shown to be wholly out
of place (see also *Guru Vachaka Kovai* verse 978).

Does He care for their service? Would not He, being Pure Consciousness, retort: 'Who are you apart from Me?'

"They say that if the individual soul be surrendered to God, the soul remains as a body of God, and the latter is the Self of that soul-body; the individual soul is called the little self and God the great Self. Can there be a Self of a self? How many selves can there be? What really is the Self? That alone is the Self, which remains over after the elimination of all that is not the Self — the body, the mind and so on; whatever is eliminated in this process is not-Self. If it be said that in this process the remainder is the little self, and that God is the Self of that little self, it only means that the process of elimination has not been carried out to the very end as it should be; if it be so carried out, then it will be seen that the little self is not the true Self — that great Self is alone the true Self; the remainder in the completed process is the great Self; it follows that they have got hold of something else, and not the real Self.

"All this confusion is due to the many meanings of the word '*Atma*', which means the 'Self'; it means the body, the senses, the vital force, the mind, the fancy, the hypothetical little self, and the real great Self; thus it is possible to describe the little self as the body of the great Self. But the verse of the *Gita*, 'I am the Self residing in the hearts of all', makes it clear that God is Himself the real Self in all; it is not there said that He is the Self of the self.

"To think of yourself as something separate from the Source, namely God, is itself theft; for by this you appropriate what belongs to God. If you want to *remain* separate even after being made pure, and to enjoy God, it is wholesale theft. Does He not know all this?"

From all this we can understand that he that wants to retain his separateness as an individual cannot make a real self-surrender; his is a surrender with a reservation, and a very big one at that.

A practical hint about the true nature of self-surrender was once given by the Sage to a young man who came to him in a disordered state of mind; he believed he had had a vision of God, in which he was promised great things if he surrendered himself; he said he had done so, but that God failed to carry out His promise; and he demanded of the Sage: "Show me God and I shall chop off His head, or let Him chop off my head." The Sage asked someone to read from a Tamil commentary on his own writings, and then made this remark: "*If the surrender be real, then who is there remaining, able to question God's doing?*" The young man's eyes were opened; he acknowledged that it was his own mistake and went away pacified. Self-surrender must be without reservations and without conditions; there is no room in it for bargaining.

The common notion of self-surrender, that it is a gift of oneself to God, is declared by the Sage to be a mistaken one. He says: "The offering of oneself to God is similar to the offering, to a Ganesh-figure made of jaggery, of a portion of jaggery taken from the figure itself; for there is no individual self apart from Him."*
This shows that the notion is, as shown before, an act of theft. And it is a continuing theft. What is really

---

* *Guru Vachaka Kovai* verse 486 (see appendix B, verse 111).

meant by the term self-surrender is just the cessation
of this theft, by the recognition by the devotee that
he himself has no separate existence.

The practical outcome of self-surrender is
indirectly expressed by the Sage as follows: *"Since
God himself is bearing the whole burden of the world,
the unreal soul that tries to carry the burden is just
like the caryatid figure (sculptured at the base of a
temple-tower) appearing to sustain the tower (on its
shoulders). If one travelling by a conveyance that can
carry heavy loads keeps his luggage on his own head
and thus suffers pain, who is to blame for it?"*† Here
two similes are employed. By the first simile we are
reminded that the so-called individual soul has no
consciousness of its own, and therefore does not really
bear the burdens of life, which are borne by God alone.
By the second simile we are shown that he that will
not surrender himself to God's grace has to suffer
worries without end, while the devotee that cultivates
the attitude of surrender is free from cares, and
therefore happy, even now.

---

† *Ulladu Narpadu Anubandham* verse 17 (see appendix A, verse 63).

Chapter 12

Some more Sayings of the Sage

HOW ARE THE conflicting views of men of different religions to be reconciled? "The real aim of all religions is to lead up to the awakening to the Truth of the Self. But the Truth of the Self is too simple for the generality of men; even though there is no one who is not aware of the Self, men do not care to be told of It; they think the Self to be of little worth; they want to hear of far-off things — heaven, hell, reincarnation and so on; they love mystery, and not the plain truth; and the religions humour them, so that ultimately they may come back to the Self. But why not seek and find and abide in the Self at once, without further wandering? The heavens cannot be apart from him that sees or thinks of them; their reality is of the same degree as that of the ego that wants to go there; hence they do not exist apart from the Self, which is the real heaven.

"A Christian would not be pleased unless he is told that God is somewhere in a far-off heaven which he cannot reach without divine aid; Christ alone knew God and he alone can take men to God. If he be told 'The Kingdom of Heaven is within *you*', he would not take the plain meaning of it, but would read into it complex and far-fetched meanings. *The mature mind alone can grasp and accept the simple and naked truth.*

"The conflict of teachings is only apparent, and can be resolved if one practises self-surrender to God; this will lead to the Self, to which everyone must come back in the end, because that is the Truth. The discord amongst the creeds can never be got rid of by discussing their merits; for discussion is a mental process. The creeds are mental — they exist in the mind alone, while the Truth is beyond the mind; therefore the Truth is not in the creeds." Therefore we must not set much store by our creeds.

On another occasion the Sage declared that a Vedantin — one that has understood the teaching of the Upanishadic lore — can understand what Jesus Christ meant by the 'Kingdom of Heaven'; he will understand what the orthodox Christian cannot, namely that the Kingdom of Heaven spoken of by that Sage is just the Egoless State.

Hence one should either go beyond the creeds by the Quest of the true Self, or take to some one of them and hold to it lightly, concentrating all effort on the *practice* of the methods taught by it; to be zealous for the beliefs inculcated is to be lax in the practice of the method; even the materialist or atheist has a creed of his own: and there is no practical difference between him and a religious one except in the purification of the mind that comes by living aright. Hence says the Sage: *"What is the use of asserting or denying that there is a real Self (other than the bodies), that it is with form, that it is one, and so on? All these disputes are in the realm of ignorance"* (*Ulladu Narpadu* verse 34).

On another occasion the Sage said: "The sacred lore is voluminous, different parts of it being adapted to the needs of different kinds of seekers; each seeker successively transcends portion after portion of it; that which he transcends then becomes for him useless and even false; ultimately he transcends the whole of it."

Original sin: Once the Sage was asked about the Christian doctrine of 'original sin' — that every man is born in sin and can be delivered from it only by faith in Jesus Christ; he replied: "The sin is said to be in man; but there is no manhood in sleep; manhood comes on waking, along with the thought 'I am this body'; this thought is the real original sin; it must be removed by the death of the ego, after which this thought will not arise." And he explained the truth of Christianity as follows: "The body is the cross; the ego is Jesus the 'son of man'; when he is crucified, he is resurrected as the 'Son of God', which is the glorious real Self. One should lose the ego in order to live." We may remember here that according to *all* the Sages the ego-life is not truly life, but death.

Is there knowledge of the Self in the Egoless State? The truth about the Egoless State is conveyed by the Sage by means of negations. "What is called Self-Knowledge is that State in which there can be neither knowledge nor ignorance; for what is commonly regarded as knowledge is not true knowledge;* the Self is Itself true Knowledge, because It shines alone — without any other that could become an object of Its

---

* The knowledge got through the mind and the senses implies the distinction between subject and object, which the experience of the Sages shows to be illusory.

knowledge or a knower of It. Understand that the
Self is not a void" (*Ulladu Narpadu* verse 12). Because
the Egoless State is not described to us in positive
terms, many people are apt to conclude that it is mere
nothingness or utter annihilation; this mistake was
committed by many of the professed followers of the
'Enlightened One', Gautama Buddha; the Sage here
provides against a similar mistake being made by
those who might become his disciples, by declaring
that it is not a void.

Since the Sage is on a plane where there is
neither ignorance nor knowledge, he has no use for
learning of any kind; even the sacred lore does not
interest him, though he may read it in order to explain
its true meaning to those who ask him about it. So
we can understand the following saying:— "Even a
learned man must bow before an illiterate Sage. The
illiterate man is simply ignorance; the learned man
is learnedly ignorant; the Sage also is ignorant,
because there is nothing for him to know."

**Fate or Free-will, which determines one's
life?** The person that puts this question expects a
categorical answer; he wants to know which of these
two is the decisive factor in life, fate or free-will. In
his writings the Sage answers as follows: "*The dispute
as to which of the two — fate and the human will —
is more powerful interests only those that are without
enlightenment about the true nature of the ego, from
which arise the two notions; he that has that
enlightenment has transcended both and is no more
interested in the question*" (*Ulladu Narpadu* 19).

To a visitor that put him this question the Sage
replied: "The answer to this question, if given, will be

rather difficult to understand. Yet almost everyone asks this question some time or other in his life. One must know the truth of him that seems to be affected, or not affected, by fate"; here the Sage evidently means the ego; since the distinction between fate and free-will exists only for the ego-mind, the truth of it is inseparable from the truth of the ego, which can be realised only by the Quest. Having said this the Sage went on explaining what fate really means; he said: "Fate has a beginning — a cause — and that is action; and that cannot be without a free-will; free-will being therefore the first cause, it is the predominant factor, and by cultivating free-will one can conquer fate." Cultivating free-will implies the process of inquiry and the Quest taught by the Sage, or in the alternative, surrendering of oneself to God as the One Reality. "What is commonly known as self-reliance is nothing but ego-reliance and hence worsens bondage. Reliance on God is alone true Self-reliance, because He is the Self."

Is not a Guru necessary? It is the common belief of the religiously minded that everyone that aspires to the state of deliverance must in due course find and attach himself to a *Guru*. The Sage was asked by someone as to whether this belief is correct. He gave the following reply: "So long as one thinks of himself as little — *laghu* — he must take hold of the great — the *guru*; he must not however look upon the *Guru* as a person; the Sage is never other than the real Self of the disciple. When that Self is realised then there is neither *Guru* nor disciple." The question arose because the Sage himself had no *Guru*, — at least no outer *Guru*. On another occasion the Sage said: "A teacher would be needed if one had to learn something new; but this is a case of unlearning."

How to overcome the worries of life? A visitor said: "I suffer from worries without end; there is no peace for me, though there is nothing wanting for me to be happy." The Sage asked: "Do these worries affect you in sleep?" The visitor admitted that they did not. The Sage asked him again: "Are you the very same man now, or are you different from him that slept without any worry?" "Yes, I am the same person." The Sage then said: "Then surely those worries do not belong to you. It is your own fault if you assume that they are yours."

Meditation and Mind-control. "Meditation (*dhyana*) is a battle; for it is the effort to keep hold of *one* thought to the exclusion of all else; other thoughts arise and try to sink that thought; when the latter gains strength the others are put to flight. Breath-regulation (*pranayama*) is for him that cannot directly control his thoughts; it serves as a brake serves a car, but one should not stop with breath-regulation; after its purpose is gained — the quieting of the mind's restlessness — one should take up the practice of concentration; in course of time it will become possible to dispense with the control of the breath; the mind will then become quiet as soon as meditation is attempted. When meditation is well established it can no more be given up; it will go on automatically even during work, play and other activities. It will go on even in sleep. The means for getting well-established in meditation is meditation itself; neither *japa* (mental repetition of words or sentences) nor a vow of silence is necessary. If one takes to selfish worldly activity there is no good taking a vow of silence. Meditation extinguishes all thoughts and then the Truth alone remains."

On another occasion the Sage said: "When camphor burns, no residue is left. The mind must be like camphor; it must melt away and be wholly consumed by the earnest resolve to find and be the real Self; by this resolve the 'Who am I?' Quest becomes efficacious. When the mind is thus consumed — when no trace of it *as mind* is left — it has become resolved into the Self."

Being asked how one can find his *Guru*, the Sage said: "By intense meditation."

People who look for specific results from meditation but do not get them, become discouraged and conclude that meditation has done them no good; to them the Sage says: "It does not matter at all whether these results are attained or not. *The attainment of steadiness is the main thing*; it is the great gain. Anyhow they must trust themselves to God and wait for His Grace without impatience. The same rule applies to *japa* also; *japa* uttered even once does good, whether the person is aware of it or not."

Some persons imagine that one must go on practising meditation even after becoming a Sage. Light is thrown on this question by the following answer. "When the mind is extinguished in the Egoless State, then there is neither concentration nor non-concentration." Referring to the same question the Sage said on another occasion: "When the Self is realised, then *samadhi* can neither be attempted nor given up."

Success in meditation comes quickly to a few, and after long practice to others; on this point the Sage

said: "Meditation is impeded by *vasanas* (proclivities
or affinities of the mind); hence it becomes effective
through the progressive weakening of the *vasanas*.
Some minds are like gunpowder which takes fire and
is consumed at once; others are like charcoal, and
some others are like wet fuel."

The following answer throws light on the secret
of mind-control: "The mind cannot be controlled by
one that takes it to be something that really exists;
in that case the mind behaves like a thief pretending
to be a policeman running after the thief; efforts made
in this way only serve to give a new lease of life to the
ego and the mind." The right method is the inquiry
into the truth of the mind and the ego, which leads
up to the Quest.

On another occasion the Sage said: "People ask
me how to control the mind. I reply: 'Show me the
mind.' The mind is no more than the series of
thoughts. How can it be controlled by *one* of those
thoughts, namely the desire to control the mind? It is
foolish to seek to end the mind by the mind itself.
The only way is to find the mind's Source and keep
hold of It. Then the mind will fade away of itself. Yoga
enjoins *Chitta-vritti-nirodha* (repression of thoughts);
I prescribe *Atmanveshana* (Quest of Oneself), which
is practicable. The mind is repressed in swoon, or as
the effect of fasting. But as soon as the cause is
withdrawn, the mind revives; that is, the thoughts
being to flow as before. There are just two ways of
controlling the mind. Either seek its Source, or
surrender it to be struck down by the Supreme Power.
Surrender is the recognition of the existence of a
Higher Overruling Power. If the mind refuses to help

in seeking the Source, let it go and wait for its return; then turn it inwards. No one succeeds without patient perseverance."

Meditation with the eyes fixed on the space between the eye-brows, the Sage warns us, may result in fear. The right way is to fix the mind on the Self alone. It is without fear.

Another thing that we learn is that there can be no meditation — in the usual sense of the term — on the real Self; meditation is usually understood to mean thinking of an object; and this implies a distinction between the subject and the object; hence no real meditation of the Self is possible; what is called meditation is no more than the dispelling of thoughts, whereby the Self is covered over; when all thoughts are dispelled, the Self shines in Its real nature; and abiding in this state is the only meditation of the real Self that is possible; hence the Sage is ever in meditation though he may seem to be often otherwise engaged. This is the truth conveyed in the first benedictory verse of *Ulladu Narpadu* (see appendix A, verse 4).

How to endure Grief. "By turning the mind inwards one can overcome the worst of griefs. Grief is possible only when one thinks of oneself as a body. If the form be transcended, one will know that the Self is eternal — that there is neither birth nor death; it is the body that is born and dies, not the Self; the body is a creation of the ego, which however is never perceived apart from a body; it is in fact indistinguishable from the body. One should consider that in sleep one was not aware of a body; one will then realise that the body is not real. On waking from sleep the ego

arises; then thoughts. Find out to whom the thoughts
belong. Ask wherefrom they arise. They must spring
from the Self, which is Consciousness. Apprehending
this truth even vaguely helps towards extinction of
the ego; and thereafter the one infinite Existence will
be realised; in that State there are no individuals —
only that one Being. Hence there is no ground for
even the *thought* of death.

"If one thinks oneself to have been born, one
cannot escape the thought of death. Let one therefore
question whether one was born at all. One will then
find that the real Self is ever-existent and that the
body is only a thought, — the first of all thoughts,
the root of all mischief."

The three moods of the mind. The mind is
alternately subject to three moods; the state of
dullness and inertia, called *tamas*, is the lowest; the
next higher is restless activity, called *rajas*; the
highest is clarity and peace, called *sattva*; the Sage
tells us that the disciple should not regret or bewail
the prevalence of the first two, but wait till the mood
of clarity comes, and then make the most of it.

Death. "The dead are indeed happy, having got
rid of the incubus of the body; the dead do not grieve.
Do men fear sleep? No, they court it and prepare for
it. But sleep is temporary death, and death is but a
longer sleep. If the man dies while alive, if he dies
the death which is not death, by the extinction of the
ego — he would not grieve for anybody's death. Apart
from this, since we know that we persist through all
the three states, with the body and without it, why
should one desire the continuance of the shackles of
the body, for oneself or for another?

"When one begins to die, hard breathing sets in; that means that he has become unconscious of the dying body; the mind at once takes hold of another body, and it swings to and fro between the two, until attachment is fully transferred to the new body; meanwhile there are occasional violent breaths, and that means that the mind swings back to the dying body. The transitional state of the mind is somewhat like a dream."

Have animals souls? The Sage treats animals as he does human beings; when speaking of an animal he uniformly uses the pronoun 'he' or 'she' as the case may be.* Once when he was asked whether animals are not inferior to men he replied: "The Upanishads say that men are just animals so long as they are subject to the ego, that is, until they become aware of the pure Self. It may even be that men are worse than animals." The Sage has also been heard to say that very advanced souls may have taken up animal bodies in order to live in the atmosphere of his hermitage. There were at one time four dogs living there, and these showed many marks of devotion; for example, when food was offered to them they would not touch it until the Sage himself had been served and had commenced his meal; as soon as he had done so they fell to, showing how particular they were on this point.

Devotional practices. "*Japa* and the like are preferred by many as being more concrete. But what is more concrete than the Self? It is within the direct experience of each and everyone, and It is experienced

---

* The Tamils regularly use the pronoun 'it' when referring to an animal.

every moment. Hence the Self is the one thing that is indisputably known. That being the case, one should seek and find It instead of seeking for an unknown something, — God or the world."

Samadhi and its interpretation. "The experience that St. Paul obtained, and which converted him to faith in Christ, was really formless; but after this experience he identified it as a vision of Christ." Replying to the objection that Paul had been a hater of Christ before, the Sage said: "It is immaterial whether it was love or hate that prevailed; anyhow the thought of Christ was there; the case was similar to those of Ravana and other demons."

How should we act in the world? "One should act in the world like an actor on the stage. In all actions there is in the background the real Self as the underlying principle; remember that and act."

The Heart. "There is no need to know where and what the Heart is. It will do its work if you engage in the Quest of the Self."

Intellect. "The intellect cannot help imagining the Self as being of the size and shape of the body."

Mind. "The mind is like the moon, deriving its light of consciousness from the Self, which thus resembles the Sun. Hence when the Self begins to shine, the mind, like the moon, becomes useless."

Helping others. "The Sage helps the world merely by being the real Self. The best way for one to serve the world is to win the Egoless State." Also this: "If you are anxious to help the world, but think that you cannot do so by attaining the Egoless State, then surrender to God all the world's problems, along with your own."

Vision of the cosmic form of God seen by Arjuna. "Sri Krishna told Arjuna, 'I am formless, transcending all the worlds.' Yet He shows Arjuna His 'cosmic form.' Arjuna sees himself, the gods and all the worlds in it. Krishna also said: 'Neither gods nor men can see Me'. And yet Arjuna sees His form. Krishna says 'I am Time.' Has Time any form? Again, if the universe be really His form, it must be one and unchanging. Why does He tell Arjuna: 'See in Me whatever you wish to see'? The answer is that the vision was mental — just according to the wishes of the seer. Hence it should not be interpreted literally. It was not a vision according to the Truth of God. They call it a 'divine vision.' Yet each one paints it according to his own views. And there is the seer also in the vision! If a mesmerist shows you something, you call it a trick, but you call this divine! Why this difference? Krishna gave Arjuna '*divya chakshus*,' — the divine eye — not '*Jnana chakshus*' — the Eye that is Pure Consciousness, which has no visions. *Nothing that is seen is real.*"

Yogic action and giving up of action (Karma-Yoga and Karma-Sannyasa). To a question about these the Sage did not reply at once, but went out into the forest on the hill, followed by the questioner, and cut off two sticks from a tree. These he fashioned into walking sticks, of which he gave one to the questioner and the other to someone else. Then he said: "The making of the sticks is *Karma-Yoga* and the gift of them is *Karma-Sannyasa*." The Sage did not make them for himself.

The Spiritual Centre is not geographical. It includes all men. Both the destructive and the constructive forces belong to It.

Reconciliation of Sankara and Ramanuja (the advocate of 'Qualified Advaita'). The latter says that the world is real, and that there is no *maya*. The former tells us to find out the Reality underlying the ever-changing world. What is called changefulness by Ramanuja is called illusion by Sankara. "The difference is only verbal, Both lead to the same goal."

Does the Sage meditate on God? "Meditation is thinking, and thinking is relative to forgetting. He that forgets God must think of God. *The Sage never forgets God, just as we never forget ourselves.* So he does not meditate on God. But as he never forgets God, it may truly be said that he is *ever* meditating on God."

On seeing God. Someone that had not studied the Sage's teaching, nor even the ancient lore, put him a series of questions, one of which was this: "Have you seen God?" The Sage answered, laughing mildly: "If anyone had appeared to me and said, 'I am Siva' or 'I am Rama' or 'I am Krishna', I could know I had seen such a one. But no one appeared to me, telling me who he was." The answer was according to the questioner's ignorance. God, who is the real Self, is formless, and cannot be seen as an object.

On another occasion, when the Sage was asked about 'seeing God in all things', which is enjoined in the sacred lore, he said: "Seeing objects and conceiving God in them are mental processes. But that is not seeing God, because He is within." The expression 'seeing God in all things' means the understanding that God is the Reality on which the world-appearance is imposed. This is called 'pravilapa drishti' — remembering the Truth underlying the variety — and is recommended by the Sage as a means of purifying and strengthening the mind.*

Why does not Revelation tell us what the Self is? "All that one needs to do to find the Self, is to peel off the non-selves, the sheaths. A man being put in doubt as to his being a man goes to someone and asks him. The latter tells him that he is not a tree, nor a cow, and so on, making it clear that he is not anything other than man. If the man is not satisfied and says: 'You have not told me what I *am*', the reply would be 'You have not been told that you are not a man.' If even then he cannot see that he is a man, it will be useless to tell him so. So too we are told what we are not, so that, by eliminating all that, we shall find the Remainder, the real Self."

How to make the Quest, 'Who am I?' "The way is subjective, not objective; so it cannot and need not be shown by another. Is it necessary to show anyone the way inside his own house? If the seeker keeps his mind still, that will be enough."

Answer to the Question, 'Who am I?' "An answer that comes in and by the mind is no answer at all." The answer is the Egoless State.

What is Direct Knowledge? "People assume that there is no Consciousness apart from the thoughts of the mind. Hence they think that sense-perception alone is direct knowledge. But sense-objects are not self-manifest. Hence sense-perception

---

* तरंगफेनादिकमब्धिमात्रां स्वाप्नं जगत्स्वप्नदृगेव यद्वत् ॥
सर्व: प्रपंचोऽप्यहमेव नान्य इति प्रतीति: प्रविलापदृष्टि : ॥

is *not* direct knowledge. The Self is self-manifest, and hence knowledge of the Self is direct. But if people be asked, 'Is not the Self perceived directly, without any medium,' they blink, because the pure 'I' does not stand in front of them with a form."

On Eternal Life. "Forgetting the Self is Death. Remembering It is Life. You desire eternal life. Why? Because the present life (in relativity) is unbearable. Why is it so? Because it is not your real Nature. you are in truth the pure Spirit; but you identify It with a body, which is a projection of the mind, an objectified thought, and the mind in its turn has originated from the pure Spirit. Mere change of body is no good, because there is only a transfer of the ego to the new body. Moreover, what is Life? It is Existence (as Consciousness), and that is Yourself. That is the true life, and It is eternal (beyond time). Life in the body is conditioned life. But you are Life Unconditioned. You will recover your true nature as Unconditioned Life, if the idea 'I am the body' dies".

Are there degrees of Reality? "There may be degrees of the *Experience* of the Reality, due to the degrees of freedom from thoughts; but there are no degrees of the Reality."

Can the Self be lost? Someone said: "The Bible says, the soul can be lost." The Sage remarked: "The ego may (and should) be lost, but never the Self."

"*Misery* is due to the great multitude of discordant thoughts that prevail in the mind. If all the thoughts be replaced by one single thought, there will be no misery. Then even the sense of doership and the consequent expectation of the results of actions will cease."

The genesis of pleasure. "When one thought occupies the whole mind, it excludes all other thoughts. Then the one thought also subsides into the Self, and the Bliss of the Self becomes manifest as 'pleasure', But this manifestation is in the *anandamaya*. Perfect bliss is realised only when all the sheaths are removed."

Identity of God with the Self. "If God be other than the Self, then He would be without a Self, which is absurd."

The True State. "Your duty is simply TO BE — not to be this or that. When the 'I' flies off at a tangent, saying 'I am this', it is egoism, ignorance. When it shines as the pure 'I' it is the real Self."

Is Dvaita to be condemned? "*Dvaita* consists in (wrongly) identifying the Self with the non-self. *Advaita* is ceasing to do so."

Heroism. "When the 'I' rises, it itself becomes both subject and object. When the 'I' does not rise (as ego), there is neither subject, nor object. For the ripe one, no more needs to be said; knowing this, he turns his mind inward, away from all this. To be able to do this, one must be a Hero, a *Dhira*. But what heroism is needed for finding Oneself? '*Dhi*' means mind and '*ra*' means the saving of its energies from flowing out in thoughts. He is a *Dhira* who can stem flood of thoughts and turn the mind inward."

Increase of relative knowledge. When someone wanted to know about his own past lives the Sage said: "Even with the knowledge of the present life you are not happy. Knowing past lives will only increase your unhappiness. All such knowledge is only a burden to the mind."

Is the Self the Witness? "The idea of the Self being the Witness is in the mind. It may be useful for helping to still the mind's restlessness. But it is not the absolute Truth of the Self. Witnessing is relative to objects witnessed. Both the witness and his object are mental creations."

"*Egolessness, Love, the Holy Ghost* and *Spirit* are all names of one and the same thing, the Self."

Happiness. "To seek happiness, identifying the Self with the body, is like trying to cross a river on the back of a crocodile. When the ego rises, the mind is separated from the Source, the Self, and is restless, like a stone thrown up into the air, or like the waters of a river. When the stone or the river reaches its place of origin, the ground or the ocean, it comes to rest. So too the mind comes to rest and is happy when it returns to and rests in its Source. As the stone and the river are sure to return to their starting place, so too the mind will inevitably — at some time — return to its Source." Thus it is promised that *all* shall reach the Goal.

"Happiness is your own nature. Hence it is not wrong to desire it. What is wrong is seeking it outside, because it is inside."

Samadhi and Ecstasy. "In *Samadhi* itself there is only perfect Peace. Ecstasy comes when the mind revives at the end of *Samadhi*, with the remembrance of the Peace of *Samadhi*. In devotion the ecstasy is anterior. It is manifested by tears of joy, hair standing on end and voice-stumbling. When the ego finally dies and the *Sahaja* is won, these symptoms and the ecstasies cease. There is no ecstasy on waking from sleep, because *Samadhi* is Sleep in the waking state."

"Buddha was interested only in instructing his disciples how to attain lasting Happiness. He refused to answer questions — which were based on and mixed up with the questioners' ignorance — about God and other matters. For this he was described as a Nihilist, *Sunyavadi!*"

The Sage who ruled a kingdom. Question: "How could Janaka rule his kingdom, being a Sage?" Answer: "Did Janaka ask the question? It does not arise in the State of Right Knowledge. It can arise only in ignorance." The questioner: "Probably he regarded his activities as a dream." The Sage: "This explanation too is in ignorance."

Washing off the mind's impurities. "The Experience of the Self (*Jnana*) will Itself wash off all the impurities of the mind."

On Annihilating Karma. "The more you prune a plant, the more it grows. So too, the more you seek to annihilate *Karma*, the more will it increase. You should seek the *root* of *Karma*, the ego, and destroy it."

On Brahmacharya. "*Brahmacharya* (continence) cannot be established by mere force of will. True *Brahmacharya* is not external. It is living in the Brahman, the Reality. If this be won, the latter will follow."

"Healthy mind in healthy body." "If you proceed on the notion that health of body is necessary for health of mind, there will never be an end to the care for the body."

The Hatha Yogis' idea of preparing the body for the practice of methods for the winning of Deliverance, by making it endure for an incredibly long time is ridiculous. They justify it by comparing the body to a screen, which has to be made fit for being painted on. The Sage said: "Which is the screen and which the painting? The *Self* is the screen and the body and the world are the painting. And what one needs to do to become aware of the Self is to erase the paintings." So *Hatha Yoga* is not intended for the *wise* disciple.

Mind-Control. "To still the incessant movements of the elephant's trunk the driver gives it a heavy chain to hold. So too, to control the mind's vagrancy, one should give it the best possible occupation. Else it will take to some undesirable kind of work. The best of all occupations to give to the mind is to engage it in seeking its own Source. The next best is meditation or *japa*."

Fasting for Spiritual Progress. "Fasting should be chiefly mental. Mere abstinence from food will do no good. It will even upset the mind. Spiritual unfoldment will come rather by regulating eating. But if during a fast of one month, the spiritual outlook has been maintained, then in about ten days after the breaking of the fast (if it be rightly broken and followed by judicious eating) the mind will become pure and steady, and remain so."

Answer to a pragmatist. Question: "If all men renounce, then who will plough and harvest the crops?"

Answer: "Realise the True Self and thus see for yourself." This is a general answer to all such questions.

Sense of difficulty. "A method will appear easy or difficult to one, according to whether one has practised it before or not."

To the levellers: "The surest way to achieve perfect equality is to go to sleep!"

Birth-Control versus Morality. Question: "Is birth-control inimical to morality?" Answer: "The Maha Bharata says that the more one yields to desire, the more insatiable it will become."

On going forward or backward. Someone remarked that it is easy to go forward, but impossible to go backward. The Sage said: "However far one goes, one is just where one always is. Where is moving forward or backward? The Isa Upanishad (verse 5) says: 'It is far, and It is also near!'"

Divine power for healing disease, etc. "There is no need to 'take in' divine power for any purpose. It is already in you. It is *You*."

Waking and dream compared. "The dream-world interests the dreamer because he takes it to be an objective reality, outside of and different from himself. The waking man is interested in his waking world for the same reason. If by Experience of the True Self he comes to know that the world is but a thought-form, it will cease to interest him."

Does the world exist? "There is a difference between the saying that the world exists and the saying that it is real," says the Sage. The latter does not contradict the seemingly opposite one, that the world is unreal, whereas the former does so. The thoroughly ignorant man confounds the Substance — the Reality underlying the world-appearance — and the appearance, and takes the mixture to be real. The disciples of the Sage know that they have to separate the appearance from the Substance, and understand that the latter alone is real, and the rest is an illusion.

God's Names. "As you respond to your name, though there was no name inscribed on your forehead when you were born, so God responds when His name is taken by His devotee, though He is really nameless.'

Renouncing family-ties. "In sleep you were not aware of 'your family.' And you are the same being now. But now you are aware of the family and feel that it binds you, and think of renouncing it. Do the members of 'your' family bind you to themselves, or do you bind yourself to them? It is enough if you give up the thought 'This is my family'. Thoughts change, but not you. Keep hold of the unchanging *you*. To do so, you do not need to stop the mind's thinking. Just remember the Source of the thoughts and be in earnest to find It."

Surrender. "The more one surrenders, the better will his surroundings become, and the more also will be his strength to work." This was said to one who was engaged in work for political independence.

"*The sacred lore* is of value only so long as one does not turn inwards, in the Quest of the Self. As soon as he does so, all that he has learnt of it will be forgotten and lost."*

Getting hold of the World. "The world being a mere shadow of the real Self, it is impossible to know it aright or get hold of it. A child tries to touch the head of its own shadow, but cannot do so, because as he moves, the shadowhead also moves. The mother then puts his hand on his own head, and shows that the shadow-head is touched. So too the world is got hold of, or known aright, only by getting hold of the Self."

---

* See *Guru Vachaka Kovai* verse 147 (see appendix B, verse 82).

On being firm and unaffected. Criticising the outlook which says 'I am like froth on the Ocean of Consciousness,' the Sage said: "To think so is the root of all worries, and should be given up. The Self is the Ocean and the world and the souls are the froth on it. If one knows and remembers this always, then one will be firm and free from doubts and worries. This truth is verified by diving into the Heart by the Quest. But even without diving inside, one is That, and nothing but That. The ideas of inside and outside can arise only so long as the right view is not accepted and adhered to. The lover of Deliverance is told to dive in, because he is mistaking the non-existent individual soul for the Self, who is infinite, including all that is seen. He that knows thus will not desire anything, but will have perfect contentment always. Even before diving inwards, the Self *is* experienced. No one can deny that he exists. That Existence is Consciousness of the Self. Unless you exist, you cannot ask questions. So you *are* aware of yourself. The fruit of your efforts to realise the Truth of the Self is just to get rid of your present errors. There is to be no new 'Realisation.'"

The Self is Light. "To know an object an ordinary light inimical to darkness is needed. To know the Self a Light is needed, which lights both light and darkness. This Light is neither light nor darkness. But it is called Light, because by It they are known. This Light is the Self, the Infinite Consciousness, of which no one is unaware. No one is an *Ajnani*, non-knower of the Self. Not knowing this, men wish to become *jnanis*!"

APPENDIX—A

(From Sri Ramana Hridayam)

———

4. अस्तीत्यस्मिन् कथं धीर्भवति यदि न सत् ? तद्विभिन्ना
   नु सच्चित् ?
   सत्यं निश्चिन्तनं तद्भवति हृदि यतस्तस्य हृन्नामकस्य ।
   ध्याता को वास्ति भिन्नो? भवति च तदिदं ध्यानगम्यं
   कथं नु?
   तस्य ध्यानं हृदन्तः प्रशमितमनसा तन्मयत्वेन निष्ठा ॥४॥

6. पश्यामो भुवनं यतो, भवति सत् तन्मूलमेकं परं
   यच्छक्ते: परिणामभूतमखिलं; नैतद्विवादास्पदम् ।
   आख्यारूपमयं च चित्रमिदमप्याधारवस्त्रं द्युति:
   द्रष्टा चेति चतुष्टयं स परमो य: स्वात्मभूतो हृदि ॥६॥

8. वादै: किं भविता जगद्भवति सन्मिथ्याभ्रमश्रिज्जडं
   आनन्दं ननु दु:खमेव तदिति ? त्यक्त्वा समस्तं जगत् ।
   स्वात्मानं समवेत्य सत्यममलं द्वैतैक्यवादातिगे
   याहन्तारहिता स्थितिर्निजपदे सर्वार्हता सैव हि ॥८॥

9. रूपी स्वो यदि रूपमस्तु जगतो रूपं परस्याप्युत
   वीक्षा केन कथं च रूपरहित: स्वात्मा यदि स्याद्धृद ?
   दृश्यं किं नु दृशोऽन्यथा वद भवेद् ? दृक् सा स्व एव स्वयं
   निस्सीमा निरुपाधिका चितिमयी सा निष्प्रपञ्चाऽद्वया ॥९॥

10. देहो यन्निखिलस्य चापि भुवने स्यात् पञ्चकोशात्मकः
कोशानामपि पञ्चकं तत इदं देहाभिधानं भवेत् ।
सत्येव वद देहतः किमु जगाद्विदं भवेत् तत्त्वत :?
किं केनापि च वीक्षितं जगादिदं देहं विना
                                             प्रोच्यताम् ॥१०॥

11. शब्दादीन् विषयान् विहाय जगतो रूपं भवेन्नो पृथक्
एवं धीन्द्रियपञ्चकस्य विषयो निश्शेषमेतज्जगत् ।
एतैः पञ्चभिरिन्द्रियैर्जगदिदं ह्येकं मनो बुध्यते
सत्येवं मनसो जगत् कथय किं भिन्नं भवेत्
                                             तत्त्वतः ? ॥११॥

12. विश्वं बुद्धिरिति द्वयं समुदियाल्लीयेत चाप्येकवत्
एवं सत्यपि भास्यते जडमिदं विश्वं धियैवाखिलम् ।
यस्मिंस्तद्द्वितयस्य जन्मविलयौ भास्वत्यनस्तोदये
सज्ज्ञानीहि तदेव पूर्णममलं चिद्रूपकं केवलम् । ॥१२॥

14. संश्रित्य प्रभवत्यहंमतिमिमां सर्वाङ्गिपुट्यस्तथा
द्वन्द्वान्यप्युत संभवन्ति तदहंनामा भवेत् को न्विति ।
अन्वेषाद्धृदयं प्रविश्य यदि तत्तत्त्वं समालोकयेत्
सर्वं तद्विगलेत् स्वयं, स च भवेज्ज्ञानी,स नैति भ्रमम् ॥१४॥

16. ज्ञातारं स्वमजानतो ऽन्यविषयज्ञानं भवे यद्भवेत्
ज्ञानं तद्विदिता कथं नु क थय ? ज्ञानस्य चान्यस्य च ।
आधारो ऽहमितीह यो भवति, तत्तत्त्वं विजानाति चेत्
अज्ञानेन समं तदा प्रविलयं ज्ञानं च गच्छेदिदम् ॥१६॥

18. आत्मा ज्ञानमयो य एष गदितस्सत्यस्स एवाद्वयो
    ज्ञानं नाम बहुप्रकारकमिदं त्वज्ञानमेवाखिलम् ।
    स्वस्माज्ज्ञानमयात् सतस्त्वसदिदं नो भिद्यते कर्हिचित्
    नानासन्त्यपि भूषणानि कथय स्वर्णात् सतो ऽन्यानि
                                            किम् ? ॥१८॥

19. भाति त्वं स इति द्वयं, समुदिताहंधी: शरीरे यदा
    तत्त्वं किं न्वहमो भवेदिति धिया स्वान्वेषणेन स्वयम् ।
    नीते ऽस्मिन्निधनं, समं तदितरप्रज्ञे ततौ नश्यतो;
    यद्द्वात्येकतया तदा, गणय तत् तत्त्वं भवेदात्मन: ॥१९॥

21. कालो देश इमौ पृथक् किमहमो ? ऽधीनास्तयो: स्मो वयं
    देहा: स्याम यदि स्वयं ; किमु वयं देहा भवामो वद ।
    सर्वत्रापि च सर्वदापि च विभात्यात्मा समानो यत:
    तस्मात्सन्तमवेहि केवलममुं तौ द्वौ निगीर्य स्थितम् ॥२१॥

23. सत्यं ह्येव जगद्वयोरविदुषो विज्ञाततत्त्वस्य च
    सत्यं यावदिदं जगत् तु मनुते सज्ज्ञानहीनो जन: ।
    ऽस्याकारविहीनमस्य निखिलस्याधारभूतं हि सत्
    भात्येवं महती भिदास्ति हि तयोस्सज्ज्ञस्य चाज्ञस्य च ॥२३॥

26. वीक्षा स्वस्य परस्य चेति गदितं ग्रन्थेषु वीक्षाद्वयं
    तत्त्त्वं किमिति ब्रवीमि; घटते वीक्षा कथं न्वात्मन: ?
    एकत्वान्न स वीक्ष्यते यदि, परं वीक्षेत को वा कथं ?
    ईशस्यौदनभावमेव गणय स्वेक्षां परेक्षामपि ॥२६॥

28. चैतन्येन विवर्जितं वपुरिदं नाहंकरोति स्वयं
    बूते नैव कदापि को ऽपि भुवने नासं सुषुप्ताविति ।
    सर्वं चाप्युदियादिदं समुदिते त्वस्मिन्नहंनामके
    तद्बुद्ध्या शितया कुतो ऽयमुदियादित्येवमन्वेषय ॥२८॥

29. ब्रूयान्नाहमिति स्वयं जडवपुः सस्या चितिर्नोदियात्
    तन्मध्ये तु वपुःप्रमाणमहमित्याविर्भवेत् किंचन ।
    एतद्ध्येव भवेन्मनो जडचितोर्ग्रन्थिर्भवो ऽहंकृतिः
    बन्धः सूक्ष्मशरीरमेतदुदितं जीवस्य तत्त्वं स्वयम् ॥२९॥

30. धृत्वा रूपमुदेति च स्थितिमुत प्राप्नोति रूपग्रहात्
    धृत्वा रूपमुतोपभुज्य विषयानुच्चैस्तमां वर्धते ।
    हित्वा रूपमुपाददीत नवमप्यन्विष्यते चेत् तदा
    धावेद्रूपविहीन एष सहसाऽहन्तापिशाचो ध्रुवम् ॥३०॥

31. एतस्मिन्नहमाख्यके समुदिते सर्वं जगच्चोदियात्
    नो चेदस्त्यहमित्यं न च भवत्येतज्जगत् किंचन ।
    तत्सर्वं ह्यहमाख्यकः स्वयमतः कोऽसौ कुतस्संभवेत्
    इत्येवं निजमार्गणं भवति यत् तत् सर्वहानं भवेत् ॥३१॥

32. तस्यामेव हि तद्वयं भवति नो यस्यामहन्तोदयः
    चेतस्तु प्रविशेदहं जनिभुवं नो चेदहन्ता कथम् ।
    नीयेतापुनरुद्भवां मृतिमियं नीता तथान्तं न चेत्
    साध्या नस्सहजा स्थितिः कथमसौ यस्यां वयं तत्
                                                  स्वयम् ? ॥३२॥

33. यत्किंचित् सलिलाशये निपतितं चिन्वन्निमज्जेद्यथा
तद्वह्वागनिलौ नियम्य जगतश्चिन्तां विहायाखिलाम् ।
अन्वेषादुदियात् कुतो ऽहमिति धीरित्येवमेकाग्रया
बुद्ध्यान्तर्हृदये निमज्ज्य विमलं विद्यात्स्वतत्त्वं

परम् ॥३३॥

34. रुध्वा वाङ्मनसी उभे, चितिरहंरूपा क्व भातीत्यलं
बुद्ध्यान्विष्य निमज्जनं हृदि निजज्ञानाप्तये साधनम् ।
देहो नायमहं स्वयं तदहमित्येवं निदिध्यासनं
अन्येषाज्ञमवेहि; किं नु भविता सोऽयं विचारो
निजः ? ॥३४॥

36. कर्तव्यं किमिहास्त्यमुष्य कृतिनो ऽहन्तां ग्रसित्वोदिते
भावे स्वे मुदितस्य तन्मयतया शान्ते तुरीये शिवे ।
स्वान्यत् किंचन वेत्ति नो निजपदे निष्ठां गतो ऽसौ यतो
मन्तुं तां पदवीं नरो वद कथं निर्मानसीं
शक्नुयात् ? ॥३६॥

37. निष्ठां तत् त्वमसीति वेदशिरसा दिष्टामलब्ध्वा निजां
को ऽहं स्यामिति मार्गणेन हृदयं बुद्ध्या प्रविश्य स्वयम् ।
धीदौर्बल्यवशात् करोति मनुजो ध्यानं तदेवास्म्यहं
नो देहो ऽहमिति; स्वयं तदनिशं भात्यात्मरूपेण
हि ॥३७॥

39. आत्मत्वेन समस्तजन्तुषु सदा सत्यं हृदन्तः स्फुरत्
अन्वेषादवगत्य तन्मयतया निष्ठामलब्ध्वा निजाम् ।
सत् किंचिद्भवतीति नेति तदिदं रूपीति नेत्येककं
द्वेधा नोभयथेति वा विवदते मायाभिभूतो जनः ॥३९॥

40. सिद्धं स्वं समवेत्य तन्मयतया निष्ठा भवेद्या निजा
    सिद्धिस्तैव हि; सिद्धयस्तदितराः स्वप्रोपलब्धा इव ।
    स्वप्रार्थः किमु सन् प्रबोधसमये ? मुक्तो ऽनृतादन्ततो
    निष्ठामेत्य सति स्वयं मुनिवरः किं तासु मोहं व्रजेत् ॥४०॥

42. यावत्साधकता नरस्य भवति द्वैतं यथार्थं भवेत्
    साध्ये त्वद्वयतेति चापि गदितं नो सत्ययुक्तं भवेत् ।
    अन्विष्यन्नपि सादरं च दशमं नष्टत्वबुद्ध्या स्वयं
    स्वं लब्ध्वापि च को बभूव दशमादन्यः कथायामसौ ॥४२॥

43. कर्तात्मा स्वयमेव चेत् कृतिफलं भुञ्जीत सोऽयं स्वयं
    कर्ताहं क इति स्वमार्गणवशाज्ज्ञानाति चेत् स्वं विभुम् ।
    कर्तृत्वं विगलेद्यतो, विगलितं तैनैव साकं भवेत्
    कर्मापि त्रिविधं स्वयं ; स्थितिमिमां नित्यां विमुक्तिं
    विदुः ॥४३॥

44. बद्धो ऽस्मीति मतिर्भवेद्यदि तदा मुक्तेर्मतिश्रोदियात्
    बद्धो ऽहं क इति स्वमार्गणवशात् स्वे नित्यमुक्ते स्वयम् ।
    शिष्टे सत्यजरे ऽमरे, वद भवेद्वन्धस्य चिन्ता कथं ?
    सा नो चेदुदियात् , तदास्य कृतिनो मोक्षस्य चिन्ता
    कथम् ॥४४॥

57. लेभे जनिं यः परमे स्वमूले
        विचार्य कस्मादहमित्युदारः ।
    स एव जातः स च नित्यजातो
        नवो नवो ऽयं सततं मुनीन्द्रः ॥५७॥

60. को ऽसौ यस्य कृतिर्विभक्तिरपि चाज्ञानं वियोगोऽपि च
    सन्तीत्यात्मविचार एव भविता कर्मादियोगक्रमाः ।
    यस्यां नास्ति विचारको ऽहमभिधो न स्यादिदं चाष्टफं
    सा सत्या स्थितिरित्यवेहि विमला स्वात्मानुभूतिः
                                            शिवा ॥६०॥

63. परे वहति भूभरं भरमिदं मृषाजीवको
        वहन् भवति गोपुरोद्वहनबिंबतुल्यो ह्यसौ ।
    भरं शिरसि   धारयन्नतिभरक्षमेणानसा
        व्रजन् भजति चेद् व्यथां भवति तत्र को
                                            दोषवान् ॥६३॥

75. गुणास्सुन्दरत्वादयो यान्ति वृद्धिं
        वसन्तस्य योगाद्यथा भूरुहस्य ।
    तथा दृष्टतत्त्वस्य तेजो बलं धीः
        निजानन्दतृप्तस्य वर्धन्त एव ॥७५॥

77. याने सुप्तिमितस्य यानगमनं स्थानं च तस्य क्वचित्
    तरयैवाश्वविय़ोजनं त्रयमिदं यद्वद्भवेदेकधा ।
    सुप्तिं ज्ञानमयीं गतस्य विदुषो याने वपुष्येकधा
    तद्वत् स्यात् त्रितयं क्रियापि वपुषो निष्ठापि निद्रापि च ॥७७॥

78. जाग्रत्स्वप्नसुषुप्तिषु स्थितिजुषां यत् तुर्यमित्युच्यते
    जाग्रत्सुषिरितीरितं स्वविदुषः शान्तं पदं शाश्वतम् ।
    सत्यं तद्धि पदं मृषेतरदिदं त्वाभासमात्रं त्रयं ;
    तुर्यातीतमतस्तदेव मुनयः शंसन्ति संविन्मयम् ॥७८॥

79. कर्मागामि च सञ्चितं च विदुषो नष्टे भवेतां ध्रुवं,
    प्रारब्धं न तथेत्युदीरितमिदं ग्रन्थेषु मन्दान् प्रति ।
    नार्येका न सुमङ्गली पतिमृतौ बह्वीषु यद्वद्भवेत्
    त्रेधा कर्म तथा विनाशमयते नाशं गते कर्तरि ॥७९॥

81. लिपिज्ञो ऽहंनामा कुत इति निजान्वेषणधिया
    लिपिं स्वां निर्मार्ष्टुं लिपिमधिगतो यो न यतते ।
    लिपिज्ञानात् किं वा फलमधिगतं तेन कथय
    समो वाग्यन्त्रेणारुणगिरिविभो ऽन्यो भवति क: ॥८१॥

82. अशान्तस्य क्लेशा विदुष इह ये सन्त्यविदुषो
    न ते सन्ति; ग्रस्तो न स मदपिशाचेन भवति ।
    न वाक्चित्तक्लेशं भवति बहुमानार्थमटनं
    न कुर्यान्नैकस्मादवितमिह जानीहि तमिमम् ॥८२॥

83. तृणतुलिताखिलजगतां करकलिताखिलनिगमरहस्यानाम् ।
    श्लाघावारवधूटीघटदासत्वं सुदुर्निरसम् ॥८३॥

84. स्वतो भवति क: पर: ? किमपि को ऽपि चेत्स्वं प्रति
    वदेद्भवति तेन किं ? गदितवत् स्वयं तद्भवेत् ।
    भिदामनधिगच्छत: स्व इति चान्य इत्यव्यये
    स्थितस्य सहजे पदे स्थिरतया परस्मिन् शिवे ॥८४॥

86. सिद्धान्तो यो भवति परम: सर्ववेदान्तसारो
    वच्मि स्पष्टं तमिममधुना तत्त्वतो ऽत्यन्तगूढम् ।
    सत्यं तत् स्वो भवति निधनाच्चेदहंनामकस्य
    शिष्येतासौ चितिमयतनु: सत्य आत्मैव विद्धि ॥८६॥

────────

APPENDIX—B

(From Sri Guru Ramana Vachana Mala)

———

4. विद्यात्मनोऽतिसुलभा हृदये सर्वस्य नित्यसिद्धस्य ।
नश्यति यदि निश्शेषं देहे लोके च सत्यताधिषणा ॥

19. नान्यद्विश्वं देहान्मनसोऽन्यो वा न विद्यते देहः ।
न मनश्रितोऽस्ति भिन्नं न सतोऽन्या चित् तदस्त्यजं
शान्तम् ॥

20. न सृष्टिरुत न प्रलयो न कोऽपि बद्धो न साधको मुक्त्यै ।
न चापि मुक्तो मनुजः परमार्थोऽयं महात्मभिर्दृष्टः ॥

21. न मनो नो वा देहो न जगन्नो जीवनामकः कोऽपि ।
शुद्धं सद्द्वितीयं ह्यजमविकारं प्रशान्तमस्त्येकम् ॥

22. पृच्छकबुध्यनुवृत्त्या यद्यपि भगवानुवाच सिद्धान्तान् ।
अजातिसिद्धान्तमिमं ब्रवीति सोऽयं निजानुभवदृष्टम् ॥

44. कामो मेरुमलब्धं करोति लाभात्परं तदेवाणु ।
श्वभ्रं दुष्पूरमतो नो जानीमः किमप्यहो कामात् ॥

82. ज्ञानदमित्यादरतोऽधीतो ग्रन्थोऽपि विस्मृतः सर्वः ।
विगलेदन्तर्मुखतां याति यदासौ विचारयोगेन ॥

82a. ज्ञानदमित्यादरतोऽधीतो ग्रन्थोऽपि साधनाभ्यासात् ।
अन्तर्मुखतापत्तौ विगलेत्सर्वोऽपि विस्मृतः साधो : ॥

96. स्व एव साक्षात्परमः स्वयं संस्तस्मात्पृथक् स्वं गणयन् मुधैव।
तेनैक्यमिच्छन् यतते तदर्थमाश्रयर्यमस्मादितरत् किमस्ति ॥

108. अहमिति तस्य यदाख्या तस्मादहमित्यनारतं ध्यायन् ।
     नीयेतान्तः साधुर्मूलस्थानं सदात्मनो लोकम् ॥

111. यथांशमादाय निवेदनं स्याद्गुडात्मकस्यैव गणेशमूर्तेः ।
     तथा परस्मै स्वनिवेदनं स्यात् स्वो नाम तस्मापृथगस्ति
                                                किं नु ? ॥

128. नरवत् प्रतीयमानं गुरुमात्मजं चिदाकृतिं पूर्णम् ।
     मन्येत देहिनं यस्तं पापिष्ठं दुराशयं विद्धि ॥

130. व्योमवदस्पृश्यस्य व्यक्तिमुक्तस्य भाति या पुंसाम् ।
     प्रतिबिंब एव सेयं द्रष्टुर्व्यक्तेर्न कर्हिंचित्सत्या ॥

131. महान्तमेनमपश्यं द्रक्ष्याम्यमुमित्युदीर्यते मोहात् ।
     महान्तमन्तःस्थं चेद्धेत्स्यथ सर्वो महान् भवेदेकः ॥

132. कुर्वन्नसदेवासत् सत्यात्मानं प्रकाशयन्नेकम् ।
     निधनं नयत्यशेषं गुरुरहमाख्यं मृषात्मकं जीवम् ॥

153. वपुरिन्द्रयाणि चेतो न त्वं प्राणोऽपि धीरहन्तापि ।
     अत्राभिमानरूपं पापं प्रथमं विवेकतो हित्वा ॥

154. कोऽस्मीत्यात्मविचारात् शान्ति नीते मनस्यलं हृदये ।
     प्रपञ्चभाने विरते भात्यहमस्मीति यत् तदेव त्वम् ॥

170. प्रमाद एव हि मृत्युस्तस्मात् तच्छान्तये प्रवृत्तस्य ।
     प्रमादवर्जनमात्रं नियमो नान्यो विचरिणो भवति ॥

172. प्रमादहेतुर्यस्मात् कर्म निजं चापि किं नु वक्तव्यम् ।
     स्वात्मविचारे युक्तो नो सज्ज्ञेतान्यकर्मणीत्येतत् ॥

176. नियमेषु सत्सु बहुधा नियताहारत्वमेव पर्याप्तम् ।
     सत्यगुणवृद्धिहेतो: गदितं साधो: सदात्मनिष्ठायै ॥

178. औदरविश्रान्त्यर्थं कालं परिपाल्य तत्परं क्षुधिते ।
     परिमितसात्विकमन्नं भुञ्जीतेति स्थितोऽन्ननियमोऽयम् ॥

182. यावन्न मृताहन्ता तावत् साधोर्विनीतिरेवाच्छा ।
     नांगीकारोऽन्येषां नमस्कृतीनां कदापि कर्तव्य: ॥

185. जलमादाय निमज्जेत् कुंभोऽनादाय दारु नो मज्जेत् ।
     सक्तो भवति निबद्ध: स्थित्वापि गृहे न बध्यतेऽसक्त : ॥

187. स्थिरतामुत्पादयितुं परेशकृपया भवति विपद् इति ।
     विश्वासधैर्यगाच्छान्त्या जय तांस्तितिक्षया साधो ॥

188. लोकस्येष्र्याजनके पदे स्थितेश्रापि संसृतौ साधो: ।
     पदमतिशोच्यं लोके वरं परस्मिन्निषक्तचित्तस्य ॥

193. सर्वत्रौदासीन्यं मनसा शान्तेन वीतरागेण ।
     अद्वेषिणापि सततं साधकलोकस्य शोभनाचार: ॥

196. विधिरिति कर्मैवोक्तं पूर्वकृतं यत्स्वयं प्रयत्नेन ।
     तस्माद्विधिं प्रमार्ष्टुं मनुज: शक्नोति साधुयत्नेन ॥

199. प्रशान्त शुद्धमनसा कर्म कृतं यत् तदेव सुकृतं स्यात् ।
     मनसा क्षुब्धेन कृतं कृतं च कामेन दुष्कृतं सर्वम् ॥

201. भारं स्वकीयं निखिलं निवेश्य तस्मिन् महेश्वरे सम्यक् ।
     विरक्तभावे शान्त्या स्थानं परमं तपोबलं विद्धि ॥

202 आश्रितवन्त: परमं न क्षीयन्ते महद्भिरपि खेदै: ।
     यद्द्घन्ते निहिता धान्यकणा: शंकुपादमूलस्था: ॥

203. सूची कान्तस्य यथा हित्वोदीचीं दिशं भजेन्नान्याम् ।
प्रेम्णा परं भजन्तो वियन्ति मार्गान्न कर्हिचिन्मोहात् ॥

204. कदापि मा कुरु चिन्तां कदाहमेतां स्थितिं भजेयेति ।
दिक्कालातीतेयं नो दूरस्था न चाग्रतो वापि ॥

205. आपूर्याखिलमेक: स्वरसेनात्मा हि तिष्ठति स्वैरम् ।
बध्येत माययासौ कथं नु ? मा गा विषादमिह साधो ॥

206. अचलस्वरूपहानात् चलजीवोऽस्मीति भावना ह्युदिता ।
एतां निरस्य मनसो वृत्तिं परमौनमाश्रयेत्साधु:॥

207. उपाय एष नेतुं नाझं चित्तस्य चञ्चलां प्रकृतिम् ।
वीक्षस्वात्माकारं दृश्यं सकलं च वीक्षितारं च ।

208. कण्टकनिरासयोग्यो यथान्य एवं ह्यशुद्धधीवृत्ते: ।
निरसनसहायभूता वृत्ति: शुद्धापि हानयोग्यैव ॥

212. व्यर्थोंऽनात्मविर्शि: स्वस्यात्मानं विहाय परमार्थम् ।
रोमसमूहावेक्षा नापितरचिता वृथा यथा तद्वत् ॥

214. यद्रन्मौक्तिकमब्धौ सहाश्मनान्तर्निमज्ज्य गृह्णाति ।
एवं वैराग्ययुतो मङ्क्त्वा ह्रादयान्ताराददीत स्वम् ।

231. प्रवहति जलधौ यद्रन्नैवोद्रन्तुं क्षमोऽल्पको जन्तु: ।
एवमहन्तोद्रन्तुं प्रवहति बोधे न शक्ष्यति क्षुद्रा ॥

247. (अ) प्रश्नोत्तराणि नाना वाचि द्वैतस्य नाद्वये मौने ॥

289. चलचित्राश्रयभूत: पट इव सद् ब्रह्म जीवजगदीशा: ।
चलानि चित्राणीव ब्रह्म विशुद्धं हि केवलं सत्यम् ॥

290. अनृतान्यपि भिद्यन्ते तस्मादेतानि नो सत: परमात् ।
भिद्येत सन्तु परमं केवलभावे वियुक्तमेतेभ्य: ॥

291. पश्यंश्चलानि तानि ब्रह्म परं नैव वीक्षते सत्यम् ।
पश्यति य: सत्परमं न चलान्येतानि वीक्षते विद्वान् ॥

292. अचलं परमात्मानं विहाय पश्यन् स्वमेकचित्रमपि ।
चित्राण्येव च जीवान् तादृग्भुवनं च मानसं भ्रान्तम् ॥

300. भवति स्व एव भूमा स्वस्मादन्यत् समस्तमत्यल्पम् ।
न वयं पश्यामोऽन्यद्युपादेयं स्वविक्रयात्किमपि ॥

310. यद्वत् तरोरधस्ताद्विरला ज्योत्स्ना सुषुप्तिसुखमेवम् ।
अनुपहतचन्द्रिकावज्जीवन्मुक्तस्य निर्वृतिर्ज्ञेया ॥

338. जीवन्मुक्तो भेदान् पश्यन्नपि तेष्वभेदमनुभवति ।
इत्यसदुक्तं ह्यद्यैः पश्यति भेदान्न कर्हिचिन्मुक्त: ।

343. यद्वत् प्रतीयमानं तस्मिन्नेक: स्व एव चिद्रूप: ।
इति विज्ञानं यत्सा समदृष्टिर्नाम मुक्तपुरुषस्य ॥

347. तिष्ठति मृतेन मनसा सर्वात्मत्वेन यच्छिवाकार: ।
अनुसन्धाय तदीयं भावं प्राप्नोति नैजसद्विद्याम् ॥

॥ ॐ नमो भगवते श्रीरमणाय ॥

———

APPENDIX-C

[The following passages are extracts from a letter which was written by Swami Tapasyananda of Sri Ramakrishna Mission and which was once published in the *Vedanta Kesari*.]

The Maharshi impressed me as a rare type of man. I do not know whether he is a *Jnani,* or what he is. For as the Vedanta says, a *Jnani* can be known only by a *Jnani,* and I am certainly not one. But this person, anyone can feel, is not of the ordinary run of men. We nowadays come across men everywhere whose one thought is world-reform and things of that kind. But here is a man who is *perfectly aware,* as one can see from his conduct and movements, who has no such idea, who has in his opinion nothing to add to the sum-total of human happiness. He simply seems to exist, without waiting for anything, without being anxious about anything. On watching him I was powerfully reminded of the *Gita* passage beginning with *'Udasinavad'* (Like one that is unconcerned)*. He seems to take, as far as I can see,

---

* "Nor do these actions bind me, O Dhananjaya; like one unconcerned, I remain unattached to these actions" — *Bhagavad Gita* 9.9; "Like one unconcerned, he remains unmoved by the *gunas;* knowing the *gunas* operate, he abides firm and moves not" — *Bhagavad Gita* 1.23. (*Publisher*)

no interest even in the Ashrama that has sprung up around him. He simply sits there; things are going on *as events and other men shape them.* The only activity of the Ashrama in which he seems to take active interest is cooking. He cuts vegetables in the kitchen, and if there is any special cooking any day he is sure to try his hand at preparing some of the dishes for that day. Spicing and other processes of the culinary art are performed there under his directions.

Another point that struck me is his *silence.* We used to ask in fun among ourselves why eminent professors who crossed the seas did not deliver their Vedantic lectures through silence. But here is a person who actually does this as far as his teaching of the Vedanta is concerned. When I asked him to tell me something of spirituality, the first thing he said was that silence is the highest teaching! The beauty of the man is that he remains faithful to that idea to the utmost extent possible. His idea is that *the Advaitin has no position to state, no Siddhanta to propound.* He regrets that in these days even *Advaita* has become a *Siddhanta,* whereas it is really not meant to be so. The reason for the existence of so much Vedantic literature is this: When doubts arise in the mind as our intellects are quickened, such literature is helpful in dispelling them. In other words, the *Advaitin* speaks only to dispel a doubt that might have arisen in himself or in another. Our saint remains faithful to this idea. He is mostly silent, and speaks but a little if questioned on any point. Of course he jokes and speaks occasionally on other things, but he has no dogmatic teaching on Vedanta to deliver.

He told me he says 'yes, yes' to everyone who
interprets *Advaita,* even to some of his followers who
interpret his ideas in the books published under his
name. When I asked, regarding a book that I
purchased in the depot there, how far the ideas stated
therein are his teachings, he told that it is very
difficult to say that, as he had no definite teaching.*
As people have understood they have written, and
they may be right from certain points of view. He
himself, he said, has absolutely no idea or inclination
to write a book; but due to the entreaties of some
people about him he has written some verses, and he
told me that he is often troubled by men who take a
fancy to translate them into this language and that,
and ask him about the faithfulness of the translation.

So mostly the Maharshi remains silent, and
people come, make prostrations, sit before him for
some minutes or hours and then go away, perhaps
without exchanging even a single world! I have got
my own doubts as to whether people benefit by this
teaching through silence. But yet people come from
long distances to hear this dumb eloquence and go
back *satisfied.*

Though he speaks but little, it is very instructive
to watch his face and eyes. There is nothing very
prepossessing about his personality, but there is a
beam of intelligence and unruffled calmness in his

---

* Refer to *Talks with Sri Ramana Maharshi* No. 107 (p.103), where
  Sri Bhagavan says that teachings or instructions must "differ
  according to the temperaments of the individuals and according to
  the spiritual ripeness of their minds. There cannot be any instruction
  en masse." *(Publisher)*

eyes that are unique. His body is almost motionless except when he occasionally changes his position or wipes his sweat in that hot place. I was carefully observing his face; I found him seldom winking and never yawning. I say this to show that I am sufficiently satisfied that the absence of activity in him is *not due to inertness.*

The third point that struck me was the absolute absence of vanity or self-importance in him. Except for his toilette confined only to a *kaupinam* a visitor may not find it possible to make out Ramana Maharshi. He eats the same food as everyone else there; there is not even a single extra item or special dish for him. I specially noticed that in conversation he is not averse to using the first personal pronoun, unlike some other Vedantins who use 'he' and things of that kind. I point out this to show how unostentatious he is. His silence, I am convinced, is not to assume a gravity of disposition calculated to keep people at a distance. And when he breaks that silence, as he does when questioned, he appears to be *the sweetest and most friendly of men.*

He makes no distinction between man and man for their wealth or position in society. I saw peasants and gentlemen in motor cars coming and being greeted with the same silence. They all sit on the floor and receive the same hospitality. In fact the Maharshi seems to be quite indifferent to any financial gain that the Ashrama may have by special treatment given to rich men.

I stayed in the Ashrama for three days. The Maharshi talked with me very kindly and quite freely on the several questions I asked him.

Although his manner of replying was not so impressive as I expected, *his thoughts are always clear, concise and free from all ideas of narrowness.* Though he has not read much, as he himself told me in some context, he has a good grasp of all the difficult points in Vedanta. My impression is this: Whether he is a *Jnani* or anything else I do not positively know. But I am convinced that *he is a sweet and lovable person who is indifferent to all things about him, who has no end of his own to gain, who is always alert even when he seems to be most deeply absorbed, and who may be said to be perfectly free from greed and vanity.* In seeing him I do believe I have seen a unique personage.*

---

* These very characteristics are, according to the ancient lore, the distinguishing marks of a *Jnani* — a perfect Sage.
                                                                    — *Author.*

INDEX

A

Action (doer, doership), 78, 175, 194, 230, 231
Advaita (non-duality), 59, 76, 114, 235
Advaiti, 86, 114, 185, 206, 207
Agency as attributed to *Jnani,* 194
'*Aham' see 'I AM'*
Analogy of::
    Alice in the Wonderland, 86
    boy catching his shadow-head, 240
    burying one's shadow, 162
    cinema-show, 129, 137, 158, 192
    dog following master's scent, 163
    dreams, 20, 65-66, 83-84, 239
    dream bridegroom, 91
    earthen pot and earth, 64
    encumbered room, 139
    gold and gold ornaments, 133, 137, 193
    jaggery offering taken from jaggery Ganesha, 217
    mirage, 65
    ordeal by fire, 152
    snake in the rope, 56, 57, 58, 65, 143
    somnolent child, 150
    temple tower-figure, 218
    thief pretending as policeman, 226
    traveller in the cart, 173
    traveller in the train and his luggage, 218
    uninvited guest, 95
Ancient lore or Revelation, 1, 7, 18, 34, 46-48, 52, 67, 92, 112, 119, 120, 121, 138, 143, 145, 146, 165, 166, 175, 183, 240

Animals, Sage's view about, 229
Arunachala, 11, 208
Arunachala; Five Hymns to, 12, 107
Atheist *(Nastika)*, 33, 57, 220
Atman: meaning of, 216
Authority, 33, 41, 52
Authority and reason, 47

B

Berkeley, 87
Bernard Shaw, 31
Bhagavad-Gita, 1, 14, 39, 52, 62-63, 103-104, 116, 154,
    184, 187, 188, 189, 198, 202, 203, 207, 216
Bheda bhava, 17, 18, 111
Birth, Real, 155
Birth and death, 78, 106, 227
'Body-am-I' Idea, 32, 80, 89, 90, 96, 104-105, 191-192, 234
Body, gross or subtle, 35, 57, 125-130, 151-152, 164
Bondage, 43, 91, 96-97, 157-158
Book-knowledge (Book-learning), 15, 28-31, 33-40, 97-99,
    235
Brahman, Para and *Apara (Nirguna* and *Saguna)*, 112
Brahmacharya, 237
Breath-control, 170-171, 224
Bucke, Dr., 43
Buddha, Gautama, 5, 26-27, 94, 115, 162, 164, 222, 237
Buddhism, 203

C

Cause, 115
Chaitanya, Sri, 209
Character-building, 202-203
Christianity, 31, 218-221
Consciousness, Pure *(chit)*, 69, 83, 89-91, 103, 109, 122,
    130-132, 136-140, 145, 154, 172, 193-194, 216, 241
Creation, 111, 133

D

Dakshinamurti, 144
Death, 111, 176, 227-228
— fear of, 5-6
Deliverance, 145, 162, 181, 182, 188, 196
— state of, 5, 8, 50, 102, 113, 117, 143, 151, 158, 181, 196
Desire and fear, 23-24, 33, 35, 50, 141, 172
Devotion, 176, 200-218
Dharma, meaning of, 116
Dream State, 73-74, 78, 83, 125-127
Dualities, 112
Dualism, dualists, 113, 184, 207
Duality and non-duality, 113

E

Ego (mind), 77, 82, 88-107, 115, 119, 120-121, 137-138, 162, 222, 228
— annihilation of, 122 to 160, 161-164, 167, 176, 179, 215, 225-7, 233
Egolessness, 107, 161, 212, 236
Egoless State or Natural State (Mindless State), 7, 10, 15, 53, 54, 100, 122 to 160
Einstein, 76
Existence, 135-136, 139-140

F

Faith and Reason, 49
Fate and Free Will, 177, 222
First Cause, the, 101
Fourth State (Turiya), 153

G

Gaudapada, 63, 133
God, 3, 13, 81, 108 to 116, 161, 177, 191, 232
— consumer of the ego, 208

— devotion to, 202, 207
— form & formless, 32
— and *Guru*, 17, 176, 185
— Personal (*Iswara*), 112, 115, 205-208
— World and Soul, 37, 86, 108, 115, 117, 137
Gospel, Sri Maharshi's, 46
Gospels, Christian, 25
Guru, 15, 50, 213
Guru, surrender to, 50
*Guru Vachaka Kovai**
— v. 99 (19), 69
— v. 100 (22), 133
— v. 119 (130), 191
— v. 121 (131), 191
— v. 147 (82), 51, 240
— v. 274 (128), 191
— v. 281 (132), 187
— v. 371 (44), 23
— v. 394 (170), 176-178
— v. 486 (111), 217
— v. 495 (182), 176-178
— v. 574 (199), 176-178
— v. 592 (181), 23
— v. 618 (187), 176-178
— v. 622 (96), 55
— v. 665 (188), 176-178
— v. 671 (153), 99
— v. 673 (154), 99
— v. 676 (208), 176-178
— v. 679 (176), 176-178
— v. 692 (196), 176-178
— v. 716 (108), 172
— v. 734 (203), 176-178
— v. 737 (202), 176-178

---

* The numbers in brackets after the verse numbers of Guru Vachaka Kovai are the corresponding verse numbers in Guru Ramana Vachana Mala (see appendix B).

— v. 781 (204), 176-178
— v. 786 (172), 176-178
— v. 823 (185), 176-178
— v. 922 (207), 176-178
— v. 931 (338), 190
— v. 978 (—), 215
— v. 1060 (300), 147
— v. 1067 (214), 176-178
— v. 1076 (212), 54
— v. 1087 (205), 176-178
— v. 1090 (193), 176-178
— v. 1092 (201), 176-178
— v. 1126 (347), 199
— v. 1142 (231), 121
— v. 1181 (247-A), 119
— v. 1216 (291), 136-137
— v. 1217 (290), 136-137
— v. 1218 (289), 136-137
— v. 1219 (292), 136-137
— v. 1220 (206), 176-178
— v. 1227 (20), 133
— v. 1250 (343), 189

Guru Ramana Vachana Mala (verses not translated from
    Guru Vachaka Kovai)
— v. 4, 54-55
— v. 21, 133
— v. 178, 176-177
— v. 310, 152

Grace, 50, 177, 187, 206, 213, 218

H

Happiness-(*Ananda*, Bliss), 14, 38, 54, 121, 129, 145, 152,
    236
Happiness, The problem of, 19-25, 29
Heart, The, 46, 146, 162-3
— diving into, 178, 241

I

I am, 153, 163, 164, 166, 167, 172, 234
I AM (*Aham*), 135, 139, 159
I am I, 172
I am That, 166, 167, 168
I AM THAT I AM, 135
Idols, 32
Ignorance, 26 to 40, 43 to 47, 59, 60, 61, 75, 101, 106, 115,
    156, 157, 158, 159
        — primary, 39, 45, 48, 57, 83, 92, 141, 152
Impersonality, 134
Individuality, 80, 89, 90, 91, 92, 97, 98, 105-107, 129, 215
Intellect, 48, 124, 187, 230

J

James, Prof., 43
Janaka, 8, 237
Japa, 229, 238
Jeevanmukti, 181, 182, 185
Jehovah, 135
Jesus Christ, 3, 7, 146, 147, 220, 221

K

Kant, Immanual, 71, 75
Karma: agami, sanchita and *prarabdha*, 182, 183, 194,
    237
Kevala Nirvikalpa Samadhi, 148, 149, 183
Kingdom of Heaven, 105, 146, 218, 220
Knowledge and Ignorance (relative), 134

L

Living Teacher or Sage, 1, 10, 25, 28, 46, 47, 51

M

Mahabharatam, 23, 139, 239
Maya, 59, 104, 159, 178, 198, 208

Maya-vada, 58
Meditation, 167, 207, 224, 225, 227, 232
Mind (*refer also* ego), 38, 42, 141, 230
Mind, body and the world, 69, 70, 71, 77, 83
Mind control, 224, 225, 238
Mind and the world, 55, 57 to 74, 81
Moses, 135

N

Names and forms, 136
Nammazhwar, 215
Natural State (*Sahaja bhava*), 7, 9, 13
    refer Egoless State
Neti-Neti, 144
Nirvikalpa Samadhi, 149
Non-becoming (Ajati Siddhanta), 133, 186, 187
Non-perception of difference, 186, 187

O

Objectivity, mere assumption, 69 to 74
Original Sin, Christian doctrine of, 99, 221

P

Parable of the tenth man, 112 to 114
    — of the pair of sparrows, 171
Perseverence, 171
Personality, 89, 115, 134, 186
Philosopher *(Pandit)*, 33-34, 36-37
Philosophy, 28, 41, 43
Pleasure as distinguished from happiness, 21, 22
Power within, 6, 172
Prajnanam, 132
Prahlada, 204, 209
Praise and censure, 17, 50, 188

Q

Quest (Self-enquiry), 40, 41, 42, 43, 48, 49, 52, 55, 101,
    102, 104, 105, 116, 119, 161 to 180, 233

R

Ramakrishna Paramahamsa, 1, 3, 10, 211
Ramanuja, 232
Reality, Degress of, 68, 234
— Experience of, 101, 130, 199, 201
— Standard of, 62, 69, 85, 115
Reason and Revelation, 47
Relativity, 75-76
Religion, 27, 51, 99, 100, 210
Religious creeds, 28, 99-100, 220
Renunciation, 170, 173, 240
Ribhu and Nidagha, 79-80
Right Knowledge, 28, 31, 130, 156, 237

S

Sage, 5, 18
Sage's activity, 8
Sage of Arunachala, 1 to 18, 25, 26, 29, 46, 118, 181-199
Sage, Saint and Yogi, Distinction between, 3, 44, 45, 46,
    47, 209, 210
Sages, Two kinds of, 1
Sahaja Nirvikalpa Samadhi (Natural State), 45, 148, 149,
    183
Saint Paul, 230
Samadhi, 230, 236
Sankara, 45, 58, 63, 92, 108, 110, 111, 123, 131, 133, 175,
    183, 186, 232
Sattva, 177, 228
Scepticism, 27
Science, 29-31
Self (Real Self), 7, 13, 35, 43, 47, 48, 49, 55, 56, 57, 58, 69,
    80, 82, 83, 94, 118-119, 133, 134, 143-144
    — Real Self identical with God and *Guru,* 13, 14
    Self, Experience of: *Ref* Reality, experience of
Sheaths, 129, 130, 131, 151
Siddhis, 157, 186, 187
Silence, 15, 144, 178

Sleep, 22, 34, 48, 54, 68, 72, 85, 104, 105, 122, 123, 124, 126, 127, 128, 141, 149, 153, 197, 224
Soul, Individual (*jeeva,* ego), 88 to 107, 133, 161-164
Suka, Sage, 8
Surrender, 107, 116, 147, 213, 214, 217, 218, 226, 240

T

Tapas, 178
Tattvopadesa, 175
Teacher and disciple, 15, 47, 52, 106, 175, 191, 201, 202
Three States, The, 122-123, 126-129, 151-153
Time and Space, 70, 76-78
Tiruvannamalai, 10-14, 173
Triads, 109-110, 204
Truth, 1, 27, 37-39

U

Ulladu Narpadu*
— benedictory v. 1 (4), 122, 227
— v. 1 (6), 159
— v. 3 (8), 53
— v. 4 (9), 82
— v. 5 (10), 124
— v. 6 (11), 71
— v. 7 (12), 68
— v. 9 (14), 109
— v. 11 (16), 30, 61
— v. 12 (17), 222
— v. 13 (18), 136
— v. 14 (19), 79
— v. 16 (21), 77
— v. 18 (23), 192
— v. 19 (24), 222

* The numbers in brackets after the verse numbers of *Ulladu Narpadu* and *Ulladu Narpadu Anubandham* are the corresponding verse numbers in *Sri Ramana Hridayam* (see appendix A).

— v. 23 (28), 104
— v. 24 (29), 89
— v. 25 (30), 95
— v. 26 (31), 102
— v. 27 (32), 161
— v. 28 (33), 169
— v. 29 (34), 167
— v. 31 (36), 196
— v. 32 (37), 167
— v. 34 (39), 38, 100
— v. 35 (40), 157
— v. 37 (42), 112
— v. 38 (43), 194
— v. 39 (44), 158

Ulladu Narpadu Anubandham
— v. 11 (57), 155
— v. 14(60), 179
— v. 17(63), 218
— v. 29 (75), 140
— v. 31 (77), 197
— v. 32 (78), 154
— v. 33 (79), 194
— v. 35 (81), 37
— v. 36 (82), 36
— v. 37 (83), 17
— v. 38 (84), 189
— v. 39 (85), 175
— v. 40 (86), 103

Upadesa Saram, 7
Upanishads, 46, 110, 111, 132, 194
Upanishad:
    Aitareya, 132
    Brihadaranyaka, 35, 103, 111, 142
    Chhandogya, 63, 122, 147
    Isa, 239
    Katha, 7, 103, 111, 146
    Kena, 81

Mandukya, 63, 102, 133, 148, 153
Mundaka, 107, 119
Taittiriya, 103, 111, 120-121, 151
Unity of God and Self, 207

V

Vasanas, 200, 226
Videha-mukti, 181
Vishnu Purana, 79
Viveka Chudamani, 45, 123
Vyasa, 8

W

Waking Sleep, 153, 197, 236
Waking State, 72, 83, 123
Wasps' bite (incident considered), 195
'Who am I?', 168
World, The, 53 to 87, 146, 147, 239, 240-241
— objectivity of the, 68 to 73

Y

Yoga Vasistham, 140, 145, 146
Yogi, Yogis, 44, 45, 183, 237

BIBLIOGRAPHY
of books in English on the life and teachings of Bhagavan Sri Ramana Maharshi

TRANSLATIONS OF THE ORIGINAL TAMIL WORKS OF SRI BHAGAVAN

Five Hymns to Sri Arunachala: an English translation of *Sri Arunachala Stuti Panchakam,* the devotional hymns sung by Sri Bhagavan.

Five Hymns to Arunachala and Other Poems: original Tamil texts of *Sri Arunachala Stuti Panchakam* and some other poems of Sri Bhagavan, with English translations by Prof. K. Swaminathan and musical notations by Smt. Sulochana Natarajan.

The Collected Works of Ramana Maharshi edited by Arthur Osborne: a collection of English translations of all Sri Bhagavan's Tamil works, including both His original works and works which He translated from other languages.

The Poems of Sri Ramana Maharshi: versified English translations by Sadhu Arunachala (A.W. Chadwick) of Sri Bhagavan's philosophical poems and stray verses.

Revelation (Sri Ramana Hridayam): a Sanskrit verse-rendering of Sri Bhagavan's *Ulladu Narpadu* (The Forty Verses on Reality) and *Anubandham* (The Supplement to the Forty Verses) with an English translation, both by 'WHO' (K. Lakshmana Sarma).

Truth Revealed (Sad-Vidya): an English translation of Sri Bhagavan's *Ulladu Narpadu* and *Anubandham.*

Words of Grace: an English translation of the essay version of *Nan Yar?* (Who am I?), the essay version of *Vichara Sangraham* (Self-Enquiry) and *Upadesa Manjari* (Spiritual Instruction), three prose works which record the teachings of Sri Bhagavan.

RECORDS OF DIALOGUES WITH SRI BHAGAVAN

Conscious Immortality: a collection of conversations with Sri Bhagavan recorded by Paul Brunton and Munagala Venkataramiah.

Day by Day with Bhagavan: a diary by Devaraja Mudaliar recording conversations and events in Sri Bhagavan's Hall during the years 1945 to 1947.

Letters from Sri Ramanasramam: a diary by Suri Nagamma, written in the form of letters narrating conversations and events in Sri Bhagavan's Hall during the years 1945 to 1950.

Maharshi's Gospel (Books One and Two): a collection of answers by Sri Bhagavan to questions covering a range of spiritual topics, arranged and edited subjectwise into thirteen chapters, forming a brief but comprehensive record of His oral teachings.

Self-Enquiry: an English translation by Dr T.M.P. Mahadevan of the question and answer version of *Vichara Sangraham,* a compilation by Sri Natanananda of answers given by Sri Bhagavan to 40 questions asked by Gambhiram Seshayyar between 1900 and 1902, most of which are questions regarding the two paths of *raja yoga* and *jnana yoga.*

Spiritual Instruction: an English translation by Dr T.M.P. Mahadevan of *Upadesa Manjari,* a Tamil work containing 70 questions and answers recorded by Sri Natanananda.

Sri Ramana Gita: Sanskrit text of 300 verses by Kavyakantha Ganapati Muni, some of which record questions by devotees and answers by Sri Bhagavan, and some of which are verses in praise of Him, with an English translation by Sri Viswanatha Swami and Prof. K. Swaminathan.

Talks with Sri Ramana Maharshi: the most voluminous collection of dialogues with Sri Bhagavan, recorded in English by Munagala Venkataramiah during the years 1935 to 1939.

Who am I?: an English translation by Dr T.M.P. Mahadevan of the question and answer version of *Nan Yar?*, a small Tamil work recorded by Sivaprakasam Pillai in 1902 and containing the essential teachings of Sri Bhagavan.

COMPILATIONS AND EXPOSITIONS OF SRI BHAGAVAN'S TEACHINGS

Gems from Bhagavan: a collection of Sri Bhagavan's teachings, compiled and edited subjectwise by Devaraja Mudaliar.

Guru-Ramana-Vachaka-Mala by 'WHO' (K. Lakshmana Sarma): an English rendering of 350 Sanskrit verses, about 300 of which are translations of selected verses from Sri Muruganar's *Guru Vachaka Kovai* (The Garland of Guru's Sayings) and all of which embody the oral teachings of Sri Bhagavan, with explanatory notes.

Reflections on Talks with Sri Ramana Maharshi by S. S. Cohen: detailed notes on selected passages from *Talks,* arranged subjectwise into fourteen chapters.

The Path of Sri Ramana (Parts One and Two) by Sri Sadhu Om: a profound exposition of Sri Bhagavan's teachings, based largely upon His original Tamil works, giving clear and detailed guidance on the practice of Self-enquiry and self-surrender.

The Teachings of Bhagavan Sri Ramana Maharshi in His Own Words edited by Arthur Osborne: selected passages from the works of Sri Bhagavan and from *Talks, Day by Day* and other books with brief explanatory notes.

COMMENTARIES ON SRI BHAGAVAN'S WORKS

Arunachala-Siva by Dr T.M.P. Mahadevan: a commentary
upon *Sri Arunachala Aksharamanamalai* (The Bridal
Garland of Letters) and *Sri Arunachala Pancharatnam*
(The Five Gems in Praise of Arunachala), two of the
Five Hymns sung by Sri Bhagavan.

Eka Sloki by C. Sudarsanam: a discursive commentary
upon the first Sanskrit verse composed by Sri Bhagavan.

Ramana Maharshi and His Philosophy of Existence by Dr
T.M.P. Mahadevan: a learned and scholarly
commentary upon Sri Bhagavan's *Ulladu Narpadu* (The
Forty Verses on Reality) and *Anubandham* (The
Supplement), and some reflections upon His life and
teachings.

Sat-Darshana Bhashya by Kapali Sastri: a commentary
upon *Sat-Darshanam* (a free Sanskrit verse-rendering
by Kavyakantha Ganapati Muni of Sri Bhagavan's
Tamil work *Ulladu Narpadu),* preceded by a record of
some dialogues with Sri Bhagavan.

Sat-Darshanam — Forty Verses on Reality: a new English
translation and commentary by A. R. Natarajan, written
in popular style.

The Cardinal Teaching of the Maharshi by Kapali Sastri:
an English translation of a Sanskrit commentary upon
Sri Arunachala Pancharathnam (The Five Gems in
Praise of Arunachala), one of the Five Hymns sung by
Sri Bhagavan.

Upadesa Saram: an English translation and commentary
by B.V. Narasimhaswami upon the original Tamil text
of Sri Bhagavan's *Upadesa Saram* (The Essence of
Instruction), with Sanskrit text included as an appendix.

BIOGRAPHIES OF SRI BHAGAVAN

A Summary of the Life and Teachings of Sri Ramana by
Sri Sadhu Om: a concise biography with a brief account
of the basic teachings, giving emphasis on practice.

Bhagavan Ramana by Dr T.M.P. Mahadevan: a sketch of Sri Bhagavan's life, reprinted from the introduction to *Ramana Maharshi and His Philosophy of Existence.*

Bhagavan Sri Ramana — A Pictorial Biography compiled and designed by Joan and Matthew Greenblatt: an aesthetically presented biography, profusely illustrated in colour and black and white, with many quotations from Sri Bhagavan and old devotees.

Ramana Maharshi by Prof. K. Swaminathan: a biography which depicts Sri Bhagavan both as a man and as a master, giving an account of His life and His works.

Ramana Maharshi and the Path of Self-Knowledge by Arthur Osborne: a popular biography which has done much to spread a knowledge of Sri Bhagavan both in India and abroad.

Self-Realization by B.V. Narasimhaswami: the earliest major biography of Sri Bhagavan, first published in 1931, and now containing an epilogue by S.S. Cohen.

Sri Maharshi — A Short Life-Sketch by M.S. Kamath: a profusely illustrated biography, written in a simple style.

REMINISCENCES ABOUT SRI BHAGAVAN

A Sadhu's Reminiscences of Ramana Maharshi by Sadhu Arunachala (A.W. Chadwick): reminiscences of an unassuming English devotee, who came to Sri Bhagavan in 1935 and who remained in Tiruvannamalai almost permanently till his passing away in 1962.

At the Feet of Bhagavan by T. K. Sundaresa Aiyer: leaves from the diary of a devotee who lived most of his life with Sri Bhagavan.

Crumbs from His Table by Ramanananda Swarnagiri (K.S. Narayanaswami Aiyer): reminiscences of a devotee who visited Sri Bhagavan several times during the years 1934 to 1936, and who noted down instructive conversations and illustrative stories told by Sri Bhagavan.

*Glimpses of the Life and Teachings of Bhagavan
Sri Ramana Maharshi* by Frank Humphreys: an
account of several meetings with Sri Bhagavan in the
year 1911, and of the teachings received from Him,
related by His earliest European devotee.

Guru Ramana by S.S. Cohen: reminiscences about
Sri Bhagavan and a record of many conversations with
Him, concluding with a diary narrating the events of
the last two years of His bodily life.

Letters and Recollections of Sri Ramanasramam by Suri
Nagamma: 31 letters which were not included in the
English version of *Letters from Sri Ramanasramam,*
together with some other reminiscences.

My Life at Sri Ramanasramam by Suri Nagamma: further
reminiscences by the author of *Letters from Sri
Ramanasramam.*

My Recollections of Bhagavan Sri Ramana by Devaraja
Mudaliar: reminiscences told in a charming and
unassuming style by the author of *Day by Day.*

Residual Reminiscences of Ramana by S.S. Cohen: a
supplement to *Guru Ramana* by the same author.

Sri Ramana Reminiscences by G.V. Subbaramayya: a
personal account of many visits to Sri Bhagavan
between the years 1933 and 1950.

MISCELLANEOUS BOOKS ON SRI BHAGAVAN

Bhagavan and Nayana by S. Shankaranarayanan: an account
of the relationship between Sri Bhagavan and His famous
devotee Nayana (Kavyakantha Ganapati Muni).

Bhagavan Ramana and Mother by A.R. Natarajan: an
account of the relationship between Sri Bhagavan and
His mother, containing many pictures in colour and
black and white.

Forty Verses in Praise of Sri Ramana: an English
translation of *Sri Ramana Chatvarimsat,* a Sanskrit
work composed by Kavyakantha Ganapati Muni in
praise of Sri Bhagavan.

Hunting the 'I' according to Sri Ramana Maharshi by Lucy Cornelssen: a collection of essays on various aspects of the life and teachings of Sri Bhagavan.

Maharshi Ramana — His Relevance Today edited by B.K. and Shashi Ahluwalia: a collection of 30 essays on the life and teachings of Sri Bhagavan by distinguished writers such as S. Radhakrishnan, C.G. Jung, D.S. Sarma, Douglas Harding, G.H. Mees and Wei Wu Wei, with an introduction by Prof. K. Swaminathan.

New Songs from Ramana Sannidhi Murai: selected verses from *Sri Ramana Sannidhi Murai*, a collection of Tamil verses sung by Sri Muruganar in praise of Sri Bhagavan, with English translations by Prof. K. Swaminathan and musical notations by Smt. Sulochana Natarajan.

Ramana-Arunachala by Arthur Osborne: a collection of essays on the life and teachings of Sri Bhagavan.

Ramana Dhyanam by N. N. Rajan: an English translation of some verses of contemplation on Sri Bhagavan.

Ramana Mandiram by Sri Muruganar: selected verses from *Guru Vachaka Kovai* and other works of Sri Muruganar, with English translations by Prof. K. Swaminathan.

Ramana Thatha by Kumari Sarada: a book for children narrating simple stories from the life of Sri Bhagavan.

Selections from Ramana Gita by A. R. Nataraj an: 42 verses selected from *Sri Ramana Gita,* with English translation and commentary.

Songs from Ramana Sannidhi Murai: selected verses from *Sri Ramana Sannidhi Murai,* with English translations by Prof. K. Swaminathan and musical notations by Smt. Sulochana Natarajan.

Sri Ramana Stuti Panchakam: an English translation of five Tamil songs composed by Satyamangala Venkataramaiyer in praise of Sri Bhagavan.

Stories from Bhagavan edited by Joan Greenblatt: a collection of instructive stories narrated by Sri Bhagavan.

The Cow Lakshmi by Devaraja Mudaliar: an account of the famous cow which attained liberation by the Grace of Sri Bhagavan.

The Liberating Question: a collection of three essays on Sri Bhagavan's Grace and teachings, by A. R. Natarajan, V. Ganesan and Kumari Sarada.

The Maharshi and His Message by Paul Brunton: a reprint of three chapters from *A Search in Secret India,* the book which first made Sri Bhagavan widely known outside India.

Thus Spake Ramana edited by Swami Rajeswarananda: a pocket-size book containing 125 passages selected from Sri Bhagavan's teachings.

SOME ANCIENT SCRIPTURES REFERRED TO BY SRI BHAGAVAN

Advaita Bodha Deepika (The Lamp of Non-Dual Knowledge): an English translation by Munagala Venkataramiah (the recorder of *Talks with Sri Ramana Maharshi)* of a Sanskrit work by Sri Karapatra Swami.

Jewel Garland of Enquiry: an English translation of *Vichara Mani Malai,* a compilation by Sri Bhagavan of salient points from the Tamil version of *Vichara Sagara* (The Ocean of Enquiry), a voluminous work originally written in Hindi by Mahatma Nischaldas.

Kaivalya Navaneetha (The Cream of Emancipation): an English translation by Munagala Venkataramiah of a classical Tamil work on *advaita* philosophy.

The Song Celestial: 42 verses from the *Bhagavad Gita,* selected and reset by Sri Bhagavan, with an English translation and explanatory notes.

Tripura Rahasya (or The Mystery beyond the Trinity): an English translation by Munagala Venkataramiah of an ancient Sanskrit work on *advaita* philosophy.

Yoga Vasishta Sara: an English translation of 230 verses from the Yoga *Vasishta.*

SOUVENIR AND JOURNAL

Ramana Smrti: a souvenir published in 1980 to commemorate the birth centenary of Sri Bhagavan, consisting of more than 60 articles by devotees both old and new, many of which contain previously unpublished reminiscences.

The Mountain Path: a quarterly journal dedicated to Sri Bhagavan, the aim of which is to set forth the traditional wisdom of all religions and all ages, especially as testified to by their saints and mystics, and to clarify the paths available to seekers in the conditions of our modern world.

Note: The above books are all published and/or available in India from Sri Ramanasramam. For details regarding current prices, please write to:

Sri Ramanasramam Book Depot,
Sri Ramanasramam P.O.,
Tiruvannamalai,
Tamil Nadu 606 603.